AF802966

Fundamental Labour Rights and the Constitution

The book reflects on constitutional balancing from the perspective of fundamental labour rights. It draws on neo-constitutional theories and builds on the assumption that fundamental labour rights, understood as rights aimed at protecting workers during their working life or after retirement, are the normative expression of founding values and can be balanced against equally axiological constitutional principles. The balancing of constitutional labour rights can be conducted by various institutional actors and by applying different techniques. This volume reviews the theoretical debates on judicial balancing and the approaches adopted by the Court of Justice of the European Union and the European Court of Human Rights, to proceed with a closer assessment of Italian and Spanish judicial traditions. In particular, it addresses the main profiles of the case law of the Italian and Spanish Constitutional Courts on labour and social law reforms adopted in the aftermath of the 2008 crisis, where balancing takes place between labour rights and economic principles. The analysis is focused on four main aspects: the fundamental labour rights in the balance; the role of the Courts; the technique applied by the Judges; and the constitutional interests subject to the balancing. It ultimately reveals that the axiological nature of fundamental labour rights is preserved and the economic and financial contingencies confirm their factual character, although they are occasionally recognised a prominent role in the *ratio decidendi*. The book will be a valuable resource for academics and researchers working in the areas of labour law, social security law, legal theory and constitutional law.

Giulia Frosecchi is researcher and lecturer of labour law and European social law at the University of Florence, Italy.

Studies in Modern Law and Policy

Series Editor: Ralf Rogowski,
Professor of Law, University of Warwick

Also in the series

Social Systems Theory and Judicial Review
Taking Jurisprudence Seriously
Katayoun Baghai
ISBN: 978-1-4094-5402-1

The EU Economic and Social Model in the Global Crisis
Interdisciplinary Perspectives
Edited by Dagmar Schiek
ISBN: 978-1-4094-5731-2

Constitutional Evolution in Central and Eastern Europe
Expansion and Integration in the EU
Edited by Kyriaki Topidi and Alexander H.E. Morawa
ISBN: 978-1-4094-0327-2

Central and Eastern Europe After Transition
Towards a New Socio-legal Semantics
Edited by Alberto Febbrajo and Wojciech Sadurski
ISBN: 978-1-4094-0390-6

Democracy, Law and Governance
Jacques Lenoble and Marc Maesschalck
ISBN: 978-1-4094-0395-1

Global Trade, Labour Rights and International Law
A Multilevel Approach
Aneta Tyc
ISBN: 978-0-367-74801-2

Cryptocurrency Regulation
A Reflexive Law Approach
Immaculate Dadiso Motsi-Omoijiade
ISBN: 978-1-032-18361-9

Fundamental Labour Rights and the Constitution
Constitutional Balancing in Italy and Spain
Giulia Frosecchi
ISBN: 978-0-367-72569-3

Fundamental Labour Rights and the Constitution

Constitutional Balancing in Italy and Spain

Giulia Frosecchi

Routledge
Taylor & Francis Group
LONDON AND NEW YORK

First published 2024
by Routledge
4 Park Square, Milton Park, Abingdon, Oxon OX14 4RN

and by Routledge
605 Third Avenue, New York, NY 10158

Routledge is an imprint of the Taylor & Francis Group, an informa business

© 2024 Giulia Frosecchi

The right of Giulia Frosecchi to be identified as author of this work has been asserted in accordance with sections 77 and 78 of the Copyright, Designs and Patents Act 1988.

All rights reserved. No part of this book may be reprinted or reproduced or utilised in any form or by any electronic, mechanical, or other means, now known or hereafter invented, including photocopying and recording, or in any information storage or retrieval system, without permission in writing from the publishers.

Trademark notice: Product or corporate names may be trademarks or registered trademarks, and are used only for identification and explanation without intent to infringe.

British Library Cataloguing-in-Publication Data
A catalogue record for this book is available from the British Library

ISBN: 978-0-367-72569-3 (hbk)
ISBN: 978-0-367-72571-6 (pbk)
ISBN: 978-1-003-15536-2 (ebk)

DOI: 10.4324/9781003155362

Typeset in Galliard
by Deanta Global Publishing Services, Chennai, India

"I certainly did not owe the suggestion of one incident, nor scarcely of one train of feeling, to my husband, and yet but for his incitement, it would never have taken the form in which it was presented to the world."
(MARY SHELLY, preface to *Frankenstein*, 1831 Ed.)

A Mara

Contents

Abbreviations

CAE	*Contrato de Apoyo a los Emprendedores*
CJEU	Court of Justice of the European Union
D.L.	Decree Law
D.lgs.	Legislative Decree
ECB	European Central Bank
ECHR	European Convention on Human Rights
ECtHR	European Court of Human Rights
EFSF	European Financial Stability Facility
EFSM	European Financial Stabilization Mechanism
EPP	Euro Plus Pact
ESM	European Stability Mechanism
EU	European Union
GDP	Gross Domestic Product
IC	Italian Constitution
ILO	International Labour Organisation
IMF	International Monetary Fund
JA	JOBS Act
MoUs	Memoranda of Understanding
RDL	Royal Decree Law
SC	Spanish Constitution
SGP	Stability and Growth Pact
TFEU	Treaty on the Functioning of the European Union
TSCG	Treaty on Stability, Coordination and Governance
WS	Workers' Statute (*Ley del Estatuto de los Trabajadores*)

Introduction

From the EU crisis to constitutional balancing

Balancing between conflicting rights and interests has long been the subject of authoritative academic debates, from various perspectives.[1] For introductory purposes, balancing can be defined as a method used by either the legislator or the courts (both ordinary and constitutional) to regulate or decide cases in which the enforcement of one right or interest comes into conflict with another right or interest. In what is called constitutional balancing, the conflicting rights and interests find explicit recognition in the constitution and their scope cannot be compressed to the point of making them void.

Before the COVID-19 pandemic brought into the limelight the controversial, and at times paradoxical, conflict between the right to health and that range of rights roughly known as personal liberties, the 2008 crisis[2] and the European legislators' reactions had already – newly – drawn attention to the delicate equilibrium between conflicting interests and rights in pluralist legal systems.

In order to tackle the effects of the economic and financial crisis of 2008, the EU institutions decided to follow the *austerity way*.[3] The austerity policies adopted by the EU have imposed a number of reforms in certain Member States, *inter alia*, labour and social security reforms, which have put social and labour

1 Among the legal theorists firmly supporting balancing as the most appropriate way to develop constitutional judgments; see Alexy 2003. In contrast, authoritative scholars such as Dworkin and Habermas reject the balancing approach; for an introduction cf. Habermas 1996 and Dworkin 1977 (see Chapter 1).

2 What is generally referred to as "the latest economic crisis" is the result of a bubble burst in the United States in 2007, with the collapse of the subprime loans and the subsequent Lehman Brothers bankruptcy (September 2008). These events rapidly hit financial markets worldwide, including EU countries, and, consequently, the real economy, too. For a comprehensive review of the 2008 crisis, see Shambaugh 2012.

3 Chieco 2015, 360, underlines how this policy option is far from being innovative. The austerity-opponents include the Nobel Prize winner Joseph Stiglitz, who has advocated, several times, against the theory that public financial constraints represent a way to foster economic development; see, amongst others, a 2014 article titled *Europe's Austerity Distaster*, available at: https://www.socialeurope.eu/europes-austerity-disaster. Tridico 2013, on the basis of empirical analysis, the author argues that countries with a less flexible labour market are those that have performed relatively better during the economic crisis.

DOI: 10.4324/9781003155362-1

rights under serious pressure.[4] Indeed, even though the flexibilisation of the labour market is not a novelty of our decade, the tendency towards increasing deregulation of the labour market was reinforced after 2008, when the bubble burst and the financial, sovereign-debt and economic crisis seriously hit a number of European countries. The way in which EU institutions have reacted to the crisis and attempted to foster a recovery is highly controversial. As a general consequence, a number of labour law reforms, adopted by several countries with the purported aim of overcoming the Eurozone crisis, have had a negative impact on workers' and trade unions' rights,[5] causing, since 2009, a deepening in the labour law crisis, within, and causally linked with, the economic and financial crisis.

The impact of post-crisis measures on workers' rights has been significantly discussed and it is often highlighted that European responses to the Eurozone crisis have threatened fundamental social rights as well as institutional balances,[6] raising constitutional issues within Member States.[7] Fundamental changes in working time regulation, an increase in atypical employment, consistent reforms of rules on redundancy and alteration of the industrial relations' structures and processes, which have affected social dialogue and collective bargaining, were observed.[8]

Barnard describes the EU crisis as divided into "three overlapping phases". In 2008, mainly because of a housing bubble and a credit boom, the *financial crisis* exploded, seriously destabilising the banking system in EU countries. In 2010, the *sovereign-debt crisis* followed, because a number of EU Member States had to face large deficits, partly due to the necessity of bailing out banks, as well as consistent debts. In order to deal with the most delicate national situations, the EU institutions encouraged the replacement of democratically elected governments with technical governments, as was the case in Italy and Greece (2011), giving rise to what the author calls the *crisis of democracy*.[9]

4 For all, Sciarra 2018.

5 Clauwaert, Schömann 2012; Bruun et al. 2014; a comprehensive review has been developed recently by Vigneau 2018. Overall, it is often highlighted that European responses to the Eurozone crisis have threatened fundamental social rights and, consequently, institutional balances, raising also constitutional issues within those Member States mostly affected by the crisis, like Portugal, Greece, Ireland, Italy and Spain. See: Kilpatrick, De Witte 2014; Caruso, Fontana 2015, which collects a series of contributions on the relationship between the 2008 crisis and fundamental labour rights.

6 Sciarra 2014; Giubboni 2016 provides a wide-ranging reflection on the impact of the crisis on the European integration process; see also Kilpatrick 2015, where the author investigates the "interaction of constitutions, sovereign debt and social rights in Europe today".

7 Tuori, Tuori 2014; see also Buekers et al. 2017. Already in 2007, Bin argued that "the decisions that impact on the enforcement of rights are taken elsewhere, in cold locations, external to the democratic circle and far from the social conflict": Bin 2007, 56 ff.; on constitutional challenges in EU sovereign debt states, Kilpatrick 2015.

8 Clauwaert, Schömann 2012; on Italy, Spain and Portugal, see the concise review by De Stefano 2013 and the critical analysis by Giubboni, Orlandini 2018; Marshall 2014 refers to a proper shifting of responsibility from the financial crisis to labour.

9 Barnard 2012, 127.

In order to respond to the financial and sovereign debt crises' effects, the EU has focused on improving the economic governance and fostering the adoption of certain shared rules, mainly directed to the containment of public deficit. In 2010, the first move to stabilise the economic situation of its area was the establishment of the European Financial Stabilization Mechanism (EFSM),[10] shortly thereafter replaced by the European Financial Stability Facility (EFSF),[11] financed by the Eurozone members, and meant to tackle the sovereign debt crisis in a temporary way, while the EU institutions were designing and working on a permanent fund. On the grounds of the EFSF, the Commission, together with the ECB and the International Monetary Fund (IMF) (a trio known as the Troika), could negotiate with the beneficiary states Memoranda of Understanding (MoUs), with the aim to release financial assistance upon compliance with terms and conditions set out therein. This procedure was applied to provide financial assistance to Ireland, Portugal and Greece, as well as for the initial recapitalisation of Spanish banks in 2012.[12] Eventually, the EFSF was replaced by the – permanent – European Stability Mechanism (ESM), which entered into force in September 2012,[13] after Art. 136.3 Treaty on the Functioning of the European Union (TFEU) was amended in order to allow the EU Member States to establish a stability mechanism as such (however, it is noteworthy that the Treaty amendment entered into force only on 1 May 2013). The main objective of the TESM is to safeguard the financial stability of the Euro area by connecting the activation of financial assistance to strict economic policy conditionality.[14]

One of the preconditions for receiving financial support on the grounds of the European Stability Mechanism consists in having ratified and implemented Title III of the Treaty on Stability, Coordination and Governance (TSCG) in the Economic and Monetary Union, an intergovernmental Treaty signed on 2 March

10 Council Regulation 407/2010.

11 A Luxemburg company, created in June 2010 by the Euro area Member States.

12 On July 2012, the Spanish Government signed with the so-called Troika the "Memorandum of Understanding on Financial-Sector Policy Conditionality" (MoU), which granted Financial Assistance for the Recapitalisation of Financial Institutions and required Spain to respect and comply with, beside bank-specific and horizontal conditionality, the recommendations intended to tackle macroeconomic imbalances, which included the need to implement the structural reforms of the labour market that had been already adopted. While Italy has not entered into any Memorandum of Understanding with the Troika; nonetheless, the Italian post-crisis management has been strongly influenced by the EU institutions.

13 On 25 March 2011, the European Council adopted the Conclusions on the establishment of the ESM; while, the proper ESM Treaty was adopted on 2 March 2012.

14 See, Tuori, Tuori 2014, 89 ff; Schoemann 2014, 11–24; specifically on the Troika, cf. Fischer-Lescano 2014, 55–81. The ESM is still an intergovernmental body – despite some attempts made in 2017 to transform it into an EU agency – and over the years it has been empowered with further functions. Most recently, on 9 April 2020, a new line of credit, the Pandemic Crisis Support (PCS), was set up in order to grant loans destined to support the Member States' health systems, with the only conditionality of using the credit line to support "direct and indirect healthcare, cure and prevention related costs due to the COVID-19 crisis"; for a critical review, see De Angelis 2022.

2012, also known as Fiscal Compact. The Fiscal Compact, which supplements the Stability and Growth Pact (SGP) (first introduced in 1997), requires the signatory Member States to comply with the debt-level rules, that is with the so-called principle of balanced budget, which entails that the general budget deficit cannot exceed 3.0% of the gross domestic product (GDP).

In the meantime, in March 2011, the adoption of the Euro Plus Pact (EPP), under the EU's Open Method of Coordination, signed by all 17 Eurozone members (and other EU Member States), was reinforcing the economic governance, by deepening fiscal coordination, with a view of complementing the Stability and Growth Pact. The EPP has been concluded having in mind, particularly, four main objectives: promoting competitiveness, which may include reviewing wage setting arrangements and fostering the decentralisation of collective bargaining; supporting employment, by promoting, among others, flexicurity; assuring the sustainability of public finances, also by limiting early retirement schemes; reinforcing financial stability. The adoption of the six-pack in 2011 and the two-pack in 2013 has reiterated, within the EU legal framework, what was provided for by the Fiscal Compact.[15]

Both Spain and Italy have decided to constitutionalise the deficit constraints, respectively in September 2011 and January 2012, even though the Treaty did not require the Member States to introduce the principle of balanced budget necessarily via constitutional revision.[16] This political choice, as shown further in this book, has an immense impact on constitutional equilibria and profoundly discomforts the work of constitutional courts, since it places a distinct choice of political economy, roughly endorsed by the respective national Parliaments,[17] at the highest level of the hierarchy of sources, *seemingly*[18] the same level as fundamental rights, which has the effect of "expunging the Keynesian [and others] instruments from the powers that can be freely exercised by the policy making bodies".[19]

The Italian legislator opted for a reform of Art. 81 Italian Constitution (IC), which entailed a proper constitutionalisation of the principle at stake.

15 The 2011 six-pack is composed by Regulation 1173/2011; Regulation 1174/2011; Regulation 1175/2011; Regulation 1176/2011; Regulation 1177/2011; Directive 85/2011. The 2013 two-pack is composed by Regulation 472/2013; Regulation 473/2013 applicable to the Euro area countries. On the economic governance effects on national labour systems see Barnard 2012, 127–140, and Chieco 2015.

16 Other Member States have, indeed, preferred other options for the implementation of the balanced budget principle, cf., *inter alia*, Ciolli 2012b.

17 Nevertheless, discussions were already ongoing both in Italy and Spain as regards the opportunity to reform the constitutional norms regulating public spending, particularly after the mid-1970s oil crisis; see, respectively, Morrone 2013 and Medina Guerrero 2012.

18 The italics wants to emphasise the only apparent comparable nature between the principle of balanced budget and fundamental rights, see the arguments elaborated in Chapter 1.

19 Chessa 2018, 281, which, in his opinion particularly contradicts a constitution, such as the Italian Constitution (but the same can be applied to the Spanish Constitution) that is intrinsically "also" Keynesian, see 282, 283. *A contrario*, Morrone 2015b, 579.

The constitutional law was approved by the Italian Parliament in April 2012: Constitutional Law 1/2012 (entered into force in May 2012, but with effect starting from 2014). However, the legislative procedure had started long before the conclusion of the Fiscal Compact. Indeed, already in September 2011 the draft constitutional reform of Art. 81 IC, as well as of Articles 97, 117 and 119 IC, was approved. Such a zeal was due to the fact that even before the conclusion of the 2012 international treaty the EU had given a clear impulse to Member States to harmonise the rules on balanced budget.[20] In order to implement the constitutional reform and the fiscal compact, Law 243/2012 ("Norms on the application of the principle of balanced budget in compliance with Art. 81.6 Italian Constitution") was subsequently approved. The result is a renewed constitution, which obliges public administration bodies, at every level, to comply with the principle of balanced budget according to European rules and the sustainability of public debt in relation to GDP.[21]

With analogous results, Art. 135 Spanish Constitution (SC) was amended in 2011 to include stringent public budget constraints upon the state, the public administrations and the autonomous communities. Given that the norm is formally considered a technical constitutional norm, to be amended it does not require a public referendum, notwithstanding its potential, but consistent, consequences upon social security and public employment. The renovated text states that public bodies must remain within a structural deficit as established by the European Union (the reference is again to the TFEU, which provides for a maximum of 3% of the GDP). Consequently, public administrations shall give "absolute priority" to the payment of the public debt.[22]

In truth, already in 2009, both Italy[23] and Spain[24] had been the targets of Council Recommendations exhorting national authorities to bring to an end the

20 Pirozzoli 2011.

21 On the constitutional law introducing the principle of balanced budget into the Italian Constitution, see the Issue edited by Carbas 2013.

22 The reformed Art. 135 Spanish Constitution gave a mandate to the ordinary law to develop further its content, the outcome was: *Ley Orgánica de Estabilidad Presupuestaria y Sostenibilidad Financiera* (*Ley Orgánica* 2/2012, 17 April). For a critical assessment, see Aparicio Wilhelmi 2016.

23 Beyond any doubt, Italy is one of the European countries most hit by the 2008 economic and financial crises. The unemployment rate has been constantly increasing since 2008, when it was at 6.7%, up until 2014, when it reached the peak of 12.7%: http://ec.europa.eu/eurostat/statistics-explained/index.php/File:Unemployment_rate_2004-2015_(%25)_new.png. Even though the unemployment trend does not seem as serious as the Spanish one, the public debt rates are quite telling about the impact of the crisis on Italy. Indeed, the public debt rate rose from 99.8%, in 2007, up to 132.6%, in 2016: http://ec.europa.eu/eurostat/tgm/table.do?tab=table&init=1&language=en&pcode=teina225&plugin=1.

24 Similarly, Spain is one of the European countries that most suffered the 2008 economic and financial crisis. In 2008 the unemployment rate was at 11.3% and in 2010 it had already risen to 19.9%. Equally striking, in 2011, the public debt was at 11%. A number of elements have

situation of excessive government deficit.[25] But it was only in August 2011 that the Italian and Spanish Prime Ministers received the letters from the ECB, where the European Bank was inviting the two governments to proceed with reforms aimed at flexibilising the labour market and wage setting procedures, favouring the decentralisation of collective bargaining, as well as cutting social expenditure and public-sector wages.[26] In other words, with an informal document, the ECB, a not-elected independent institution, has dictated, with impressive success, the policy line to two national governments.

Overall, the European institutional responses to the 2008 crisis, which led to the amendment of the Lisbon Treaty, the setting up the European Stability Mechanism and the signature of the so-called Fiscal Compact, have influenced national labour laws, which have "undergone profound reforms marked by a blatant explosion of inequalities and insecurity for workers, in many cases heedless of fundamental social rights".[27] In Italy, the "parallel legal system", represented by the new tools and institutions of the European economic governance, has strongly influenced the labour reforms under both the Monti (2012) and Renzi (2014–2015) Governments,[28] which have allegedly attempted to shift the protection of workers from the contract to the market and have exposed the industrial relations model to considerable pressure.[29]

---

been considered the causes of the 21st century great recession, see Rocha 2014, 175; as well as Clasen et al. 2012, 17–19.

25 Council Recommendation 15757/09, of 30 November 2009 to Italy with a view to bringing an end to the situation of an excessive government deficit; Council Recommendation 15764/09, of 30 November 2009 to Spain with a view to bringing an end to the situation of an excessive government deficit.

26 Tuori, Tuori 2014, 83; Countouris 2020, 364–365; Ridaura Martínez 2012.

27 Bruun et al. 2014, 325; see also Kilpatrick, De Witte 2014. Similar conclusions are reached by Leschke 2012 and Sciarra 2016. Tuori and Tuori suggest that the EU crisis management has confirmed "the fundamental imbalance between Treaty provisions on social and economic issues": Tuori, Tuori 2014, 233. For a critical reflection around prospects for social rights in the EU and Social Europe following the 2008 crisis, see the rich anthology edited by Countouris, Freedland 2013; Giubboni 2013; Garben et al. 2017; Kilpatrick 2018. While Dorssemont 2014 adopts the social partners' point of view to address the EU legal framework.

28 The EU pressure did not only strongly influence the subsequent reforms, but it also led to the resignation of Berlusconi's Government and the appointment of a technical government led by Mario Monti, see Biasi 2014; cf. also Pizzoferrato 2015. Nevertheless, before resigning, and as a consequence of the ECB letter, on 13 August 2011 (eight days after the ECB letter was received) the Berlusconi Government approved a norm in support of decentralised collective bargaining (Art. 8, Decree Law 138/2011).

29 For an introduction to the post-crisis reforms, see Pizzoferrato 2015; Carinici 2015; Carinci et al. 2016. For a wide-ranging reflection on the current status of Italian labour law, see, among others, Lassandari 2015; Caruso 2016 and the academic dialogue between Mariucci 2015 and Caruso Del Punta 2016. For a focus on d.lgs. 81/2015, Nogler 2015. The social security perspective is provided by Cinelli 2015a. On the factual impact on the Italian industrial relations system see, instead, Colombo Regalia 2016; see also Clawert, Schoeman 2012, and, from a more legal perspective over the Italian industrial relations, Leccese 2012; Chieco

Likewise, in Spain, austerity measures have reduced welfare rights, led to a decentralisation of collective bargaining and eased the termination of the employment relationship.[30] In the crisis context, legislators have often tried to justify threats to the rule of law and foundations of democracy under the state of emergency argument.[31]

Some of the national norms implementing austerity policies and policies oriented towards the flexibilisation of the labour market have been challenged before national constitutional courts, which have sought to resolve the conflict between the fundamental labour rights tackled by the reforms and economic interests, through balancing exercises.[32]

An assessment of the relevant Italian and Spanish constitutional post-crisis case law can contribute to defining the current status of the constitutional conflict of fundamental labour rights with other interests of an economic nature, in national legal systems strongly influenced by the EU policies in the aftermath of the 2008 crisis. The constitutional case law of the two southern European countries is well suited for inspiring a joint reflection, inasmuch as both Italy and Spain have adopted a centralised system of constitutional review – albeit with certain differences – and the respective constitutions are rich in principles and programmatic norms that both the Parliament and the Constitutional Court have to translate in directly applicable legal terms.[33] And, as concisely reviewed

---

2015, addresses the reforms of 2012 and 2015, with a view of stressing the role of the Charter of Fundamental Rights to enforce labour rights. Guarriello 2016 assesses the changes imposed to the collective bargaining system following the economic crisis. However, there is not absolute consent over the criticisms made to these reforms: Caruso 2016 observes that the opinions over the JOBS Act are various and range from total disappointment, to an optimistic attitude that sees in this reform the trigger for a new way of regulating employment relations. See also Tega 2014a.

30 Baylos Grau 2012a; Baylos Grau 2012b; Merino Segovia 2012; Baz Rodríguez 2012; Gómez-Millán Herencia 2012; González Pascual 2014; Rodríguez 2014; Gil y Gil 2014; Villalón 2016. A broader analysis of the EU impact on national labour law from a Spanish perspective is provided by Casas Baamonde 2014; on collective bargaining, cf. Ojeda Avilés A. 2013; Cruces Aguilera et al. 2016; Cruz Villalón 2016.

31 Sciarra 2014; Giubboni Lo Faro 2013.

32 The courts have been blamed for having applied "judicial restraint and displayed far-going understanding of government defences invoking economic emergency"; Tuori, Tuori 2014, 240. A remarkable exception is represented by the Portuguese Constitutional Court case law, appreciated for having been extremely defensive of the fundamental labour rights concerned, see Cisotta, Gallo 2014; Butturini 2016. For a first and comprehensive analysis of the constitutional post-crisis case law, see the contributions published in Kilpatrick, De Witte 2014; Fasone 2014; also Guazzarotti 2013.

33 Italy and Spain are characterised by the same system of centralised constitutional review of ordinary legislation, inspired by Hans Kelsen theories. Indeed, both the Italian and the Spanish systems adopted the Kelsenian model of constitutional review, which was originally implemented by the Austrian Constitution. This model provides for the establishment of a separate constitutional tribunal, which is the sole court entitled to solve all disputes concerning the constitutionality of secondary legislation, in order to effectively grant the rigidity of the constitution (for a review see Comella 2004). However, the Austrian model was not fully

above, in the aftermath of the 2008 crisis, the two countries have been subject to considerable pressure from EU institutions to implement austerity policies and liberalise the labour market.

In Italy and Spain, the so-called post-crisis reforms have been adopted in a political (*e.g.* exchange of letters, recommendations by the EU institutions), economic (economic and financial crises) and legal (overuse of urgency legislation, constitutional reforms of the public budget constraints) context, which is increasingly calling into question the content and enforcement of constitutional (from now on, either called constitutional or fundamental) labour rights.

Although the Spanish and Italian judicial cases are neither parallel in normative terms, nor perfectly comparable, all of the selected constitutional post-crisis judgments on labour and social security reforms have addressed norms that have limited the scope of fundamental labour rights. For the purpose of this research, labour rights refers to rights aimed at protecting workers, either during their working life or after retirement. In the Spanish and Italian legal systems, these rights are *fundamental* inasmuch as they are recognised and protected at constitutional level, thus representing – a part of – the foundation of the respective societies.

Notwithstanding the relevant similarities in both the 2008 crisis's impact and the constitutional structure – in terms of fundamental social rights and centralised system of constitutional review – the assessment of the legal reasoning in the selected judgments is conducted under the assumption that we are not in a "global age of balancing".[34] Even though the technique of balancing labour and social rights with other interests and rights, in order to decide upon the constitutionality of an ordinary norm, is a common feature of all courts, *balancing* can take different names and shapes depending on the court and the legal tradition concerned.

The book concentrates on the legal reasonings of the Italian and Spanish Constitutional Courts in the post-crisis case law with the aim to understand if the arguments used to justify a reduction in the scope of the fundamental labour

transplanted in those European legal systems, which adopted it at a later stage. Indeed, both the Italian and the Spanish Constitutions are rich in principles and programmatic norms and the Constituent Assemblies have given the role to translate in directly applicable legal terms principles and values enshrined in the constitution to both the Parliament, entrusted with the legislative power, and the Constitutional Court, which is entitled to oversee the ordinary laws; Modugno 1982. Nonetheless, the Italian and Spanish systems of constitutional review present substantial differences, one for all, while the Italian system does not envisage a procedure that allows citizens to appeal directly before the Constitutional Court, the Spanish Court can receive the so called *recurso de amparo* (appeal for constitutional protection of fundamental rights); for an introduction to *recurso de amparo*, see Arroyo Jiménez, Ortega Carballo 2014.

34 The expression "age of balancing" was coined by Aleinikoff 1987 and it refers to the widespread use made by the courts, all over the world, of the balancing technique. The author, writing at a time when balancing was less pervasive, warned against a too facile use of balancing and invited judges to consider also alternative ways to solve constitutional conflicts.

rights concerned and – as has occurred on certain occasions – authorise their infringement retain a structural character that shapes the understanding of the constitutional models lying behind such fundamental labour rights, or, rather, may be understood as circumscribed arguments that do not upset the understanding of such rights as normative expression of founding values. Ultimately, I argue that, although a number of profiles of the case law addressed legitimately raise concerns as to the enforcement of fundamental labour rights and the resistance of the social state designed by our constitutions, the two courts do not question the axiological character of those rights, nor the contingent character of the economic and financial factors raised by the legislator to justify the contested provisions.

What this book aims to value in respect of the constitutional post-crisis case law is that, notwithstanding its impact on specific constitutional norms and on the respective fundamental labour rights, it does not upset the constitutional equilibria *to the core* and does not question the different ontological nature of the various factors at play in the *ratio decidendi.* If the courts have built a pattern for future decisions on fundamental labour rights, that pattern consists in the corroboration of the axiological character of fundamental labour rights and the contingent and ancillary character of economic and financial arguments.

Although Italy and Spain present consistent similarities in their constitutional organisation, as well as in the structure and functioning of the constitutional courts, the crucial differences do not allow for a comparison of the case law.[35] What makes a parallel analysis of the Spanish and Italian cases noteworthy is the shared necessity to enforce constitutional labour rights, in the economic crisis context.

In the Spanish constitutional post-crisis case law, the proportionality test is either not applied at all, or only allegedly applied, as properly demonstrated by the dissenting opinions of Judge Valdés Dal-Ré. The decisions of the Court have been accused of being oriented to support economic interests at the detriment of fundamental labour rights, in order to uphold the government's choices slavishly. On the other side of the Mediterranean, the Italian Court offers a rich case law which appears not always consistent and coherent, and it has been accused of having failed to develop a structured and convincing legal reasoning, which can satisfy the demands for transparency. However, the same case law has also been prized as an active defence of labour rights and a correct understanding of the constitutional court's role in a democratic system based upon a rigid constitution that enshrines a wide range of fundamental labour rights.

35 It is shared that "[E]ach court, be it national or supranational, is grounded on different premises and carries specific competences, which also imply the adoption of different arguments and techniques of adjudication. For this reason, it is informative to enrich the inventory of such techniques and to expand the research on arguments offered by judges, when they are faced with the pressures of measures adopted in exceptional circumstances"; Sciarra 2018, 138.

The first question that a labour lawyer approaching topics such as constitutional balancing, traditionally addressed by constitutional lawyers, is tempted to ask is whether priority should be given to the structure of the legal reasoning, or to the effective protection of the fundamental labour rights at issue.

On the one hand, certain legal scholarship seems to suggest that the application of a rigid proportionality test is a priority, in order to assure transparency and consistency of the constitutional legal reasoning. Yet, that literature undermines the prominence of an effective enforcement of fundamental labour rights, which is instead the central argument of several labour lawyers. On the other hand, the missed application of the proportionality test is beclouded, mainly by the Spanish labour scholarship, by the reflections on the missed protection of the fundamental labour rights concerned by the Spanish judgments.

While the arguments in favour of the application of a systematised technique as the proportionality test are intriguing and consistent, it is legitimate to wonder whether a fundamental rights discourse, as long as it is well framed and structured, should prevail over a systematised and rigid technique. Therefore, it is necessary to investigate if legitimate alternatives, in terms of legal reasoning, on how to supervise the balancing of fundamental labour rights with other constitutional interests and principles exist, bearing in mind the urgency to enforce fundamental labour rights and comply with the values of a social constitution.

Even though the rights and principles tackled and discussed by the courts do not perfectly coincide, the judgments inspire the same questions: to what extent and under what type of arguments can fundamental labour rights be limited by the legislator in the context of an economic crisis? And, what role is left to the constitutional court?

I claim that the assessment of the fundamental labour rights' enforcement by constitutional courts cannot avoid an accurate understanding of the techniques employed by the same courts to decide the case, since the two profiles inevitably interact. As a consequence, the book wants to represent a step towards a paramount reconciliation between constitutional and labour law in light of the necessity to guarantee a full enforcement of fundamental labour rights, independently from the economic arguments and the ever-changing labour-market policies.

For that reason, Chapter 1 addresses balancing as a method. It starts by introducing the concept of pluralist constitution and by reviewing the neo-constitutional theories that explain the relationship between fundamental rights and principles as a relationship between founding values that have been legally positivised. These principles and rights, which are expression of values, are absolute, in abstract terms, but they may enter into conflict in the legislative practice, if the implementation of a fundamental right risks violating another – conflicting – constitutional right and can only be solved through the balancing exercise. The key profiles of this method, such as the balancing actors and the proportionality principle theories are addressed, with an eye to both the international and the Italian and Spanish literature, so as to capture the main theoretical arguments around the key features of the legal reasoning conducted by the Italian and Spanish Constitutional Courts and build a solid basis, well rooted in the national judicial traditions and legal dogmatics, for the analysis of the relevant post-crisis judgments. Notwithstanding the authoritative critiques to the balancing method, the analysis of the case law carried out in the following chapters is, indeed, based upon the assumption that balancing is necessary to solve conflicts axiologically grounded. Before concluding by introducing the social state theory, which clarifies the lenses used in the assessment of the constitutional judgments conducted in the following sections, Chapter 1 reflects on the essential content criterion and on its relationship with balancing.

Chapter 2 focuses on balancing techniques, with a view to identifying and discussing the hermeneutic tools applied by constitutional courts to conduct the judicial balancing. Beyond any doubt, the proportionality test is the most widespread technique. Its application by both the Court of Justice of the EU (CJEU) and European Court of Human Rights (ECtHR) is addressed, mostly from a labour rights perspective. The proportionality adjudication in supranational courts provides food for thought as far as concerns the main features of proportionality, making evident its flexible character. But, most of all, if the assumptions of legal dogmatics reviewed in Chapter 1 hold true, whether constitutional balancing can be conducted in a supranational legal order such as the EU must be seriously questioned, precisely because it is questionable whether the latter constitutes a proper "constitutional" system. This sort of scepticism surely does not arise as regards the Italian and Spanish legal systems, which offer remarkable insights into, respectively, the principle of reasonableness and the proportionality test, *i.e.* the hermeneutic criteria invoked by the courts to scrutinise norms allegedly infringing upon fundamental (also labour) rights. The chapter concludes with some considerations about the use of financial and economic arguments in the constitutional case law, particularly focusing on the principle of balanced budget and the economic crisis argument.

Chapter 3, first, provides an overview of the contested measures in both the Italian and the Spanish case law and, with introductory purposes, briefly traces the judgments' conclusions, second, reflects on the fundamental labour rights concerned and on the contribution given by the post-crisis case law in defining their scope and content. The Italian judgments can be divided into three clusters. Judgment 223/2012, Judgment 178/2015 and Judgment 124/2017 concern the reduction of public employees' wages; Judgment 70/2015, Judgment 173/2016 and Judgment 250/2017 regard the reduction of the revaluation of retirement benefits; Judgment 194/2018 has addressed a precise element of the 2015 reform on unjustified dismissal. Only two Spanish judgments are relevant for our discourse, Judgment 119/2014 and Judgment 8/2015; nonetheless they deal with numerous norms of Royal Decree Law 3/2012, approved with the purported aim to promote companies' flexibility and employment in a context of serious economic crisis. This chapter aims to contribute to the discussion around the status of fundamental labour rights under a crisis without providing conclusive answers in that respect, being aware that any attempt to ultimately define such status without a careful assessment of the development such rights have undergone over the years, in the respective legal contexts, would be inaccurate and misleading. The right to work and the right to collective bargaining are concerned by both the Italian and the Spanish post-crisis case law, whereas the right to a sufficient and proportionate remuneration and the principle of adequacy of pensions are peculiar to the Italian post-crisis case law.

The framework provided in Chapter 3 is paramount to appreciate the analysis conducted in Chapter 4, which studies the Italian and Spanish constitutional post-crisis case law from three profiles: first, the role of the court; second, the technique adopted; third, the constitutional interests balanced against fundamental labour rights. The analysis of the two streams of judgments follows the same structure. Indeed, even though the book does not attempt to compare the two cases in a rigorous way, given that the units of analysis are too complex for allowing a proper comparison, structuring the analysis by focusing on the same elements is functional to emphasise similarities and differences and develop a joint reflection. In the post-crisis case law assessed, the Italian Court performs the role of supervisor of the balancing conducted by the legislator. However, a considerable exception is represented by Judgment 178/2015, where the Court actively balances the right to collective bargaining against the public financial interest, in light of the reformed Art. 81 IC, with a ruling of supervening unconstitutionality. The Court strongly and consistently relies on the principle of reasonableness, which is understood as the hermeneutic principle to be applied jointly with the fundamental – labour – rights at issue. Only some of the challenged norms pass the scrutiny of the Italian Court; those are the cases in which the financial arguments advanced by the legislator prevail over a full enforcement of fundamental labour rights. The two Spanish judgments are coherent under various profiles. In both cases, the Court recognises a wide margin of freedom to the legislator and stresses its extensive discretional power. Consistently with its recent trend, the Spanish Constitutional Court refrains from scrutinising the norms under a rigorous proportionality test. While in Judgment 119/2014 the proportionality test criteria are not even mentioned, in Judgment 8/2015, the three sub-tests are only formally invoked. None of the norms of Law 3/2012 scrutinised by the Spanish Court is found constitutionally illegitimate and the fundamental labour rights concerned are not properly valued. The Court mostly argues that the contested provisions are justified on the grounds of other constitutional norms, such as the freedom to conduct a business (Art. 38 SC) and, especially, the public authority's duty to conduct a policy aimed at full employment (Art. 40 SC), which are the winners of the confused balancing exercise to the detriment of fundamental labour rights.

The concluding chapter concisely outlines the main theses supported in this book, by eventually emphasising those elements of the Italian and Spanish constitutional post-crisis case law that allow an understanding of the judgments which does not upset the nature of the respective constitutions and values the primacy of fundamental labour rights, axiologically grounded, over other factors that merely express a contingency.

1 Constitutional balancing of fundamental labour rights

1.1 Introduction

"Proportionality test" and/or "principle of proportionality", as well as "reasonableness" are frequently used with levity by labour law scholars. Equally, it is very rare to perceive a conscious use of the term "balancing", not only as far as concerns its application and the terms at play, but also as regards the institutional actor entitled to conduct the constitutional balancing.

Even the labour law perspective that addresses constitutional judgments, by focusing on the effective enforcement of fundamental labour rights, needs to approach the post-crisis (but not only) constitutional case law by taking seriously the analytical categories traditionally belonging to constitutional studies, in order to cleanse the analysis of the constitutional interpretation of fundamental labour rights of clichés and inaccuracies and increase the value of a perspective usually more prone to support the enforcement of fundamental labour rights and widen their scope.

This chapter starts by assessing constitutional balancing as a method to adjudicate fundamental rights and traces its theoretical justifications, which, drawing on neo-constitutional theories, are to be found in the axiological nature of fundamental rights that implies that constitutional balancing is possible only among rights/principles expression of values. Second, it emphasises the unquestioned axiological nature of fundamental labour rights. Third, the balancing of fundamental social rights, which poses specific problems, is addressed. In particular, the focus is on the relationship between the principle of proportionality and the essential content of such rights, as well as on the relationship between fundamental social security rights and public spending constraints. The concluding paragraph traces the main elements of the social state theory, as the preferred lens of analysis, in order to introduce the perspective adopted in the assessment of the constitutional case law.

DOI: 10.4324/9781003155362-2

1.2 Constitutional balancing as a *method* and its theoretical justifications

The increasing compression of constitutional labour rights requires a reflection upon the role that constitutional balancing and hermeneutic principles – as those applied in the Italian and Spanish cases – have, or may have, to constrain this tendency and foster the dialogue between written norms and their context, through a "solid awareness of the purposes and a fine argumentative technique".[1]

It has been argued that, differently from the legal reasoning that applies in the domain of ordinary law, where balancing is used only to found the premises of the decision, in constitutional adjudication it constitutes "the form of the decisions, which consists of either a judgment of prevalence between different principles, which are in conflict in the concrete case, or a judgment of coexistence and competition (*concorrenza*), where there is reciprocal limitation".[2]

The assessment of the balancing of conflicting rights, principles or interests in the two national legal systems selected needs to be introduced by a discussion on the legal theoretical debates on modern constitutionalism and fundamental rights. In this respect, it shall be acknowledged that the balancing of fundamental rights and principles is a judicial *method* deemed essential by neo-constitutional theories. Neo-constitutionalism has various shades and grades, and this concise review does not go into detail about the diverse and articulated neo-constitutionalisms; only the key points of the theory are traced.[3]

One of the core aspects of neo-constitutional theories is the relevance recognised, in constitutional legal systems, to constitutional *principles*, which are firmly distinguished from *rules*.

Certainly, in several legal systems, the application of general principles represents an efficient way to adapt rights to the changing economic and social context; in this sense, the combination of rules and principles constitutes a key feature of modern constitutional states.[4] In the principles' cluster, *fundamental* – or *constitutional* – *principles*, that affect any branch of ordinary law, retain a prestigious position.[5]

If it is true that "only principles [and not rules] play a proper constitutional role, which is 'constitutive' of the constitutional system", the centrality of constitutional principles can hardly be questioned.[6] In modern constitutions, as in the Italian and Spanish ones, fundamental rights are formally expressed by norms, but they retain the structure of and act as principles, inasmuch as they express a preference

1 Mengoni 1986, 165–178, my translation.
2 Mengoni 1996a, 122, my translation.
3 On the distinction between "neo-constitutionlism" and "neo-constitutionalisms", see Ratti 2015.
4 Loi 2016, 169; see also the review on neo-constitutional theories by Ratti 2015.
5 Chiassoni 2015, 52.
6 Zagrebelsky 1992, 148, my translation.

for protecting certain interests over others.[7] Hence, constitutional principles make values enforceable and underpin rights and interests that are constitutionally protected,[8] and if principles realise values, rules realise principles.[9]

Various theories have been developed in order to justify and frame the distinction between principles and rules, which is further complicated by the terrific debates around the very concept of principle, where the only uncontroversial feature seems to be its indeterminacy.

The main distinction between rules and principles can be identified in the different jurisprudential treatment the two concepts undergo. Indeed, only rules are interpreted through methods and general clauses, which assess the wording of the legislative act, while in the case of principles "there is not much to be interpreted", given that their lexical meaning is plain.[10]

Rather than being interpreted, principles shall be understood in terms of the values they express. While we must obey rules, we adhere to principles, hence there is a necessity to understand the set of values to which they belong.[11]

The *value* is a pre-legal concept that becomes legal – is *positivizzato* – once it is incorporated in a principle or in a fundamental right.[12] Fundamental principles and rights are norms, albeit weaker norms, which need to be recognised and enforced.[13] No need to specify that the norm in a strict sense is a "strong" legislative requirement, which demands obedience.

Under the neo-constitutional perspective, the circumstance that a difference between rules and principles exists does not mean that principles are ancillary to rules and only have an integrating function in the legal system – as a positivistic

7 See Bin 1992, 1–8; Pino 2009. On fundamental rights theories, see also Cruz Villalón 1989; Fernández Segado 1993.

8 Modugno 2007, 33.

9 "[L]as reglas son formas de realizar los principios y los principios son formas de realizar un valor", Preciado Domènech 2016, 84, my translation. The author widely refers to Pérez-Luno 2017. The theory is also known as "teoría de la Constitución por valores", Ruggeri 2003, drawing on Baldassarre 1991.

10 Zagrebelsky 1992, 148, my translation.

11 However, a relationship between principles and interpretation seems to exist and to be bidirectional, so that principles are both functional to the interpretation and deriving from the hermeneutic activity, see Loi 2016, 168.

12 Values are "freezed" in constitutional principles, according to Bin 2007, 31.

13 For instance, the value of *freedom* is legally expressed in a series of fundamental rights, see Mengoni 1993, 257 and Mengoni 1996b, 56, where the scholar adopts the expression "meta-legal values" to identify superior parameters to control the legitimacy of ordinary law; the same expression is employed by the Italian Supreme Court of Cassation, that declares that fundamental principles have a "contenuto assiologico di metavalore" (Suprema Corte di Cassazione, Sezioni Unite Civili, n.14201/2008), as emphasised by Lipari 2010, 635, 638. Also Zagrebelsky 1992, 147, 149; and Zagrebelsky 2008, 210, where he clarifies the distinction between rule and principle, on the grounds that the first is a norm with closed antecedent, which clearly identifies the facts that trigger the application of the norm, while the principle is a norm with open antecedent, hence the norm does not make the triggering facts explicit.

approach would support.[14] To the contrary, principles have a direct impact on reality and are able to shed a normative light over the factual case, so that "each principle underpins the imperative: 'you will take a stand on reality, on the grounds of what I am stating'".[15]

Dworkin, one of the pioneers of the neo-constitutional approach, claims that a rule is a norm that sets a goal, while a principle does not entail the achievement of a specific aim, but it can influence the final decision depending on the weight the judge assigns it. In practice, if two rules are in conflict, one of them is simply not valid, since the rule has an absolute weight. To the contrary, if two principles are in conflict, both are still valid and the weight of one principle has to be decided in relation to the other, for this reason they can (must) be applied by the judge in the most controversial cases.[16]

Drawing on Dworkin's theory, Alexy articulates that, while a rule is a norm that can be simply complied with or not, as definitive command (***definitive Gebote***), a principle represents an ***optimisation requirement*** (***Optimisierungsgebote***), which is in a structural and indissoluble relationship with values, inasmuch as a judgment based on principles entails a reference to values, whether explicit or implicit. Under the optimisation theory, norms require "that something be realized to the greatest extent possible, given the factual and legal possibilities at hand".[17] Principles can only be applied in relation to the judicial and factual possibilities of the legal system, in the sense that the enforcement of a principle requires an assessment of both the concrete case at stake and the legal possibilities (that is other principles and rules). Therefore, a conflict of principles is inherent in a constitutional system providing for fundamental principles and it can be solved by taking into account each relative weight, hence, by balancing the relevant principles. As a result of this rational process, no principle is declared inapplicable (as it would happen in case of conflict of rules), but simply slightly recessive compared to the other, nor is an absolute prevalence of a principle over the other established.[18] Where values compete against one other, they cannot be jointly maximised and we have to resort to a "balanced maximalisation".[19]

14 Nor does the neo-constitutionalism correspond to natural law; besides Zagrebelsky 1992, see the accurate distinction made by Mauro Barberis on the various philosophies of law, *inter alia*, neo-constitutionalism and natural law: Barberis 2011. On legal positivism, one for all, Bobbio 1997.

15 Zagrebelsky 1992, 163, my translation. Lipari 2016, 31, goes further and, with a view of overcoming the positivistic approach, argues that "principles not only play an interpretative or integrative role, but they have an autonomous normative role", my translation; on the other hand, constitutional norms constitute direct sources of law also in civil law disputes, Camardi 2017.

16 Dworkin 1967, 22 ff.

17 Alexy 2010b, 21.

18 Alexy 2000 and, most recently, 2021. Although Alexy's theories on principles and rights are widespread and extensively accepted, they do not fail to raise controversies; see, *inter alia*, Ramião 2018.

19 Sartor 2010, 176.

Under this view, the constitutional court has a pervasive role in the continuous construction of the legal system. On the grounds of Dworkin and Alexy's theories, Luigi Mengoni similarly advocates for the application of constitutional balancing.[20] According to the Italian scholar, the normative structures expressing values – that is both hermeneutic principles, as the principle of equality, and fundamental rights – differ from the traditional legal norms, especially in their application, which occurs through the balancing of "corresponding goods and interests". Therefore, it is up to the judge to conduct a scrutiny, which puts in an equality order the concurring values (*giudizio di equiordinzione*).[21] Indeed, the balancing of principles requires a theory that circumscribes rigorously the discretional power of the judge and avoids the "apparent collisions", which, according to the author, are the result of the introduction of extraneous ideological factors. The "apparent collision" is not the direct outcome of the application of the balancing method, but it rather stems from a weak analysis of the normative scope of application of fundamental rights and principles, which should consist in the first phase of this type of constitutional judgment, in order to detect when a real collision occurs.[22]

The protection of several and diverse interests by the Italian and Spanish Constitutions makes the balancing of conflicting principles – and respective rights or interests – a crucial moment of the constitutional judgment in both legal systems addressed in this dissertation. Indeed, "[T]he constitutional judgment rather consists in the identification of the relevant constitutional principles and their balancing, in order to evaluate the compatibility of the ordinary norm under scrutiny, with those principles".[23] In this sense, balancing guarantees that each value expressed by each principle is protected and enforced at least to a minimum extent.[24]

Most of the continental constitutions, differently from the constitutions of the 19th century, have embedded the conflict of values, rather than providing a solution. In other words, they do not freeze the conflicts among interests by determining a definitive point of equilibrium; thereby they qualify as *pluralist* constitutions, which is the feature that makes modern constitutions able to face the social complexities of modern societies.[25]

An absolute hierarchy of principles would contradict the very nature of a *principle*, which is the legal expression of a value and, hence, does not accept to be classified, considering that a value cannot be considered higher than any other. "As *in abstract* principles are never logically incompatible, *in abstract* it is not

20 Mengoni 1993 and Mengoni 1992.
21 See also Pino 2008, 134 ff., who holds that the scrutiny over fundamental principles and rights shall be based upon the application of the proportionality criterion.
22 Mengoni 1993 and Mengoni 1992.
23 Modugno 2008, 229, my translation.
24 Modugno 2008, 250.
25 Bin 2007, 23–24, who refers to the Italian Constitution, but the same easily applies to the other continental constitutions, first of all the Spanish Constitution.

possible to establish an order of preference",[26] differently from the norms in a strict sense, which can be organised hierarchically. The political character of the constitution implies that its provisions cannot be translated into neutral concepts responding to a pre-ordered scale of values (*concetti assiologicamente neutrali*). Indeed, the relationship between the person and the society/state cannot be predetermined in light of a static hierarchy of values.[27]

At the same time, principles *per se* are not absolute either, since "a right is relative whenever the extent of its protection is narrower than its entire scope",[28] meaning that the potential scope of a right, or principle, is more extended than what is legally protected when such right, or principle, comes into conflict with another right of equal value.

1.2.1 Against constitutional balancing

This work assumes the neo-constitutional distinction between rules and principles, as well as the axiological nature of principles as the correct premises and, consequently, adheres to the theory that balancing is the appropriate method to adjudicate fundamental rights. Nonetheless, it is noteworthy to acknowledge the existence of diverse, thoughtful and influential theses that contest the theoretical framework designed above.

Among those arguing against an assimilation of values and rights or principles, crucial is the contribution by Jurgen Habermas, who denies the rationality and, hence, the applicability of balancing altogether. The distinction between values and rights/principles is supported by the argument that once a value is translated into a norm – that is a principle – its meaning changes, by acquiring a legal significance. In a nutshell, Habermas identifies four core distinctions. First, norms show the correct behaviour, while values simply recommend the most suitable behaviour. Second, norms can only be either valid or not valid, while values establish preference relationships. Third, principles are universally binding, while values provide for a general estimation of what is good for the society. Last, and crucial, while norms can never contradict each other and shall be coherent to frame the legal system, values are in a constant struggle to prevail.[29]

The renowned philosopher advocates for a more limited role of the judicial constitutional body, which should be confined to grant the proper functioning of the democratic mechanisms.[30] As with Alexy, Habermas also grounds his reflec-

26 Bin 1992, 33, my translation, italics in the original text.

27 Mengoni 1996a, 122–123.

28 Barak 2012, 32. The author accepts the existence of a limited number of "absolute rights", as rare exceptions, for instance the right to human dignity enshrined in the German Constitution, 27 ss. On the specificity of the principle of human dignity, see also Bäcker 2021. On the possibility to admit that certain rights are absolute and cannot be subject to balancing adjudication see also Sieckmann 2021, 113–125.

29 Habermas 1996, 243 ff.

30 Habermas 1996.

tion upon the German constitutional case law, but differently from his colleague, he criticises the role of the court as interpreter of constitutional values. In his opinion, given that principles, as norms, are not optimisable and cannot be balanced but have to be entirely applied, empowering the court with such faculty causes an overlapping with the democratic decisions. Furthermore, he does not foresee any possibility to grant rationality in the application of the balancing technique, which he considers a subjective procedure,[31] with the result that a similar judicial approach undermines the solidity of constitutional rights, in favour of other legally recognised interests.[32]

Yet, Habermas agrees that principles, compared to rules, are undetermined norms, which, anyway, does not imply an incoherence of the overall legal system. Indeed, the principles' indeterminacy exclusively entails that legal argumentation is necessary, in order to understand which principle is applicable. In the end, only one norm (one principle) can be valid, in relation to the factual case, and applicable to the case at stake.[33]

Further criticism has been moved towards the neo-constitutional approach by a number of authors. Among them, Luigi Ferrajoli, in a remarkable essay, elaborates a critique of both the neo-constitutional distinction between rules and principles, and the respective theory on constitutional balancing. Ferrajoli claims that the sharp differentiation between rules and principles does not reflect a structural feature of the constitutional system, but it is rather a mere stylistic choice, which, however, has a notable practical effect: it weakens the normative power of principles, that is fundamental rights. The scholar proposes an alternative distinction, between *principi direttivi* (that provide for general guidelines) and *principi regolativi* (which content is imperative), with the result that a constitutional norm can either express a *principio regolativo* or a *principio direttivo*, but also both of them, in the sense that it can be *regolativo* as to the *an* and *direttivo* as to the *quomodo* (*e.g.* Art. 38.1 IC). "Behind every rule there is a principle",[34] and the *principi regolativi*, if violated, act as rules.[35]

As a consequence, the appropriateness of balancing adjudication, as conducted by the constitutional courts, is also put into question. In this respect, he openly opposes what he calls *costituzionalismo principialista* to *costituzionalismo garantista*. Ferrajoli introduces its argument in favour of *costituzionalismo garantista* by sharply distinguishing between judicial balancing and legislative balancing. The balancing conducted in the law-making process is welcomed, albeit only between *principi direttivi*, and the same is true when fundamental social rights that include both types of principles come into question, so that the full application of the *principi regolativi* expressed therein cannot be put into question

31 Habermas 1996, 303 ff.
32 Haberma 1996, 254.
33 Habermas 258 ff.
34 Ferrajoli 2010, 2799.
35 Ferrajoli 2010, 2794–2805.

(see again the example of Art. 38 IC). This is necessary because fundamental rights mutually reinforce each other, so that if social rights are not guaranteed, liberty rights cannot be properly exercised and, as a consequence, also political rights remain unenforced. Different is the case of judicial balancing. Indeed, the *costituzionalismo garantista* understands the judicial power as tightly limited by the law and the constitution, and requires the court to balance exclusively factual circumstances and not also the norms, of any kind.

The author advocates for the *costituzionlismo principialista*, insofar as constitutional balancing must be conducted on a factual case-by-case basis; factual circumstances, not principles, are subject to the balancing exercise, given that principles, in Ferrajoli's view, have an absolute and not relative weight and therefore cannot be sacrificed, neither partially, nor occasionally. If this were to happen, the constitution would be dis-applied and the legislator authorised to exercise its power in conflict with the primary source, thus overly widening the court's discretion and, hence, raising controversies over a political role of the constitutional court. In light of the constitutional judicial tradition, judicial balancing seems to be slightly more than a new word to call the old "'systematic interpretation' [...] which consists of the interpretation of the meaning of a norm in light of all other norms of the legal system";[36] on this ground the scholar criticises what he considers to be an excessive emphasis on the idea of judicial balancing that has become a "terminological bubble".[37]

1.2.2 The balancing actors

Even from a perspective that accepts constitutional balancing as the most appropriate method to solve value-based conflicts in pluralist systems, the issues raised by Ferrajoli as regards the moment in which constitutional balancing is conducted and, hence, the entitled public power are noteworthy and deserve to be explored.

In a recent publication, Roberto Bin discusses a number of profiles around the understanding and enforcement of rights. Among the various matters addressed, theconstitutional lawyer devotes a chapter to answer a question, which is a crucial precondition to analyse the balancing method: whose job is it to balance rights?

The concise reflection helps to clarify an aspect that, so far, has not been explicitly addressed by the traditional academic literature on balancing, even though it is of paramount importance to evaluate both the legal reasoning of a constitutional court and whether the court remains within its constitutional competence, or it trespasses on the political domain, pertaining to the legislative power (even Roberto Bin himself, in his popular book on balancing published in 1992, did not make this element clear). The main argument cannot be misunderstood, as it is reiterated clearly several times: "it is up to the legislator to set the balancing

36 Ferrajoli 2010, 2809, my translation.
37 Ferrajoli 2010, 2806–2815, my translation.

terms"[38] and "reconcile different interests".[39] The balancing is conducted by the legislator in abstract terms, the same legislator sets the (material) point of equilibrium in ordinary laws, according to its political vision. The constitutional court may be called upon "to verify if the balancing that the legislator has translated into legal terms remains within the tolerance limits".[40] Indeed, national constitutional courts do deal with the balancing of interests to verify their constitutional consistency, but they do not directly conduct the balancing, since in a proper constitutional judicial balancing, the balancing conducted by the legislator is the object of the constitutional legal reasoning.[41]

In a certain sense, balancing can be understood as a competence of three different subjects. First, the constitution itself, where the constitutional norm already provides indications on the fair balance; second, the legislator; third, courts, mostly constitutional courts (which is the profile addressed in this book), who can either balance directly conflicting principles, or conduct a "second level" balancing by which they review the balancing designed in an ordinary norm,[42] by applying specific techniques, such as the principle of proportionality or the principle of reasonableness.

This distinction overcomes the risk that balancing may become just a "terminological bubble", as, in fact, something like "judicial balancing", strictly speaking, does not exist under neo-constitutional terms, but it must be understood as a terminological abbreviation of *supervision from the judiciary of the balancing conducted by the legislator*,[43] which becomes *constitutional balancing* if the responsible body is a constitutional court. In addition, the terms that can be subject to such an interpretative method are not just all principles written in a constitutional text, but also principles that express values and contribute to composing a pluralist legal system.

Adhering to the suitability of judicial balancing to adjudicate fundamental rights implies sharing the understanding of such rights as expression of founding values. And vice versa, understanding principles, such as fundamental rights, in terms of values necessitates balancing adjudication. Therefore, the following section is devoted to illustrating the axiological nature of fundamental labour rights, in order to justify – and explain – the application of balancing to this domain.

1.2.3 *The axiological nature of fundamental labour rights*

Social rights are rights intended to allow a full integration of the individual into a society and realise substantial equality for all; labour rights contribute to

38 Bin 2018, 28, my translation.
39 Bin 2018, 52, my translation.
40 Bin 2018, 54, my translation.
41 Bin 2018, 55.
42 Pino 2014, n.p.
43 This is the meaning given to "judicial balancing", when it is used over the course of this book.

achieving this goal by covering the necessities connected to the employment status. Both become "fundamental" once they are enshrined in charters with a constitutional nature.[44] Adopting a broad definition, fundamental labour rights can be understood as rights aimed at protecting workers, either during working life or after retirement. Under this view, they include both fundamental social security rights, ontologically conditioned by economic resources, and labour liberty rights, which cannot be conditioned by an alleged economic sustainability, in relation to the community or to a single company.[45]

Consistently, fundamental labour rights are traditionally included in the fundamental social rights cluster.[46]

Social rights are (post-)modern rights: their recognition belongs to the late era of modern constitutions, adopted after the Second World War, and are the result of a process of affirmation that overcame the bourgeois constitutions, unhinging the conception of a legal system as the ideal framework for the exaltation of personal liberties, through the recognition (and promotion) of property rights.[47]

Modern constitutions, originally founded only upon liberty rights, normatively endorsed social rights as a consequence of the acknowledgement of equality as an essential value of modern societies and, nonetheless, compatible with the value of liberty.[48] And if the principle of equality does not correspond to egalitarianism, since inequalities characterise the individuals, the advent of the principle of equality and the urgency to solve the social question it carried along could not simply entail the levelling of property rights; instead, it

44 This definitional note exclusively aims to clarify the scope of the discourse articulated in this book. We do not dare to enter the theoretical debate on the relationship between human rights and the law. For a first encounter with the theme, see the paramount work by Amartya Sen, *e.g.* Sen 2006. The debate is massive, also when it comes to social right and labour rights; for instance, King 2012, 20 ff., plainly considers social rights as human rights; on the controversies over "labour rights as human rights", see the critical review by Mantouvalou 2012. An interesting reading of the relationship between labour rights and human rights has been offered lately by Dawkins 2022.

45 An alternative taxonomy is provided by Ales 2015, who distinguishes social rights, which include the right to work, the right to pension and social assistance, the right to housing, etc., from labour liberty rights, which do not imply any financial burden on the state.

46 One for all, Baldassarre 1989. Even though "social rights and labour rights have an history in common, but not the same history", Bavaro 2018, 244.

47 The codifications of the 19th century were notoriously bourgeois, *inter alia*, Speziale 2022, 122. Modern constitutionalism was founded upon liberty as a way to overcome authority, both in the public and private sphere, see Laforgia 2018, particularly 16 and 19. Not even the Weimar Constitution, which introduced the legal recognition of workers' organisations, industrial action and arbitration, at a very early stage compared to other legal systems, provided for fundamental social rights with binding legal content (Bongiovanni 2001, 79 and Contiades Fotiadou 2012, 664); on this unique constitutional experience see, *inter alia*, Dukes 2014, 33–45. On the history of rights, you might want to read the brilliant reconstruction by Rodotà 2011.

48 Amongst the many, Laforgia 2018, 20–23, and bibliography cited. For an insightful review of the Italian academic debate around fundamental social rights, see Caretti Tarli Barbieri 2017, 504.

must consist in "offering possibilities otherwise precluded",[49] thus in recognising a competence and a duty upon the legislator to adopt social reforms, not exclusively aimed to guarantee the provision of services, but, most importantly, aimed to create the most favourable conditions for the expression of everyone's personality, in individual and collective terms.[50] Consistently, the constitutions adopted in the aftermath of the Second World War, albeit rejecting the approaches taken by the totalitarian regimes of the first half of the 20th century, still adopt the view that the economic sphere must be regulated by politics (in its highest sense).[51]

The path towards a constitutional recognition and a full legal status of social rights has been obstructed by a number of arguments, related to the difficulties in identifying the accountable actors, the doubts over the justiciability of those rights,[52] the concerns over the political role that would have been allegedly recognised to the court responsible for adjudicating social rights.[53]

Different arguments prevailed and were eventually expressed in all modern constitutions, so that social rights are now enshrined in fundamental principles, which are understood as norms with full legal status, and a programmatic character, that are deemed to direct the political action.[54]

As a result, social rights became "a decisive part of the axiological horizon enshrined in the Constitution".[55]

Theoretically, the distinction between first-generation and second-generation rights, which included political and civil rights in the first cluster and social and

49 Costa 1997, 294, drawing on the theories developed by Lorenz Stein, between 1841 and 1850, who advocated for the overcoming of the conflict between capital and labour through a positive collaboration between state and society, expressed at its best by the adoption of social reforms and the improvement of working and social conditions, which is possible as long as capitalists accept a containment of their profit expansion, in exchange for social peace. A visionary theory that, in the end, prevailed over an equally visionary theory, that of the full control of the means of production by the public power led by the proletariat, envisaged by Karl Marx and Friedrich Engels, in the same years.

50 It has to do with a qualitative understanding of the social rights, see Longo 2017, 222.

51 It is the attempt to reconduct "l'economico all'interno del politico", Zagrebelsky 1992, 136.

52 For an introduction on the justiciability of social rights see Langford 2008; Saura Estapà 2011 and Aa. Vv. 2010. Cf. also Rey Pérez 2007.

53 Which are also the arguments that have been raised during the Italian Constitutional Assembly by those who were supporting the inclusion of social rights in a programmatic preamble to the Constitution, instead of in constitutional norms, Bongiovanni 2001, 79.

54 A full recognition of social rights does not undermine the role of economic rights in constitutional texts that hold pluralist societies, see the comprehensive assessment by Jung et al. 2014. On the crucial role and value of constitutional social rights, see Ferrajoli 2001.

55 Bongiovanni 2001, 81. Bongiovanni's proposition was made with regard to the Italian Constitution, but is applicable to all modern constitutions that provide for a catalogue of fundamental social rights. On the qualification of social rights as fundamental rights see also Prieto Sanchís 2016. To take a leap forward in time, we may move to the perspective of fundamental labour rights as a key component of the global constitutionalism, for a reflection see Fudge 2015.

economic rights in the second, has been overcome.[56] Exemplar is the Charter of Fundamental Rights of the European Union (the Charter), adopted in 2000 and reviewed in 2007, that disregards the traditional categorisation in favour of a taxonomy based on core values: dignity, freedom, equality and solidarity.[57] Among legal scholars, the understanding is now shared that civil and liberty rights also necessitate an active engagement of the state to be fully enforced, which includes public spending.[58] Furthermore, by endorsing an integrated interpretation of fundamental rights, social rights may be even understood as necessary preconditions to the effective enjoyment of liberty rights.[59] On the other hand, it is recognised that, in practice, economic downturns primarily damage social rights, thus creating a hierarchy *de facto*.[60]

This does not undermine the assumption that social rights express the values that uphold democratic systems.[61]

Above all, fundamental social rights enshrined in modern constitutions represent the normative expression of the core value of solidarity[62] and the labour principle, as articulated in the relevant fundamental labour rights, is the concretisation of solidarity at the economic and social level.[63] But fundamental labour rights are also the normative expression of "justice, liberty, equality", whose enforcement ultimately guarantees "human dignity".[64] Such values are eventually translated

56 On the compatibility of social rights with political and civil rights, in terms of structure and scope, see Pino 2016.

57 Schiek 2017, 627.

58 "Very few rights are inexpensive, especially in the complex contemporary socio-political systems": Ruiz Miguel 1994, 660, my translation.

59 See the discussion reviewed by Bongiovanni 2001.

60 As demonstrated by the 2008 crisis, Longo 2017, 207–208 and bibliography cited.

61 Baldassarre 1989, 7.

62 Caretti Tarli Barbieri 2017, 503; also Sciarra 2019, 266; solidarity "evokes an ancient concept, a primeval moral feeling of empathy, coessential to the intrinsic sociality of mankind and, therefore, to the same idea of law and social and legal order", Giubboni 2022, 18, according to whom the value of solidarity, consecrated in Art. 2 IC, on the wave of Art. 1 IC, represents the cement of all fundamental principles entrenched in the Italian Constitution, 33.

63 Bongiovanni 2001, 78; the concept of solidarity was first brought to the fore in the ascending phase of the conflict between capital and labour by Pierre Leroux in 1840, see Costa 1997. On the value of labour in modern Constitutions, cf. the latest book by Ruth Dukes, where the author reflects on the meaning of "labour constitution" in current times and in the EU context, drawing on Sinzheimer's and Kahn-Freund's theories about the economic constitution as a way "to meet the need for the organisation of economic life, to put to an end to the anarchy of so-called 'economic freedom', and to ensure that the economy was run so as to fulfil social ends", Dukes 2014, 18. For national insights: on fundamental labour rights in the Italian Constitution, cf. Gaeta 2003; on fundamental labour rights in the Spanish Constitution, Palomeque López 1991.

64 Perulli 2018, 697. "Human dignity" found a formal constitutional acknowledgment with the Basic Law for the Federal Republic of Germany (1949); its endorsement in Art. 1 of the Charter has surely promoted its conceptual autonomy, at least in the theoretical debate, nev-

into labour law, *i.e.* a systematic corpus of ordinary norms able to provide them with a concrete character.[65]

Fundamental labour rights, which, traditionally, stand in defence of those norms protecting the weak part of the employment relationship that form labour law,[66] express a certain understanding of the human being. The human being around which labour law develops is concrete and immersed in the reality of power relations, where he normally has a dependent status.[67]

But if we look back at the origins of values, we must wonder on what grounds they are selected by a society.[68] In other words, drawing on Sinzheimer, how the understanding of the human being changes over time and what forces drive this change.

Values, even before rights,[69] need a social conflict[70] to be affirmed and gain the socio-political consent that allows them to achieve a constitutional status.[71] First

ertheless it remains an extremely controversial notion. As regards the debate on the essential content, see also chapter 1, para. 4.

65 Perulli 2018, 696. Definitely, values justify labour law while, in the meantime, guide its development. Del Punta argued that they can be considered either valid *per se* or valid as long as they are, simply, actualised or, more radically, reinterpreted, Del Punta 2022c, 24; the author was inclined to prefer a reinterpretation of the traditional axiological foundation of labour law, mainly relying on the approach of capabilities, which draws on Amartya Sen's theories. Other leading scholars constantly question themselves and the whole labour law community around the most feasible, and successful, perspectives for labour law, just to quote some: Supiot Meadows 2001; Davidov Langille 2011; Rogowski 2013; Davidov 2016; Caruso et al. 2020; Perulli Speziale 2022.

66 Labour law is a rationaliser of the asymmetries of power created by the market, Perulli Speziale 2022, 79. One of the first scholars who has discussed the possibility to extend the protective norms beyond the classical dichotomy strong (employer) and weak (employee) part of the employment contract, *i.e.* to self-employed workers, is Lyon-Caen 1991.

67 These thoughts are based on a lecture given by Hugo Sinzheimer in 1932, recently translated into Italian by Luca Nogler. Sinzheimer's theses, however, were built around ordinary branches of law (civil law, labour law and the law of economics); indeed his analysis, for obvious historical reasons, could not be based on fundamental rights as understood in relation to the constitutional texts adopted after the Second World War. Precisely, he divided the status of dependency into material dependency; collective dependency; personal dependency (Sinzheimer 2022, 47). Similarly, Bogg 2017, 16, differentiates labour law from private law, as the first "has generally been conceived in more functional terms". On the *abstract* character of the individual addressed by liberal constitutions, which is overcome in post-war constitutions, see Laforgia 2018, 20 and 27–30.

68 Pennacchi 2018, 70, 71, assimilates "values" to "preferences" and "tastes". Mengoni 1996b, 75–81, without assigning a pervasive relevance to history in relation to values, still observes that the axiological awareness is conditioned by the passage of time.

69 Longo 2017, 226.

70 Or "Rivendicazione umana" – to borrow the expression used by Sinzheimer in 1932 – which follows a change in power relations and affirms what the leading German scholar identified as a new conception of the human being (Sinzheimer 2022, 53, translated into Italian by Luca Nogler). Also, Rodotà 2012, 56, and Baccelli 2014.

71 The normative legitimacy of values stems from the socio-political consent crystallised in the constitutional pact, Grandi 2006, 362. On perspectives of constructive social conflict in the near future, Baccelli 2014.

were the bourgeois values of liberty and property,[72] claimed by the respective social class. Then it was the turn of that set of values that can be summarised with the whole-comprehensive concept of social values, which established themselves following social unrest and collective claims. It is now time for environmental movements that are bringing to the forefront the value of environmental sustainability, in an attempt to shift the paradigm from economic growth, to (no less than!) survival of the human species.[73] It is only at a second stage, when values are widely recognised by the society, that the lawyer and the legislator intervene and transform those values into norms, which take the primary form of fundamental principles.[74]

The path towards labour law is no exception: it starts from an exemplary social conflict between capital and labour which affirms the social ("socialist" one would have said in the early 19th century) values in modern societies, which is progressively enshrined into positive norms and, once deeply rooted and fully recognised by the society, finally achieves the higher normative recognition through catalogues of fundamental labour rights embedded in constitutional texts.[75]

Although the discussion around the axiological dimension of labour law carries along infinitive controversial profiles,[76] which cannot be addressed here, this concise reflection still allows to conclude that, incontestably, fundamental labour rights constitute the legal expression of values. Therefore, the legal dogmatics arguments that underly and justify constitutional balancing naturally apply to adjudication of fundamental labour rights.

72 Which, ultimately, were endorsed by civil law norms: Sinzheimer 2022.

73 Where social and environmental values integrate with each other, as demonstrated by the growing scientific interest of labour lawyers towards issues that intersect the labour and the environmental perspective:

Transfer: European Review of Labour and Research first addressed this profile already in 1996 (2:3) and again in 2022 (28:3); see also Doorey 2017. In Italy, scientific reviews are showing growing interest in the topic among them, *Lavoro e Diritto*, with Issue n. 1/2022, *Giornale di Diritto del Lavoro e di Relazioni Industriali*, Issues 2, 3 and 4/2022, *Diritto delle Relazioni Industriali*, Issues 3 and 4/2022. Remarkably, with Constitutional Law 11 February 2022, n. 1, the Italian Parliament has approved an amendment to Art. 9 and Art. 41 of the Italian Constitution, to include the protection of the environment, also in the interest of future generations.

74 Not by chance, Pennacchi 2018, 9, in introducing her book on values in the post-neoliberal era emphasises the interdisciplinary approach that guides her reflection and calls into question "philosophy, economy, anthropology and sociology", but not law. Which does not contradict the rational character of values, see Grandi 2006, drawing on Luigi Mengoni's thesis.

75 This perspective is surely controversial, especially if, to justify the adoption of protective labour norms, the human rights argument is preferred. On this challenging debate, see Alston 2005, Mantovalou 2012 and Atkinson 2018.

76 The relevant academic discussion is tremendous; just to mention some of the thesis shared in the last decade: the insightful contributions in Collins et al. 2018; Bavaro 2018; Del Punta 2019; the remarkable essays in Del Punta 2022a. Not to mention that even whether labour is a value may be questioned, one for all: Russels 2017 (originally published in 1935).

To address the balancing of fundamental labour rights, from an axiological perspective, in relation to judgments that have scrutinised the legitimacy of norms approved in the aftermath of the 2008 crisis, is even more pregnant as these reforms respond to the highest moment of the neoliberal logic,[77] which entails an urgency to deal with values in labour law,[78] especially where they are eroded by the "law of the market", which "seeks to incorporate and define even the conditions for the recognition of rights".[79]

1.3 Balancing *technique(s)*

Assuming the argument that rights and principles are both expressions of values and have a relative character in their relationship with other rights and principles of an equal nature, it has been fairly argued that "[L]imitation clauses, and the principle of proportionality at their core, reflect the relativity of the right".[80]

The "principle of proportionality" has now become of common use in several legal orders. It is widely understood as the ideal, or even the sole, technique to conduct judicial constitutional balancing. The affirmation of this principle in courts all over the world is, indeed, a reality.[81] Even though numerous authors have confronted themselves with the assessment of proportionality, its theoretical construction is originally due to Robert Alexy, who has recently reiterated his thesis, according to which, first, "the rational application of constitutional rights necessarily presupposes proportionality analysis" and, second, "proportionality analysis can be rational only if it is embedded in a theory of legal argumentation".[82] This thesis is also expressed with the notion of "necessity connection" between constitutional rights and the principle of proportionality, as opposed to the "contingent connection", which understands the relationship between constitutional rights and proportionality as dependent on the intentions of the framers of a specific constitution.[83]

According to the "necessity connection" thesis, the test of proportionality can be explained as a simplification of a model of optimisation, which solves the conflict of principles by finding the optimal solution through the determination of the priority among normative arguments, through the application of a mathematic formula, also called the "Weight Formula".[84] In this adaptation of the

77 Del Punta 2022b, 8, refers to the post-2008 crisis as the "golden years of neo-liberalism".
78 Del Punta 2022c. Although is undeniable that "economic crisis" is the traditional companion of labour law, Palomeque López 2004.
79 Rodotà 2012, 94. On the impact of the increasing valorisation of economic aims on labour rights (and, hence, values), see Perulli 2018 and, along the same lines, Speziale 2022. Cf. also Del Punta 2019, 7–13, who identifies in the *social market economy* a possible answer to the turbulent relationship between labour and economic instances.
80 Barak 2012, 32.
81 On the principle of proportionality as *lingua franca* in constitutional law, see Chapter 2.
82 Alexy 2021, 1.
83 On the debate, see Alexy 2014 and Andrade Neto 2018.
84 Alexy 2021, 4.

Pareto-optimality formula "[A] solution is optimal if it results in a state of affairs where the conflicting arguments are considered to be of equal weight, that is, where one is indifferent between the respective gains and losses in the fulfilment of the conflicting requirements. Accordingly, there is no reason to change the situation and look for a better solution",[85] where it is not the position of persons to be weighted, but just the normative arguments.

Under this view, the application of the optimisation approach to judicial balancing – which is expressed in every sub-test of the proportionality test – is justified precisely by the nature of principles, which are optimisation commands.[86]

Alexy's thesis is not the sole theory on proportionality. Andrade Neto, drawing on the relevant constitutional literature, has identified three different theses, which "set out practical reasons for borrowing the proportionality test".[87]

According to Andrade Neto's classification of normative theses, Alexy is the initiator of the "necessity thesis" or "strong thesis", which understands proportionality as unavoidable in a constitutional system; other authors, like Andrade Neto himself, hold that proportionality is not endemic to whatever constitutional system, but it ought to be applied only if certain conditions occur (the moderate thesis); while those supporting the weak thesis argue that judges should use proportional adjudication because it enhances the effectiveness of fundamental rights.

The latest thesis deploys teleological arguments, as it considers proportionality the best technique to fulfil the social goal of given norms, which is justified on the grounds of its consequences and on a precise assumption of what is good. The strong thesis, as postulated by Alexy first, also known as "principle theory", draws on deontological arguments and holds that the application of proportionality is "conceptually necessary" in a system based upon fundamental rights, since there is a conceptual identity between rights and principles (identity thesis)[88] and every legally developed system is necessarily based upon fundamental principles (incorporation thesis).[89] Under this view, if principles, as seen above, are optimisation commands that need to be satisfied at the maximum possible extent, proportionality is the only possible tool to determine the correct degree of satisfaction, which implies that independently from the existence of a specific norm providing

85 Sieckmann 2018, 14. "The Pareto-optimality defines as optimal those states of affairs that one cannot change without deteriorating the position of at least one of the individuals involved", Duarte Silva 2018, 15.

86 Alezy 2021, 2.

87 Andrade Neto 2016, 8.

88 Others propose to distinguish fundamental principles and fundamental rights, *e.g.* Camardi 2017.

89 Among the numerous scholars adhering to this thesis, Pino 2014, who argues for the intimate connection between the structure of constitutional rights and the "age of balancing", understood as the unavoidable recourse to balancing and the proportionality test in current times.

for the principle of proportionality, constitutional courts are bound to apply it, due to the very structure of the system.[90]

The moderate thesis, supported by Andrade Neto, derives the necessity of the proportionality test from the existence of certain premises, a sort of conditional-necessity thesis. According to the author, this thesis is more respectful of the specificities of each national legal system and does not foresee a case for legal underdevelopment in those systems which do not meet the conditions for considering the proportionality test necessarily applicable.[91] "The normative conditions are the same implied by the principles theory: that principles are deemed as optimization requirements, fundamental rights as possessing wide scope, and courts as argumentative representatives of the people", but, according to the moderate thesis, these conditions recur if the interpretative practice and the institutional framework, together with the constitutional text, have progressively designed the constitutional system accordingly. The American model provides a glaring example of a system where fundamental rights are interpreted as having a narrower scope and, therefore, proportionality adjudication is not necessarily the ideal tool.[92]

Remarkably, notwithstanding the relevant differences, the three theses reviewed plainly identify constitutional balancing with the principle of proportionality, without questioning that the principle of proportionality – still defined in a variety of ways – may constitute just one possible tool to engage in the scrutiny of the balancing of fundamental principles.

1.3.1 The proportionality test, a critique

Albeit this book argues against an understanding of the proportionality principle as the only possible argumentative path to solve conflicts between constitutional rights and principles, its scope and expansion require a reflection upon its origins, function and structure.

To discover the origins of the proportionality test, we must locate ourselves in Germany, more than a hundred years ago, when in Prussian administrative law, the term "proportionality" was first used to identify a precise positive legal concept, at the time applied and developed by the Supreme Administrative Court of Prussia to censure the conduct of the police, when it was disproportionate compared to the citizen's infraction.[93] Notwithstanding the protagonism of the Administrative Tribunals, the first development of the legal concept at issue is also due to German political philosophy, legal theory, private and public law, which kept contributing to the affirmation of the proportionality principle throughout

90 Andrade Neto 2016, 10–12, drawing on Alexy 2010b.
91 For extensive argumentation on the moderate thesis, see Andrade Neto 2018, 283 ff.
92 Andrade Neto 2016, 13–17.
93 Barak 2012, 178, 179.

the Weimar Republic.[94] The second phase of the historical development of proportionality starts after the Second World War and is marked by the constant and coherent use by the German Constitutional Court of the proportionality principle as the preferred argumentative path to adjudicate fundamental rights, despite the absence of an explicit provision on proportionality in the Basic Law for the Federal Republic of Germany.[95]

To recapitulate, the function of the proportionality principle is to provide a rational argumentative path to the constitutional courts that ought to solve conflicts between fundamental principles, with a view to both identifying the optimal solution for both principles concerned and rationally justifying their limitation.[96] In order for this principle to serve its rationalisation purpose, a proper test has been elaborated. The main point of reference is again Robert Alexy, who defines the structure of the proportionality test by studying the German Constitutional Court jurisprudence.

The three sub-tests that compose the proportionality test are the suitability test, the necessity test and balancing in a strict sense (or proportionality in the narrower sense), where the application of the first two sub-principles aims to avoid unnecessary interferences with fundamental principles, while the third sub-principle intervenes when a certain cost for principles is not avoidable, but it ought to be constrained. Indeed, the three sub-tests are placed in a strict order. Only the ordinary norm that passes the first test can undergo the second test and the same applies between the necessity test and balancing in a strict sense.

"The first sub-principle, the principle of suitability, precludes the adoption of means that obstruct the realization of at least one principle without promoting any principle or goal for which it has been adopted".[97] The reasoning assumes that a norm that obstructs the realisation of a principle must be, on the other hand, apt to promote another principle. The very first stage of the assessment requires the judge to evaluate if the contested provision that realises a cost for the implementation of a principle is suitable to implement the content of another principle. If this does not occur, then "there are no costs either to P1 [the principle to be allegedly promoted] or P2 [the principle obstructed] if M[the contested norm] is omitted".[98]

The practical relevance of the suitability test is considered poor, as the legislator hardly fails to associate a legitimate aim, in application of a fundamental principle, to a norm. To the contrary, according to Alexy, the necessity test, that is, the second step of the evaluation, may represent a problematic testing ground.[99]

94 Andrade Neto 2018, 36.
95 Barak 2012, 180.
96 On the rational justification, see Barak 2012, 458–460, and bibliographic references cited therein.
97 Alexy 2021, 2.
98 Alexy 2021, 2.
99 Alexy 2021, 3.

The necessity test, also known as "the requirement of 'the less restrictive means'",[100] "requires that of two means promoting P1 [the principle promoted] that are, broadly speaking, equally suitable, the one that interferes less intensively with P2 [the principle obstructed] has to be chosen [...]. Under this condition, P1 and P2, taken together, require that the less intensively interfering means be applied", the cost of fulfilling a principle via ordinary law would then be eliminated.[101]

The reasoning is plain, and it can be undoubtedly associated with a mathematical formula (at least in the abstract). However, it seems to mis-consider the limited role given to the judge, who is not in possession of the extended power needed to go beyond the evaluation of the contested norm to the point of assessing the legal system as a whole, even in its potentialities.

Even though Alexy does not express it openly, the necessity sub-test assumes that the judge is entitled to detect and evaluate possible alternative means to the one proposed by the legislator, thus confronting the contested norm with others, which may be either already existing in the legal system or potentially adopted, and indicate the "necessary" one among them.[102] One of the crucial weaknesses of the proportionality test arises at this stage: should the judge truly search for alternative means capable of fulfilling the purpose of the law and suitable to the aim, therefore implementing a precise fundamental principle, its activity would constitute an excessive intrusion into the sphere of action of the legislator, with the result that the judge becomes the main actor of the balancing, rather than the supervisor.[103]

100 Barak 2012, 317.

101 Alexy 2021, 3.

102 See also Barak 2012, 323–324. Contiades Fotadou 2012, 676 ff. rather suggest that necessity means that the lawmaker has to demonstrate that he has looked for possible alternative measures.

103 On this profile, see the arguments by Bernal Pulido 2014, 203–264; the author carefully dismisses several critiques to the proportionality test, including the lack of legitimisation of the constitutional court to apply the proportionality principle. According to this critical view, every time the constitutional court addresses the legal questions by balancing fundamental rights and interests constitutionally protected extends its competence in an illegitimate way and, hence, reduces the – legitimate – scope of action of the legislator, democratically elected. Bernal Pulido argues that the conflict is not between the legislator and the constitutional court, but it is endemic of the democratic legal systems that, on the one side, provide the legislator with the competence to produce normative acts, but, on the other, bind it to respect the fundamental rights. These two elements (fundamental rights and democratic principle) enter into conflict during the scrutiny of the constitutional court, which cannot be empowered with an unlimited competence; on the other hand, such competence cannot be denied and it inevitably intervenes in the legislative action, inasmuch as the limits to the legislative competence are always determined in advance and in abstracts terms. In his view, the principle of proportionality represents the best solution to manage the endemic tension that arises in the concrete cases, since it reduces as much as possible any doubt as to the legitimacy of the constitutional court to apply this technique.

The two sub-tests reviewed optimise the fundamental principles in relation to the factual possibilities, while the last phase of the assessment, "proportionality in the narrower sense", "tells us what optimization relative to the legal possibilities is".[104]

The Weight Formula in a strict sense is conceptually more complex than the first two sub-tests.[105] It requires the interpreter to weigh principles and the intensity of interferences, by associating such values to a precise number, which can then be integrated into a mathematical formula that allows the identification of the concrete weight of one principle in relation to another, colliding, principle. "It is a type of cost-benefit analysis which brings the aim and the right into relationship with each other" and "requires the court to identify the gain and the loss respectively".[106] Alexy's suggestion is to assign the values "light", "moderate" and "serious" to the intensity of interference and to the abstract weights and express the values by using, respectively, numbers 1, 2, and 4.[107] Such a formula should allow to understand the benefits gained by a constitutional principle and the harm caused to another constitutional principle by an ordinary norm,[108] through the weighting of the principles concerned; the interference on those principles; the "degree of reliability of the assumptions concerning what the measure in question means for the non-realization".[109]

However, Alexy's solution has been criticised on the grounds of the shareable argument that "the choice of these values is completely arbitrary". One could have chosen 1, 10, and 15 instead, which would lead to different outcomes of the mathematical operations. There is not a single argument that Alexy can make to justify why his numerical operationalisation of the weight formula is superior to any alternative operationalisation.[110]

The feasibility of such a proportionality test is questionable also on the grounds of recent studies of the German Constitutional Court's jurisprudence that have revealed that only the Court's reasoning that confirms the constitutional legitimacy of a norm easily reflects Alexy's conceptualisation of proportionality adjudication. Even a decision which might be politically controversial does not pose many issues in this case, since the Court simply confirms

104 Alexy 2021, 4.
105 This is the proportionality test's phase that is mostly criticised, as noted by Silva Sampaio 2018, who, instead, supports its application.
106 Rivers 2006, 200.
107 For the precise formula, cf. Alexy 2003 and, lately, Alexy 2021, 4–5. For a further, critical and constructive reflection on the values to be attributed to the various elements of the Weight Formula, most recently see Silva Sampaio 2021.
108 Barak 2012, 340.
109 Alexy 2021, 5. Duarte 2021, 4, criticises Alexy's Formula, holding that it does not fulfil the Pareto Optimality, although it admits that it constitutes a "wonderful piece of legal engineering", and elaborates an alternative formula, still grounded on a mathematical approach to balancing legislation and adjudication.
110 Petersen 2020, 165. For a critique of Alexy's scale of interference, see also Juan Moreso 2012, 38.

the legislator's choice. To the contrary, "[I]n the vast majority of decisions in which the Court declares a statute to be unconstitutional, the structure of the reasoning does not follow Alexy's Law of Balancing".[111] According to this assessment of the German constitutional case law, in the 80% of cases the Court's argumentative framework is more restrictive or more creative, as when it "second-guesses the motives of the legislature by highlighting inconsistencies in the conception of the legislation".[112] While only in a minor group of rulings it consistently applies the proportionality test, as constructed by Alexy. The self-restraint concretely operated by the Court, in fact, overcomes the risk of a judicial decision that trespasses the boundaries of the judiciary, to invade the legislative power.

Similarly, a more ductile attitude of a constitutional court, even without impinging on the rationality of the arguments that can be achieved in alternative ways to the Weight Formula, surmounts the reserves as concerns the possibility to adopt an approach based on mathematic models and assumptions, where the premises, *i.e.* the constitutional principles in play, are not the outcome of the same mathematical logic.[113] Solving a conflict between elements which do not reflect a mathematic structure, hardly even a rational structure, with a mathematic model is indeed disputable, as it creates "a false illusion of rationality and determination".[114] Even though a similar approach can support the coherence of a reasoning, as well as the strength of a judicial argument, by contributing to its rationalisation.[115]

Yet, a strict reliance on a mathematical formula risks resulting in a claim of absolute and crystallised justice, unbearable in a legal system which is not the outcome of mathematical discourse, but rather of a political dynamic and compromise.

The need for a rational argument is not put into question, but the reliability of precise procedural rules in the development of the rational discourse, especially given that these rules, if applied rigorously, are inevitably "intrusive" of the legislator's competences, is rather contestable. The necessity to overcome the understanding of the balancing method as a "black box" in which judges take decisions without shedding light on the underlying argumentative steps cannot justify the switch to a rigid test, based upon a weight formula that "remains without any satisfactory methodological foundation", which "precision is revealed to be a mere illusion, a methodological chimera".[116]

111 Petersen 2020, 168.
112 Petersen 2020, 171.
113 The mathematical approach is described by Tsakyrakis 2009 as the "illusion of some kind of mechanical weighing of values similar to that of weighing apples and oranges", 475. Tsakyrakis's passionate critique to the proportionality test is contested by Khosla 2010.
114 Petersen 2020, 165.
115 Undoubtedly, one of the strengths of the proportionality test, Jestaedt 2012, 157–158.
116 Jestaedt 2012, 165. Indeed, "[D]opo Kant noi sappiamo che la forma della conoscenza matematica non è ripetibile dalle altre scienze, e in particolare dalla scienza giuridica, le cui

1.4 Balancing in fundamental social rights' adjudication and the essential content dilemma

Fundamental labour rights adjudication makes no exception in respect of the criteria and the theories reviewed so far, notwithstanding their peculiar features.

The enforcement of fundamental social rights is dependent upon either the competing interests with a constitutional status or the resources available;[117] the same applies to the narrower group of fundamental labour rights.

The debate on the possibility of admitting the balancing of fundamental social rights with public spending necessities is extensive and partially concerns our perception[118] as regards the items that can enter the constitutional balancing and those that remain in the background, as a further condition that the legislator has to consider when adopting a law which implements fundamental social rights, consistently with the indications provided by the court to achieve the appropriate point of equilibrium. Some could even question the very legitimacy of compressing these rights and, eventually, the extent of the compression allowed. Indeed, admitting that these rights can be balanced means accepting that they can be compressed.

This discourse becomes especially relevant face to an economic crisis, when policy reactions demand constraints in public spending and redistribution choices, as demonstrated by the judgments assessed in Chapters 3 and 4, which represent the constitutional judicial round of a saga initiated with the EU policies adopted with the aim to face the effects of the 2008 economic crisis.[119] In a similar context, the axiological perspective plays a major role. Particularly, solidarity, being one of the founding values of fundamental social rights, is destabilised by the impact of the economic downturn on its key component: societal cohesion.[120]

Addressing the topic at stake requires evaluating if social rights, thus including fundamental labour rights, can be compressed only to the point of preserving their essential content, under what conditions they can be potentially compressed further and if such essential content is immutable, or even the fundamental social rights' nucleus changes over time, to adapt to the mutating economic, political

---

proposizioni possono dirsi dommatiche propriamente in via di distinzione dai *mathemata*", Mengoni 1996b, 29.

117 This profile is emphasised by, *inter alia*, Contiades Fotiadou 2012, 667; Bilchitz 2014, 710. The compression of the content of rights is also the object of Bin's reflection, who repeatedly argues that financial means and content of rights are strictly related, or, more precisely: "the limitation of means corresponds to the compression of rights": Bin 1992, 102–107.

118 The word "perception" is not used with levity. Indeed, it expresses the understanding that at one point of the legal reasoning rational arguments fail to be enough to support a standpoint, and the sensory sphere, influenced by everyone's personal history, becomes predominant. Surely, the ambition of the lawyer lies in moving forward the moment when the sensory sphere prevails, or, rather, remains the only available argumentative tool.

119 See the Introduction to this book.

120 Contiades Fotiadou 2012, 664.

and social context. The function attached to the hermeneutic principles in this respect is crucial, as it may either jeopardise the very convenience of employing the essential content criterion or contribute to its definition.

When it comes to the adjudication of fundamental social rights, the international literature is mostly interested in discussing its relationship with the principle of proportionality, widely understood as the ideal hermeneutic tool to adjudicate fundamental social rights and, simultaneously, grant them at the utmost.[121]

The understanding of the relationship between the alleged core content of social rights, which identification may be conceived as essential to assure their justiciability, and the principle of proportionality, reflects different approaches, which are well expressed by the scientific diatribe published by the *International Journal of Constitutional Law*, between Contiades and Fotiadou, on the one hand, and Bilchitz, on the other.

Contiades and Fotiadou – who develop arguments that could be partially transferred to other judicial balancing techniques – argue for the proportionality principle to be applied by courts also in order to provide social rights with a tangible content,[122] assuming that the proportionality review is rigorous and relies on judicial precedents. The main reason that supports this function of proportionality adjudication is its characteristic feature, that is its flexibility,[123] as well as its attitude to stimulate dialogical exchange between public powers that, according to the scholars, renders the proportionality test perfectly suitable to define the content of social rights, which is not fixed, but rather elusive and in constant dialogue with other fundamental rights. Under this view, a crystallisation of the core content of fundamental social rights is not desirable, while the application of proportionality also in this domain, hence at all stages of social rights' adjudication, allows a protection which goes way beyond a hypothetical essential nucleus, an outcome to be particularly praised in times of economic crisis, since "[I]nsisting

121 *E.g.*, Contiades, Fotiadou 2012; Bilchitz 2014; Clérico 2018; De Fazio 2021, who argues that there is structural identity between the proportionality test regarding norms interfering with positive rights (omissions) and negative rights (excesses); while Loi 2016, 63, observes that "proportionality and balancing appear as indispensable tools of redistributive justice", as these instruments are seen as an efficient way to avoid the "unequal distribution of rights". Fundamental labour rights being a cluster of social rights, the academic debate reviewed above applies also to fundamental labour rights' adjudication. The application of balancing and, more precisely, of the proportionality principle by ordinary courts to decide upon employment cases, hence not constitutional balancing, belongs to a different domain, see, *inter alia*, Loi 211 and Alon-Shenker Davidov 2013.

122 A view shared by Caruso 2015, 73–75, who is confident that the proportionality principle (understood as a corollary of balancing, a distinction not endorsed here), if assisted by a persuasive reasoning, represents the ideal system to guarantee the best possible enforcement of fundamental social rights and a reliable control of the political balancing operated by the lawmaker. Differently, Giubboni 2017, 25, invites to giving priority to a re-constitutionalisation of the European economic governance; see also Sciarra 2013.

123 A feature that blatantly emerges in Chapter 2.

on defining a minimum core content as a prerequisite for the justiciability of social rights is an updated aspiration, which risks the very enforceability of these rights in the context of a global economic crisis, that is, at times when they are needed the most".[124]

Still without denying the crucial role of proportionality adjudication, Bilchitz argues against its autonomy, and holds that it should be supplemented by the minimum core approach.[125] In his view, the "weak approach to the content of socio-economic rights"[126] implies a very low protection of social rights, precisely, in times of crisis. Exposing rights to proportionality adjudication in times of crisis, without the shield of an essential content, would expose them excessively to economic downturns, while the minimum core approach protects them, at least to a certain degree, even in these phases. Consequently, basic socio-economic needs, which are the overriding priority, are met at any time through the redistribution of available resources. The definition of such "relative minimum threshold"[127] is a responsibility of courts and international bodies (the author refers to the United Nations Committee on Economic, Social and Cultural Rights, to the European Committee on Social Rights of the Council of Europe and to the International Covenant on Economic and Social Rights), according to the following criteria: "[T]he first threshold or minimum core can be formulated as involving the general conditions necessary to be free from threats to survival; the second 'sufficiency' threshold concerns achieving the general necessary conditions to be in a position to realize one's purposes or to live a life of dignity".[128] Under this construction, the minimum core is not inviolable, but, in order to be limited, an adequate justification by the legislator is required. In other words, proportionality adjudication allows a strict scrutiny of the legislator's choices, on the grounds of a precise understanding of what is the essential nucleus.[129]

The essential content of fundamental social rights poses a dilemma – that even precedes the discussion around the relationship between the latter and

124 Contiades Fotiadou 2012, 686, who also reject the idea that categorical rules better protect social rights.

125 Smilarly, Lenaerts 2019 and Rivers 2006, 184, hold that "Absolute core [...] is to be understood as an extreme infringement, rather than merely an exemplary one. They thus try to create a clear limit to state action without balancing. The idea of an absolute core finds a counterpart in European Convention case law in the idea of the "very essence" of a right. If the notion of essences or cores is to be of any use, it must be definable independently of proportionality and perform a distinct role in preventing certain forms of state action.

126 Bilchitz 2014, 738.

127 Bilchitz 2014, 733.

128 Bilchitz 2014, 730.

129 Bilchitz 2014; see the answer by Contiades Fotiadou 2014, who contest a number of arguments posed by Blichitz, most of all that proportionality is understood just as a limitation to limitations, 742. Joining the debate, Kilpatrick 2015 emphasises that "the assumption underpinning [Biltchitz] analysis - that crisis constitutional challenges are focused on meeting basic needs – is wrong in Europe", where the focus of contestations is rather on "cuts to existing entitlements", 9–10.

proportionality adjudication – as its understanding depends primarily on whether the interpreter conceives it as absolute, or rather relative.[130] In the first instance, which implies that "[P]roportionality begins where essence stops",[131] the essential content of a social right should be considered applicable in any circumstance, to any person, independently from the relevant social, political, economic conditions, so that the essential content of fundamental social rights would nearly correspond, in its function, to those social rights that are understood by some as integrating human rights, to which everyone is entitled for the sole fact of existing.[132] While, if the essential content is interpreted as relative, it means that it is dependent upon the social, political and economic context of the state that recognises the fundamental social right at issue. This theory strictly connects the essential content to the justification of the provision that imposes the sacrifice, with the result that the essential content is the portion of that right that survives and its definition is destined to vary often, or even constantly,[133] since it "conceptualises a right as a progressive entitlement where the greater the infliction, the greater the need for justification and scrutiny"[134] and can be more easily combined with the principle of proportionality.

Bernal Pulido, in his book on the principle of proportionality and fundamental labour rights,[135] discusses the *teoria mixta del contenido esencial*,[136] a further theory on the essential content,[137] which combines the absolute theory with the

130 See, *inter alia*, Messineo 2010, 55–60 and Prieto Sanchis 2000, 70, 71.

131 Tridimas Gentile 2019, 803; which seems also the approach of Modugno 2008, 251: "[T]he interferences take place at the principles' margins, which remain untouched in the nucleus" (my translation).

132 Which seems to be the approach adopted by Blichitz 2014, 732, when arguing that the minimum core approach may be particularly useful "in developing countries where ensuring a minimum threshold for everyone represents an improvement from a situation where people may literally starve to death or be completely homeless", but also in developed countries, where those living under the minimum threshold are ignored because of "incorrect factual assumptions that everyone in the society is living above that basic minimum standard".

133 Interestingly, the Italian Constitutional Court refers to collective agreements for the identification of the sufficient remuneration, that is the essential content of the right to a fair remuneration, thus strongly attaching the essential content to the factual reality of industrial relations and labour market, see Andreoni 2006, 122.

134 Tridimas Gentile 2019, 803. The interpretation of the nature of the essential content may also depend on the choice to apply the concept strategically, as Kilpatrick 2015 seems to suggest, explicitly referring to the appropriate understanding of the essential content in times of crisis in the EU.

135 Bernal Pulido 2014, for whom a full objectivity in determining the essential content of fundamental rights is nothing but a fascinating utopia, while the principle of proportionality offers the most rational interpretative method, Bernal Pulido 2005, 68; in a similar way see also Stone Sweet Mathews 2008.

136 Supported by renowned Spanish scholars, such as Perejo, Prieto Sanchis and Medina Guerrero.

137 Bernal Pulido assesses and develops counterarguments on a number of theories on fundamental rights and their essential content, one for all Habermas's theory, see Bernal Pulido

proportionality principle. Under this view, the hard core of the fundamental right remains stable and cannot be sacrificed for any reason and to any extent, to the contrary the peripheral zone can be affected by ordinary norms and the proportionality principle is applied to assess whether the intervention of the legislator on the peripheral zone complies with the criteria of suitability, necessity and proportionality in a strict sense. According to Bernal Pulido, while the *teoria mixta del contenido esencial* has the merit to improve the absolute theory by envisaging a method to protect the fundamental right beyond the essential content, it does not overcome a crucial shortcoming of the absolute theory. In particular, a rational criterion that allows one to separate sharply the essential content from the periphery of the fundamental right does not exist.[138] In conclusion, according to the scholar, the theory of the essential content and the proportionality principle are incompatible in terms of theoretical structure. Therefore, it is necessary to get rid of the abstract idea of essential content and apply plainly and exclusively the principle of proportionality. However, the mixed theory can inspire a rule to be applied in the course of the proportionality assessment, especially in the phase of the balancing in the strict sense: the most intense sacrifices to fundamental rights can be admitted only exceptionally.[139]

As introduced by reviewing the debate between Contiades Fotiadou and Bilchitz, disagreement, and more often approximation, can be found as far as concerns the technique that a legislator, or a court, should apply, or the principle they shall invoke in order to determine the scope and substance of the essential content, especially if adopting the absolute theory, which disengages the definition of the essential content from the legislative justification upholding the contested norm.[140] This second profile is clearly dependent also upon the choice made as concerns the first one, *i.e.* the relationship between proportionality and essential content.

Neither is the theory of Preciado Domènech of any help to clarify how the core content can be determined and whether a proper technique exists to this end. In his view, the essential content is determined at an earlier stage, "at the moment of the delimitation of the content of the right", which is conducted by

2014, 509–621.

138 Bernal Pulido 2014, 452–544.

139 Indeed, according to Bernal Pulido, the theory of the principle of proportionality offers a stronger protection to fundamental rights and binds the legislator more tightly than the essential content theory, see Bernal Pulido 2014, in particular 551.

140 "In short, although the concept of essence as a legal threshold must be understood as an autonomous limit, in effect, it is impossible to determine it without engaging in a balancing process which is best carried out through a proportionality analysis. Therein lies a conundrum that limits the utility of essence as a tool of judicial methodology", Tridimas Gentile 2019, 804; even if the authors still seem to rely on the use of the essential content, understood in absolute terms, to give substance to Art. 52.1 of the Charter, 805. More peremptory is Barak's thesis, which acknowledges the difficulties in defining the "core" of a right and seems to suggest getting rid of such notion in favour of proportionality, particularly proportionality *strictu sensu*, Barak 2012, 498.

the constitutional court; secondly and consequently, the proportionality of the norm can be evaluated.[141] Here, a norm may respect the essential content of a fundamental right, but, at the same time, be disproportionate, while the other way round is not as true: a norm not fulfilling the essential content of a fundamental right cannot be proportionate.[142]

1.4.1 Italian and Spanish insights on the notion of essential content

In the latest decades, the notion under discussion has increasingly gained attention, mostly due to the adoption of the Charter that refers to the essential content of fundamental rights in Art. 52.1 and has, thus, formalised at the EU level a concept already embedded in a number of Member State's constitutions and in the Court of Justice case law, but it still has little prominence in the international literature.[143] The Spanish and Italian legal systems offer two emblematic alternative examples.

The Spanish Constitution expressly refers to the protection of the essential content of rights and freedoms.[144] Indeed, Art. 53.1 SC states that the exercise of rights and freedoms recognised by the Constitution can be regulated "only by an act which in any case must respect their essential content".[145] It has been argued, by the supporters of the principle of proportionality (applied in the Spanish constitutional case law), that in light of a constitutional norm establishing that fundamental rights are characterised by an essential content that must be respected in any event, the application of the principle of proportionality also serves the

141 Preciado Domènech 2016, 143, my translation.

142 Preciado Domènech 2016, 143; see also González Beilfuss 2015, 86–88.

143 Dawson et al. 2019; Tridimas Gentile 2019; the debate around the essential content of fundamental labour rights was revitalised in Italy by Veneziani 2016; on this wave see the extensive analysis by Laforgia 2018. The Court of Justice, so far, has barely invoked the essential content of fundamental labour rights to support its argumentations, Castelli 2021, 469–473; for a viewpoint that takes into account both the national and the EU legal systems, see Lenaerts 2019; while the relationship between the EU jurisprudence and the international perspective is the focus of Thielbörger 2019. Earlier, Young 2008.

144 The legal scholarship has clearly borrowed the concept of "*contenido esencial*" or "nucleus" from the sciences, where it has a concrete and tangible meaning (*e.g.* the nucleus of a cell), while in law it acquires a metaphoric significance; see Bernal Pulido 2014, 512, on the "*contenido esencial*" of fundamental rights, also Medina Guerrero 1996.

145 The norm was inspired by Art. 19 of the Basic Law for the Federal Republic of Germany. The Basic Law for the Federal Republic of Germany, the constitutional law, was approved on 8 May 1949. The Spanish Constitutional norm, however, differs from the German provision, in two crucial aspects. First, Art. 53.1 SC allows the ordinary law to interfere in the exercise of any freedom, independently from the existence of specific norms expressly providing for such legislative capacity. Second, and more subtle, in the Spanish Constitution, the norm on the essential content seems to be addressed to any legislative act, including – but not only – those that limit rights and freedoms, Prieto Sanchis 2000, 70. The concept of essential content can be found also in the Constitutions of other European Member States, such as Estonia (Art. 17.2), Hungary (Art. I.3), Poland (Art. 31.3), Portugal (Art. 18), Romania (Art. 53.2) and Slovakia (Art. 13.4).

purpose of providing the legislator with an understanding of which duties must be fulfilled in order to enforce the fundamental rights, at least in their nucleus.[146]

The Spanish Constitutional Court, with Judgment 11/1981, provided crucial insights on the essential content of a fundamental right, which turns out to be "that part of the right's content, which is absolutely necessary so that the interests legally protected, that enliven the right, result real, concrete and truly protected". This content is not general, but "essential" in the sense that it concerns the elements which are paramount to legally recognise the right at issue, both in its meaning and in its justiciability. In addition, according to the 1981 Constitutional Court, the essential content must be understood in relation to the historical context in which the judicial case is decided;[147] it constitutes an "undetermined legal concept", which becomes a tool for the assessment and protection of a fundamental right, with due regard to both its original meaning, that is the intention and the will of the constituent assembly, as well as the "evolutionary adaptation" that it has undergone over the years.[148]

In order to decide whether the essential content of a fundamental right is violated, the Constitutional Court deploys two methodological options. The first technique lies on the assumption that the interpreter shall be able to identify the "*tipo abstracto del derecho*", which pre-exists the legislative act, in the ordinary law under scrutiny. However, the "*tipo abstracto*" is not fixed and absolute but reflects the collective idea in a precise historical context, which is shaped by the legal scholarship and the case law. Therefore, the judges have to conduct a comparison between what the legislator has produced and how the right at stake is normally understood. The second step does not concern the internal dimension of the fundamental right, but rather the beam of faculties that emanate from a given right, that is the various elements that compose the interest protected. Therefore, in light of the two key elements pointed out (the consistency with the "abstract type" and the satisfaction of the interest protected), the essential content is violated when the ordinary law does not comply with the abstract category of the said right, or when, even if the abstract category of the constitutional right is reflected in the ordinary norm, the latter limits or complicates the exercise of the said right, or its justiciability, in an unreasonable way.[149]

146 Bernal Pulido 2005; Villaverde 2008; Prieto Sanchis 2003, 105, 106, according to whom judicial balancing comes after the legislative balancing operated by the legislator during the legislative phase.

147 The relevance given to the historical content is discussed by Bernal Pulido 2014, 531, 532, who emphasises that this element implies that the court has rejected the absolute theory.

148 Parejo Alfonso 1981, 186–190, my translation.

149 Parejo Alfonso 1981, 186–190. Also Solozabal Echavarria 1991 refers to Judgment 11/1981, to identify the scope of the essential content of constitutional rights. However, the meaning and interpretation of the concept of "essential content" of fundamental rights is controversial, for an attentive review of the traditional academic literature, Rodríguez-Armas 1996. On the topic, see also Martìnez Pujalte 1997; Prieto Sanchís 2003 and 2000 and, of a different view, Medina Guerrero 2008; Aguiar de Luque 1993.

The Italian Constitution recognises every right together with its limits and, often, the limited character of a fundamental right emerges explicitly from the provision in which it is enshrined, but neither a general norm on the essential content of fundamental rights nor a general limitation clause were included in the 1948 Constitution.[150] The Italian Court has made occasional reference to concepts that can be assimilated to the essential content of fundamental rights,[151] mostly defining it in terms of human dignity,[152] a connection that may be interpreted in the sense that "the essential content of social rights is an expression that refers to the services which are necessary to realize the processes of inclusion of the single person into the dynamics of the community".[153]

The attempt to solve the indeterminacy of the essential content criterion by recurring to the notion of "dignity"[154] is equally problematic, given that, playing with words, "dignity" is equally undetermined. In our cultural models, the content of "dignity" is apparently self-evident, however when the interpreter strives to transform it in a legal paradigm it becomes an "hermeneutic enigma".[155]

Albeit undoubtedly fascinating from a theoretical perspective, operatively it risks leading the interpreter to either an opportunistic use, or to an argument *ad abundantiam*[156] or, worse option, to an impasse, unless the reference is clearly identified in the norms provided by international tools, or in basic human rights, widely accepted as such by the international community, hence a minimum, inalienable, floor.

Unsurprisingly, the possibility to evaluate and define the essential content of a fundamental right is strongly questioned in the Italian context, as well. Recently, it has been argued that "the content of rights cannot be determined, rather we must investigate the origin, justification and scope of their limits",[157] since "none knows exactly" what is the minimum essential content that cannot be compressed,

150 It must be acknowledged that, in 2001 a reform of Art. 117 IC has entitled the state to determine the "essential levels" of services implementing civil and social rights; on the point see Simoncini 2003.

151 Such as *misura minima essenziale*, *parte ineliminabile*, *nucleo invalicabile* (the latest employed in ICC, Judgment 256/2016), see Castelli 2021, 475–482.

152 *E.g.* Judgment 1146/1988, Judgment 85/2013. On the notion of dignity in Art. 36 IC, see Messineo 2010, Vallauri 2010 and Laforgia 2018.

153 Messineo 2010, 95, my translation.

154 See, *inter alia*, Messineo 2010 and Laforgia 2018, 91, who declines the discourse around "social dignity", with an attentive assessment of the Italian legal system's foundations of the notion, and, yet, denies social dignity the status of super-value, always exempted from judicial balancing. In fact, the Italian Constitutional Court, in its erratic use of the essential content criterion, has been significantly linking it to dignity, as noted also by Tridimas Gentile 2019, 806, although without clarifying its meaning; see Chapter 2.

155 Lipari 2010, 638, according to the scholar only the judges' evaluation of the concrete case, consistent with the relevant jurisprudence and aware of the supranational charters that guarantee fundamental rights, can unravel the content of "dignity".

156 Vallauri 2010, 681.

157 Bin 2018, 34, my translation; Giuliano Amato's work to which Bin refers is Amato 1967.

therefore the protection of a fundamental right cannot be constrained to the recognition of its essential content.[158]

Indeed, thinking in operative terms, a minor engagement in the search for a notion that serves the purpose to crystallise the untouchable, in either absolute or relative terms, is to be favoured, for two reasons. On the one hand, doubts should be raised about the convenience of employing the essential content criterion understood as the guarantee of dignity in human rights terms, to ensure the enforcement of fundamental social rights, particularly, in times of crisis and particularly in legal systems structurally very protective towards such rights, since it may risk transforming – through an imperceptible corroboration of the case law, due to the not unlikely rise in the scarcity of resources – what is born to be a minimum floor of guarantees, in a ceiling.[159] On the other hand, it is impossible not to admit a discomfort in accepting that an alleged essential content of fundamental social rights, which evokes a protection of the individual that is constitutive of the social system, may be manipulated at the mercy of the choice of political economy made according to the contingency or every time the word "crisis" is strategically articulated in a law.[160]

1.5 Conclusions

The thoughts shared in this book are based upon the doctrinal assumptions developed in relation to the social constitutions that have emerged after the Second World War,[161] as opposed to the liberal constitutions of the early 20th century that ignored the equality principle and the relevance of fundamental social rights as a key to promote social integration.[162]

158 Bin 2018, 44, 45. Doubts on the essential content criterion for fundamental social rights are raised also by Chessa 2018, 280.

159 The implicit reference to the literature discussing the posting of workers directive and the relevant case law of the Court of Justice is self-evident.

160 The refusal of an approach prone to favour the "contingency of rights" does not deny the historicity of rights, see Viola 1989; Lipari 2010; Baccelli 2013.

161 Or "socially oriented" constitution, Bavaro 2018, 261, in a gripping essay on the relevance of the material constitution for the enforcement of labour – social – rights. The theory on fundamental rights adopted, that is the lenses with which constitutional labour rights are addressed, has a significant, or even decisive, role in the interpretation of the fundamental rights enshrined in a constitution. The same can be said when the analysis of the Constitutional Court's arguments is conducted, in the sense that the interpretative framework selected, as regards fundamental rights, constitutes a strong underlying assumption, which conditions the assessment of the Court's legal reasoning, as well. In other words, certain steps of the analysis of the constitutional balancing of fundamental rights certainly hinges on a specific understanding of the constitution, and, precisely, of the value and role of the fundamental rights provided therein.

162 Besides the references cited above, see Ewing 2012. Constitutional interpretation as a broader field of analysis is beyond the scope of this book. The theories to be addressed in this respect would be endless. Just to provide an example, while some support the need to adopt a purposive interpretation of constitutional rights, which requires the judge to

The social state theory, the theory that permeates the social state, implies an understanding of the constitution as the tool that grants substantial equality among citizens, where equality is the linchpin of the pluralist system and social rights its main operational means.[163] In both the Italian and Spanish legal systems, the social state nature is foremostly expressed in the constitutional norms that provide for the duty of the public authorities to grant substantial equality among citizens, which overcomes the mere "non-interference" and requires positive actions by the state bodies (see Art. 3.2 IC, and Art. 9.2 SC). If *equality* were not elaborated also in substantial terms, rights and freedoms would be purely declarations and they would fail to become effective.[164] The establishment of a society founded upon substantial equality allows the construction of both positive freedoms and social equality. Here hinge fundamental labour rights, understood for the purpose of this book as rights aimed at protecting workers, either during their working life or after retirement, that encompass both financially conditioned rights and liberty rights of workers.[165]

---

take into account both "the intention of the text's creators (subjective purpose) as well as the system's 'intention' as a whole (objective purpose)" (Barak 2012, 48), therefore trying to combine the intention of the constitution's authors with the system as a whole (on the purposive approach applied to labour rights, see Davidov 2016); others suggest interpreting the constitutional text only in light of its original understanding, since a "modernisation" of their meaning would simply reflect the current majority's understanding of a right, thus betraying the very function of a constitution, that is to protect the minority, cf. Scalia 1989.

163 Preciado Domènech 2016, 108, drawing on Böckenförde 1993, 44–83, reviews four other theories of fundamental rights, beyond the social state theory, which are not independent and self-standing, but complement each other. The liberal theory, grounded upon the *favour libertatis*, entails that the state has the exclusive competence of guaranteeing the enjoyment of constitutional freedoms, on the other hand, the citizens shall simply comply with the generic rule that "everything that is not forbidden is allowed" and, under this view, fundamental rights work as the "law of the jungle" (my translation). While, according to the institutional theory, a statute or any legal provision that concerns a fundamental right, on the one hand, facilitates the exercise of the liberty enshrined in that right, but, on the other, directs that liberty to a specific goal, so that the law becomes the framework of that liberty. The axiological theory puts emphasis on the values expressed by each fundamental right, which are crucial and coherent tools that lead the state in the construction of an integrated and homogeneous society, insofar as they inspire every normative intervention. The functional-democratic theory (an evolution of the institutional theory), divided into functionalist-institutional theory and multifunctional theory, in brief, stresses the institutional dimension of public freedoms, cf. Preciado Domènech 2016, 107–112. See also Künkler Stein 2017 and Bernal Pulido 2007, 352–402.

164 Bin 2007, drawing on Karl Marx's arguments (Marx 1974) observes that this was one of the features of the French Constitution of 1848, which was, indeed, a mere declaration of rights and freedoms.

165 Bin also notices that "the Constitutional Court often identifies in the constitutional provisions a favour for social interests, which are not among the traditional fundamental rights, as, inter alia, the favour for employees recognized in Art. 35 (Judgment 180/984) and Art. 38.2 (Judgment 286/1987)": Bin 1992, 4, my translation.

Both these clusters of rights necessitate the intervention of the state in order to be effective. The public authority has to intervene not only to allocate the resources for the effective enjoyment of welfare rights, but also to "remove the obstacles" (the expression is used in both by Art. 3.2, IC, Art. 9.2, SC) that hamper the full enjoyment of the liberty rights; in fact, an abstentionist attitude from the state towards labour liberty rights would lead to greater power inequality and would fail to balance in an equal way the interaction of social forces. Contemporary democracies, based upon the social state, do not consider economic rights as absolute and immune from democratic rights. In order for this principle (which stems from various constitutional norms) to be applied, the active participation of workers and their organisations must be not only allowed, but also granted and favoured. Therefore, public powers must actively promote collective participation, which means that, for instance, in order to allow the exercise of the trade union freedom, the state cannot simply adopt a tolerant and abstentionist attitude.[166]

The very first sentences of the two Constitutions, albeit far from being exhaustive of the constitutional social coverage of the two legal systems, are demonstrative of the dualistic dimension of the legal systems they are designing, which is built around both the individual and the collective dimension of labour: Art. 1.1. SC declares: "Spain is hereby established as a social and democratic State"; in a similar way, Art. 1.1 IC states that "[I]taly is a democratic republic, founded on labour".[167]

The promotion of the collective dimension of labour has been likewise at the centre of the development of what is usually called "Social Europe", under the guidance of Jacque Delors.[168] Yet, the EU enlargement and the austerity policies that have followed the 2008 crisis have been blamed for causing a significant change of course.[169]

166 See the essay by Antonio Baylos Grau on the relationship between private powers and fundamental rights in Baylos Grau 2017, 10.

167 For all, Mengoni 1998; Nogler 2009 and Nogler 2020.

168 Also named, by some, "European Social Model", it was firmly supported, *inter alia*, by Jacques Delors, who, still in 2013, argued "the European social model exists" (as quoted in Vaughan-Whitehead 2015, 1); an assumption challenged by the diversities of national social state systems, see Scharpf 2002. The critical literature on the social dimension of the EU is extensive, to mention only a few: Bercusson 2009; Countouris Freedland 2013; Rogowski 2016; Giubboni 2017, 1–32.

169 On the EU enlargement effects, see Vaughan-Whitehead 2003; for a particularly negative evaluation of the effects, especially on collective bargaining, of the EU austerity measures (and else), see Bruun et al. 2014. Whereas Sciarra 2008 reflects on the challenges posed to European trade unions following, on the one hand, the EU enlargement, on the other, *Viking* and *Laval* judgments. Cf. also Ewing 2015, who emphatically titles his essay "The Death of Social Europe"; on the risks for the welfare systems following a transformation of the EU into an "asocial Europe", Moreno Fernández 2013; for a national, thoughtful, perspective, Katsaroumpas 2018.

The EU institutions, in the various forms and with the diverse legal tools addressed in the Introduction to this book, have significantly contributed to – not to say determined – what has been called a "narrowing" of national constitutions,[170] threatening the apparently solid labour constitutions of, especially, Southern European countries, through the pressure to adopt a series of measures, with a direct and indirect impact on the social equilibria guaranteed by the constitution,[171] affecting the values of equality, solidarity and social justice, which had been incorporated into the EU genetic code.[172] The structural reforms that have followed have concerned not only constitutional provisions, particularly public budget constraints,[173] but also the domains of flexibilisation of the labour market, privatisation policies and, not least, decentralisation of collective bargaining.[174]

Part of the "narrowing" process of national social constitutions pursued with the alleged aim of managing the disturbing effects of the 2008 crisis has been eventually brought before constitutional courts under the guise of constitutional challenges of ordinary law reforms.[175]

This chapter has introduced the analysis of the constitutional adjudication of fundamental labour rights in two EU Member States in times of crisis, by addressing the doctrinal assumptions underpinning constitutional balancing in a social state democracy, *i.e.* the axiological nature of fundamental rights, and the techniques applied by the courts to adjudicate, particularly, fundamental social rights. Judicial balancing is the adjudication method necessary to decide cases of conflicts between principles, that is constitutional provisions that have provided values with a normative character.

Fundamental labour rights recognised by national constitutions serve the dualistic purpose of making substantial equality effective[176] – thus being a cluster of the wide category of fundamental social rights – and expressing values in normative terms;[177] therefore, that constitutional balancing is an applicable adjudication method even in this domain can be hardly contested. The same cannot be

170 Countouris 2020; on the same line, Losurdo 2016 and Taschini 2019, 1–86. A change in national constitutional settings, which, according to Menéndez Menéndez 2012, has followed a "constitutional mutation" of the EU itself, more prone to favour a dismantling of national social states. See also the anthology edited by Caruso and Fontana 2015.

171 Both the formal and the material constitutions (drawing on the thesis developed by Mortati in 1940, see Mortati 1998) have been affected by the pressure of EU institutions, for instance, by favouring, in Italy, the replacement of the elected government, with a technical one.

172 Veneziani 2016, 232.

173 On this profile, see the essays collected in Beukers et al. 2017.

174 Busch et al. 2013.

175 And "it seems evident from the case-law of the highest Courts that the crisis relaunches and consolidates balancing", Caruso 2015, 73.

176 On the principle of equality in employment relations see, *inter alia*, Palomeque 1983.

177 They are "fundamental" precisely because of their "*stretta immanenza e coessenzialità ai valori fondanti dell'ordinamento democratico repubblicano*", Giubboni 2006, 3.

equally certainly asserted when other constitutional provisions come into play, namely those interests that are conveyed by constitutional norms but doubtfully reflect constitutive values, such as the reformed constitutional norms on public budget constraints.

Given that the main purpose of this book is to assess the Italian and Spanish constitutional judgments on the reforms adopted as a response to the 2008 economic crisis, and firmly promoted by the EU institutions, with a focus on the balancing techniques adopted by the two Constitutional Courts, in order to appreciate the consequences in terms of effectiveness of the fundamental labour rights concerned and reflect on the weight recognised as given to the post-crisis policies adopted by EU institutions, the assessment of the relevant constitutional judgments needs to be preceded by an assessment of the balancing techniques.

2 Constitutional balancing techniques in the world

A glimpse

2.1 Introduction

Notwithstanding the common legal sentiment, fundamental rights adjudication does not necessarily entail constitutional balancing and alternative methods may be preferred. On the other hand, judicial balancing may be construed by using argumentative frameworks that do not necessarily correspond to the proportionality test. In other words, proportionality is not the only suitable technique for a constitutional court to balance conflicting rights and interests. Inasmuch as, balancing, as a fundamental right adjudication method, is not inextricably linked with a unique technique.

Indeed, if proportionality can be broadly defined as "*a legal tool* designed to resolve conflicts between constitutional rights, or conflicts between constitutional rights and the public interest"[1] nothing prevents judges from developing different tools to achieve the same goal. Moreover, where the fundamental principles adjudication is not understood as a conflict of rights and/or principles, not only the legal tool changes, but the overall approach to the constitutional decision does, as well.

The alternative theories of fundamental rights adjudication go from understanding the legislative power as the only one that can determine the scope of a fundamental right and its boundaries, since it expresses the enduring process of negotiation within a given society and, consistently, rejecting constitutional balancing in itself; to the categorisation-based alternatives, applied in several areas of American constitutional law.[2]

Conversely, proportionality can be operationalised in unaccountable different ways.[3] This is what has occurred following the dissemination of the proportionality principle around the world.

1 Barak 2012, 493, italics added.
2 A comprehensive assessment of the alternatives to proportionality is provided by Barak 2012, 493–527, who admits that the "most important alternative offered to proportionality, by far, is categorization", 502. Nevertheless, and albeit recognising that room for improvement exists in both cases, he remains a defender of the proportionality principle, 527.
3 Gardbaum 2010, 83.

DOI: 10.4324/9781003155362-3

The literature that addresses the operationalisation of balancing and proportionality in the constitutional jurisprudence, from national, transnational or supranational perspectives is countless and covers an extensive number of countries and legal systems. A comprehensive analysis of the relevant and vast theoretical profiles, as well as of all the legal systems where the application of proportionality has been documented is beyond the scope of this chapter, which discusses the principle of proportionality with a view to introducing this principle theory in its main elements and to providing an introductory picture of the widest theoretical and operative judicial context of multi-level protection of fundamental rights, in which the Spanish and Italian jurisprudence operates. Therefore, after a concise overview of the balancing in the world, the chapter concentrates on, first, the balancing of fundamental labour rights in the Court of Justice of the EU and the European Court of Human Rights, second, the techniques and the criteria applied by the Italian and Spanish Constitutional Courts and, third, the controversial profile of the role public financial factors play in the constitutional courts' case law.

2.2 A worldwide panoramic of constitutional balancing

The territorial expansion of the principle of proportionality is extraordinary, enough to render the search for an alternative balancing technique in modern legal systems particularly challenging. As shown in the following chapters, Italy provides a rare example of a possible alternative to the proportionality test, *i.e.* an alternative – although not opposite – balancing technique.

The migration-phase of the principle of proportionality, started in the 1970s, has been cautiously traced by Barak.[4] First, the Court of Justice of the European Union (CJEU) and the European Court of Human Rights (ECtHR), respectively in 1970 and 1976, endorsed the proportionality principle of German origins.

The ECtHR subsequently influenced the Canadian Jurisprudence (1986), which, in turn, impacted on New Zealand and Australia, where the proportionality principle was adopted as a procedure to adjudicate fundamental rights in 1992.[5] In the mid-1990s also South Africa and Israel joined the judicial globalisation process, by adopting the same adjudication technique.[6]

The application of the proportionality test by the CJEU and the ECtHR contributed to spreading the technique in Central and Eastern European

4 Barak 2012, 181 ff.

5 Even if, Bernal Pulido 2013, 488, holds that in Australia the proportionality test is not properly applied, while there is a discussion at judicial level, on whether a justification for borrowing proportionality exists and, hence, if proportionality should be accepted as a standard in judicial practice.

6 Barak 2012. Although others claim that the South African Constitutional Court argues in terms of reasonableness, Young 2017. These diverse conclusions demonstrate the ambiguity that still remains around the principle of proportionality, notwithstanding the attentive studies of authoritative scholars.

Countries, such as Russia (1993) and Poland (1997), as well as in numerous Western European Countries, where Austria was the first country of endorsement, in 1978, also due to its legal familiarity with the German system, and UK and Greece the latest, in 2001.[7]

Not even Brazil and Latin America have been immune and since 1992 the principle of proportionality found its way also in these legal contexts.[8]

As a result, *proportionality* is a key component of the *lingua franca* of comparative constitutional law.[9] The diffusion that proportionality adjudication has undergone is known as migration and/or borrowing,[10] or even as a proper legal transplant. While migration and borrowing are technically not interchangeable terms, nor can be used as synonymous strictly speaking, they render an image which is appropriate for concisely depicting the phenomenon at issue. Obviously, in fact, the principle of proportionality has migrated precisely because other legal systems have decided to adopt it, *i.e.* borrow it.[11] The proportionality migration has not always occurred in full awareness of the receiving courts. Stone Sweet and Mathews observe that "courts first moved toward proportionality tentatively, before embracing it as an overarching principle of the legality".[12]

With migration, the proportionality principle has experienced the influence of each environment in which it has been embedded. Following the particular circumstances of each national context, the operationalisation of the principle of proportionality has acquired different formulations, contents and nuances, depending on the receiving legal culture.[13]

It has been observed that common law judges are still not familiar with balancing in the strict sense, and continental courts tend to strongly rely on the third

7 In Barak's list of countries that have adopted the proportionality test figure also: Portugal, Ireland, Switzerland, Belgium, the Netherlands and Spain (which is assessed further on in this book), Barak 2012, 182.

8 An attentive review of the paths taken by the proportionality principle in space and time is offered Barak 2012, 182 ff. See also Stone Sweet Mathews 2008, 111–158. For an early assessment of proportionality in the European context, Emiliou 1996; while Andrade Neto 2018 devotes a thoughtful analysis to the proportionality migration in Brazil.

9 Andrade Neto 2016, 5; "*constitutional Esperanto*", according to Contiades Fotiadou 2012, 670.

10 See, *inter alia*, Bernal Pulido 2013 and Andrade Neto 2016 who use both expressions; while Stone Sweet Mathews 2008 and Barak 2012 tend to prefer "migration".

11 On the debate around the reasons that justify the migration of proportionality, Bernal Pulido 2013, who specifically claims that the migration of the proportionality principle does not simply derive from a conceptual necessity, according to which proportionality is necessarily entrenched in constitutional rights adjudication, but is supported by a proper normative justification, which is developed by the author by addressing what he identifies as the six phases of the proportionality migration across European countries and legal fields.

12 Stone Sweet Mathews 2008, 160.

13 "[I]n terms of operationalization, different systems employ somewhat different concrete or doctrinal tests", Gardbaum 2010, 83; in a similar way, Stone Sweet Mathews 2008, who refer to "important differences in how judges use PA [Proportionality Adjudication]", 162; see also Harbo 2010, 171.

prong of proportionality adjudication,[14] while in Canada "the three sub-tests that comprise proportionality in Germany are only performed once the measure passed an additional legality test"[15] and judges engage in "balancing in the strict sense" in rare hypotheses.[16]

The US Supreme Court substantially departs from the German test, since it applies a form of judicial balancing, but rejects "the (single) concept of proportionality in favor of separate tiers of means-end scrutiny, strict scrutiny, intermediate scrutiny, undue burden, and so unincorporating different presumptions and tests depending on the particular right at issue".[17]

Perhaps, the notion of "legal transplant" is more suitable to describe the fortune of the principle of proportionality,[18] as it is proper of the comparative method, and it precisely refers to the employment of legal features native to other countries. "Legal transplant" immediately leads to the lecture given at the London School of Economics on 26 June 1973 by Otto Khan-Freund, who conclusively remarked that "any attempt to use a pattern of law outside the environment of its origin continues to entail the risk of rejection",[19] which calls upon legislators and interpreters that avail of the comparative method to carefully consider the social, economic and legal context of origin. Accordingly, it is possible to accept that a hermeneutic principle, as the principle of proportionality, ductile by its very nature, is ontologically more prone to adapt to a new receiving context and successfully deal with the "environmental obstacles",[20] compared to a legal institute.

2.3 Balancing in supranational courts

2.3.1 The CJEU way of balancing: a labour reading

Even at EU level, it is claimed that "[T]here are few areas of Community law, if any at all, where [the principle of proportionality] is not relevant,"[21] but then, which is the content of the proportionality principle applied in the EU context?

Even though the principle of proportionality was not verbalised in the constituent documents of the European Community, it was subsequently developed by the Court of Justice and is now used as a ground for review of EU measures

14 Gardbaum 2010, drawing on Rivers 2006.
15 Andrade Neto 2016, 6.
16 Stone Sweet Mathews 2008, 163. Even the terminology used to identify the three-prong tests is different: rationality, minimal impairment and proportionality, a comparative analysis of German and Canadian application of the proportionality test can be found in Grimm 2007.
17 Gardbaum 2010, 83; Barak 2012, 503 ff.
18 See Bernal Pulido 2013 and, primarily, Kumm 2004, 595, who speaks of "the most successful legal transplant of the twentieth century".
19 Kahn-Freund 1974, 27.
20 In this way Kahn-Freund 1974, 10, 13 and 17, drawing on Montesquieu's theory.
21 AG in CJEU, C-120/94, *Commission v Greece*, opinion delivered on 6 April 1995, 70.

and national measures and is equally relevant in the adjudication of fundamental rights and freedoms provided for by the Charter of Fundamental Rights of the European Union, although less judicial practice exists on this side.[22]

In the earlier stage of judicial application, the proportionality principle was mostly invoked to evaluate market regulation measures with an impact on economic freedoms.[23] One of the first occasions in which the Court of Justice has referred to the concept of proportionality dates back to 1977, when it had to decide upon the legitimacy of an agriculture policy measure. With a calculation based on precise economic factors, it concluded that the burden imposed upon the interested manufacturers was "disproportionate".[24]

An early application of the principle of proportionality to the labour law field regarded Council Directive 93/104/EC, concerning certain aspects of the organisation of working time.[25] The United Kingdom had contested the legitimacy of Council Directive 93/104/EC, mainly supporting that it would go beyond the competence recognised to the Council by Art. 118a of the Treaty (of Maastricht), since the Directive at issue would not be limited to impose "minimum requirements for gradual implementation". The applicant argued, among others, that the improvement of health and safety protection of workers required by the Directive could not be regarded as corresponding to the definition of "minimum requirements" and that "less restrictive measures" could have equally achieved the "desired level of protection".[26]

While the UK understanding of "minimum requirements" is quickly dismissed, since the expression cannot be understood as a "lowest common denominator",[27] "[A]s regards the principle of proportionality, the Court has held that, in order to establish whether a provision of Community law complies with that principle, it must be ascertained whether the means which it employs are suitable for the

22 Tridimas 2006, 137, adds that the principle "governs the exercise by the Community of its legislative competence", while he does not accentuate the role in the Charter's rights adjudication, likely because, at the time, the Charter's legal status was not defined, yet.

23 Especially as far as concerns agricultural policies, Jacobs 1999.

24 CJEU, C-114/76, 5 July 1977, *Bela-Mühle Josef Bergmann KG v Grows-Farm GmbH & Co. KG*, 7, here the "Written observations submitted to the Court" had introduced and elaborated on the content of the principle of proportionality even more than the Court itself. Although others prefer to emphasise CJEU, C-11/70, 17 December 1970, *Internationale Handelsgesellschaft mbH v Einfuhr- und Vorratsstelle für Getreide und Futtermittel*, a case still concerning the common agricultural policy, where the AG's argument that the principle of proportionality found a sufficient basis in the EU Treaties was accepted the Court, which applied in practice the suitability and the necessity tests, without, however, naming the proportionality principle as such: Barak 2012, 185; Sauter 2013, 446.

25 CJEU, C-84/94, *United Kingdom of Great Britain and Northern Ireland v Council of the European Union*, 12 November 1996. Nevertheless, the first occasion ever in which the Court of Justice used the proportionality principle to assess the consistency of a national act with EU law has been identified in CJEU, C-120/78, 20 February 1979, *Rewe-Zentral AG v Bundesmonopolverwaltung für Branntwein*, *inter alia*, Suter 2017, 446–447.

26 CJEU, C-84/94, 51, 52.

27 CJEU, C-84/94, 56.

purpose of achieving the desired objective and whether they do not go beyond what is necessary to achieve it".[28]

It is also stressed that the judicial review of the compliance with the principle of proportionality, "must allow a wide discretion" to the Council. The Court explains the argumentative consequences for the judicial review process: "[J]udicial review of the exercise of that discretion must therefore be limited to examining whether it has been vitiated by manifest error or misuse of powers, or whether the institution concerned has manifestly exceeded the limits of its discretion".[29]

The Directive is finally found suitable to achieve the aim pursued[30] and it is notable that, in applying Art. 118a, the Council does not have to produce scientific proofs to demonstrate the suitability of the measure to achieve its aim, but it is enough that a clear justification is provided.[31] At the same time, no manifest error was found and the Court supported its conclusion by reviewing the merit of the labour norms at stake.[32]

Not even a misuse of powers was met, where, by "misuse of powers" is meant "the adoption by a Community institution of a measure with the exclusive or main purpose of achieving an end other than that stated or evading a procedure specifically prescribed by the Treaty for dealing with the circumstances of the case".[33]

In reviewing Community acts, the Court controls the exercise of the EU public power. The intensity of the scrutiny varies over the years and from case to case,[34] but it is now settled that for a Euro-unitarian norm to be respectful of the principle of proportionality, the discretion of the legislator must be exercised so that the means the provision employs to achieve its aim correspond to the importance of the aim (suitability test), are necessary for its achievement (necessity test) and no less restrictive means can be preferred (LSR test[35]).[36]

The tendency to apply only two stages of the proportionality test, avoiding the balancing in a strict sense test, is deemed to be the consequence of "an axiological pre-conception favouring market freedom",[37] which, being the pillars of the internal market, do not accept a counter-weight that may obstruct their application.

28 CJEU, C-84/94, 57.
29 CJEU, C-84/94, 58, it is the "manifestly inappropriate" test, Tradimas 2006, 143–149.
30 CJEU, C-84/94, 59.
31 CJEU, C-84/94, 79
32 CJEU, C-84/94, 60 ff.
33 CJEU, C-84/94, 69.
34 Jacobs 1999, 5. For a review of the principle of proportionality in EU law in the review of Community measures, cf. Tridimas 2006, 136–174.
35 That is an element of the test applied by the CJEU particularly emphasised by some authors, as Sauter 2013.
36 Tridimas 1996, 84 ff.
37 Scaccia 2019, 20.

Proportionality *stricu sensu*, the third, and last, sub-test of the proportionality adjudication, may become relevant at a further stage, *i.e.* when a conflict between fundamental rights or freedoms arises,[38] that is the stage where the principle of proportionality implies "[the] establishment of a link between the seriousness of the interference found and the seriousness of the reason that could justify the interference".[39]

The principle of proportionality in the EU serves the further purpose of checking on the compatibility of national measures with the Treaties, in order to determine whether and to what extent they interfere with fundamental freedoms. In this context, proportionality becomes an instrument to promote market integration.[40] In fact, it has been observed, there is a difference in the Court's application of the proportionality principle when an economic fundamental freedom is restricted by a national norm or by an EU measure. While in the first case the Court is more rigid in its evaluation and more prone to disregard the national prerogatives, when an EU measure is at stake "the Court is more readily prepared to defer to the discretion of the Community [now EU] institutions",[41] by applying a "mild form of balancing".[42] Although there are differences depending on the fundamental freedom at issue, access to the market remains the key criterion that guides the Court.[43]

The elaboration of the so-called Gebhard-formula, which systematises the previous Court's case law, represents a turning moment for the application of the principle of proportionality in the assessment of national measures. National measures, to be legitimate even if hindering or making less attractive the exercise of fundamental freedoms, must comply with both the principle of non-discrimination and the principle of proportionality. In practice, "they must fulfil four conditions: they must be applied in a non-discriminatory manner; they must be

38 Gutiérrez-Fons 2021, 235, as clearly expressed in CJEU C-283/11, 22 January 2013, *Sky Österreich*, 60: "[w]here several rights and fundamental freedoms [...] are at issue, the assessment of the possible disproportionate nature of a provision of [EU] law must be carried out with a view to reconciling the requirements of the protection of those different rights and freedoms and a fair balance between them". On this stage of application of the proportionality test see also Pino 2007

39 Opinion of AG in CJEU, C-207/16, *Ministerio Fiscal*, delivered on 3 May 2018, 82. However, at EU level, "a truncated test is generally used", Sauter 2013, 445. Overall, the scholar develops a slightly different reconstruction of the proportionality test in the Court of Justice's case law, by assessing a number of judgments, covering various fields of EU law.

40 Harbo 2010, 172; Tridimas 2006, 193.

41 Tridimas 2006, 193 and case law cited therein; in a similar way De Búrca 1993, 146. A tendency to be stricter towards national acts can also be explained with the argument that "it is for the EU legislator to strike the right balance between European unity and national diversity", Gutiérrez-Fons 2021, 232. A positive stand towards the application of the proportionality principle in EU law, specifically in the field of administrative law is taken, for instance, by Schwarz 2006, 664–665.

42 Sauter 2013, 447.

43 Still more relevant than the anti-discrimination principle, which is anyway established, Tridimas 2006, 206.

justified by imperative requirements in the general interest [justification principle]; they must be suitable for securing the attainment of the objective which they pursue [suitability principle]; and they must not go beyond what is necessary in order to attain it [necessity principle]".[44] Where this latter criterion is expressed in "the 'less restrictive alternative' test".[45]

With the *Laval* quartet,[46] the international labour lawyers' community extensively confronted itself with the practical application of the Gebhard-formula and, generally, with the proportionality test in the EU context.[47]

Not that a judicial balancing between economic freedoms and fundamental labour rights by the CJEU had not occurred before. Emblematic is *Schmidberger*,[48] where the Austrian authorities had allowed a demonstration that had the effect of blocking the Brenner Pass between Austria and Italy. However, presumably, the *Schmidberger* case did not give rise to the same academic and political stir since the fundamental right of expression and the right of assembly (as enshrined in Art. 10 and Art. 11 of the ECHR) prevailed, mostly because the Austrian authorisation passed the less restrictive means test.

The explanation of the reason why the Court has adopted a different approach in *Schmidberger*,[49] compared to *Laval*, given by Harbo, does not convince, since "the idea that there exists a hierarchy of rights, where freedom of expression and human dignity have a high standing, whereas the right to strike does not" is not supported by any strong argumentative basis; not even the classification of the right to strike "as an economic right" can be shared. The difference should rather be found in the central relevance the norms of the posting of workers Directive have played in *Laval*,[50] or, rather, in the change in the composition of the Luxemburg Court that followed the 2004 enlargement.[51]

44 CJEU, C-55/94, 30 November 1995, *Reinhard Gebhard v Consiglio dell'Ordine degli Avvocati e Procuratori di Milano*, 37.

45 Tridimas 2006, 209–220.

46 Expression used to identify four landmark CJEU judgments on freedom to provide services and posting of workers, namely: CJEU, C-438/05, 11 December 2007, *International Transport Workers' Federation and Finnish Seamen's Union v Viking Line ABP and OÜ Viking Line Eesti*; CJEU, C-341/05, 18 December 2007, *Laval un Partneri Ltd v Svenska Byggnadsarbetareförbundet, Svenska Byggnadsarbetareförbundets avdelning 1, Byggettan and Svenska Elektrikerförbundet*; CJEU, C-346/06, 3 April 2008, *Dirk Rüffert v Land Niedersachsen*; Cjeu C-319/06, 19 June 2008, *Commission of the European Communities v Grand Duchy of Luxemburg*.

47 Although the Court refrains from using this wording. Only to mention some of the authors that have addressed the four controversial cases: Orlandini 2008; Van Peijpe 2009; Davies 2008; Ales Novitz 2010; Zahn, De Witte 2011; Giubboni 2017, 55–96. For a focus on the balancing in *Laval*, *Viking* and *Omega* see also Sybe 2013. See also Maduro 1999, 449.

48 CJEU, C-112/00, 12 June 2003, *Eugen Schmidberger, Internationale Transporte und Planzüge v Republik Österreich*.

49 As well as in CJEU C-36/2002, 25 June 2020, *Omega Spielhallen- und Automatenaufstellungs-GmbH v Oberbürgermeisterin der Bundesstadt Bonn*.

50 Also Harbo 2010, 176; Orlandini 2013, 52.

51 *Inter alia*, Naômé 2008; Belavusau 2008.

The balancing exercise is particularly interesting in the *Laval* Judgment, where the Court has balanced the freedom to provide services against the right to collective action, which must "be recognised as a fundamental right which forms an integral part of the general principles of Community law" and "[A]s is reaffirmed by Art. 28 of the Charter of Fundamental Rights of the European Union, it is to be protected in accordance with Community law and national law and practices".[52] However, "the exercise of that right may none the less be subject to certain restrictions".[53]

Here, the criteria adopted by the Court are reiterated as follows: "since the freedom to provide services is one of the fundamental principles of the Community [...] a restriction on that freedom is warranted only if it pursues a legitimate objective compatible with the Treaty and is justified by overriding reasons of public interest; if that is the case, it must be suitable for securing the attainment of the objective which it pursues and not go beyond what is necessary in order to attain it".[54]

The CJEU formally recognises that the European Community does not only pursue market-oriented aims, but also a "social purpose", so that the objectives followed by economic freedoms must be balanced against the aims pursued by social policies. That is the reason why, in principle, a collective action, taken in order to ensure a certain level of working terms and conditions to posted workers, can be considered as falling within the objective of protecting posted workers.[55]

However, this was not the case in the *Laval* dispute. In fact, according to the Court the blockade organised by the Swedish trade union went beyond what was necessary to attain a legitimate objective, since the aim of the collective action, namely the signature of the collective agreement for the building sector, did not correspond to the objective of protecting posted workers.

The collective actions organised by the Swedish trade unions could not be justified in light of the public interest objective either, since the negotiation on pay was not imposed by a legislative act.

The balancing applied by the CJEU has been extensively blamed as being unfair.[56] In *Laval*, the right to strike and the freedom to provide services have been placed by the CJEU on two different footings, thus showing an evident

52 CJEU, C-341/05, 91

53 CJEU, C-341/05, 91. The proportionality test in the CJEU case law is especially criticised when used to adjudicate cases dealing with fundamental rights; see, *inter alia*, De Witte 2009; Loi 2011; De Vries et al. 2012.

54 CJEU, C-341/05, 101.

55 CJEU, C-341/05, 105 ff.

56 On the balancing conducted in *Laval* cf. Beucker et al. and, also, Ballestrero 2008, 379, who metaphorically illustrates how the competence on strike action (excluded by Art. 153 TFEU) left the European Union from the main door and the CJEU, in *Viking* and *Laval*, let it in again from the economic freedoms' window. Orlandini 2013, 49–61, denounces, with a well-articulated argumentation, not the results of the balancing conducted by the Court, but the very choice of deciding through judicial balancing the case at issue, since he does not share the assumption that economic freedoms can be applied in the context of an industrial

liberal approach of the European judges, still prone to promote the primacy of the *Economic* Union.[57]

In a recent essay, Sacha Garben reflects on whether the problems arising from *Laval* and *Viking* have been most lately resolved by the CJEU, with the aim to eventually discuss the ways in which economic and fundamental social rights can find a more appropriate balance.[58] In his analysis, conducted adopting a positive conception of the internal market in itself, as a potential valuable instrument for social progress, *Viking*, *Laval* and *Rueffert* are defined "game changers"[59] of the balance between economic and social interests.

Albeit some positive leaps have been identified, the author does not find a significant improvement in the economic-social imbalance, even without denying the acknowledgement of the activism demonstrated by the Court in the case law on equal treatment and the relative improvements in specific aspects of working-time, which, however, do not pose sensitive problems from our perspective. An optimistic stand is expressed about *Regiopost*, but that cannot be shared.[60] Indeed, in *Regiopost* the Court interprets the norms of Directive 96/71/EC consistently with its case law, and not by chance it is often referring to *Rueffert*, with the effect of confirming that the discretion of a public authority to impose the application of a given wage to a company winner of a public tender is limited to the wages imposed by law, administrative acts or collective agreements declared universally applicable.[61]

In *WABE*, the tensions between the economic and the social dimension of the EU came into play once more with a case of conflict between religious freedom at work and freedom to conduct a business. This paragraph is not the place to assess the judgment, which mostly turns around anti-discrimination law. Nevertheless, it is worth using a few words to focus on the terms balanced by the Court: "the principle of non-discrimination enshrined in Article 21 of the Charter and the right to freedom of thought, conscience and religion guaranteed in Art. 10 of the Charter" are understood as being in conflict with "the right of parents to ensure the education and teaching of their children in conformity with their religious,

---

dispute aimed at advocating for the signature of a collective agreement, especially where the right to strike is recognised also by Art. 28 of the Charter.

57 And similar conclusions can be drawn for *Viking*. See, *inter alia*, Eklund 2007–2008; Reich 2008, 159; Davies 2008; Barnard 2014. Recently on the topic, Hartzén et al. 2022.

58 Garben 2020, eventually the author argues that there is a need for a consistent framework, constitutionally and democratically legitimised, which allows a coherent and predictable adjudication of fundamental rights that overcomes the case-by-case approach.

59 Garben 2020, in the same essay, CJEU, C-426/11, 18 July 2013, *Mark Alemo-Herron and Others v Parkwood Leisure Ltd* and CJEU, C-210/15, 21 December 2016, *Anonymi Geniki Etairia Tsimenton Iraklis (AGET Iraklis) v Ypourgos Ergasias, Koinonikis Asfalisis kai Koinonikis Allilengyis*, where the freedom to conduct a business is at stake, are reviewed.

60 Garben 2020, 376 ff.

61 CJEU, C-115/14, 17 November 2015, *RegioPost GmbH & Co. KG v Stadt Landau in der Pfalz*; skepticism confirmed also by CJEU, C-549/13, *Bundesdruckerei GmbH v Stadt Dortmund*, 18 September 2014, cf. Frosecchi, Orlandini 2020.

philosophical and pedagogical convictions recognised in Article 14(3) of the Charter and the freedom to conduct a business recognised in Article 16 of the Charter".[62] It is hardly conceivable that the right to religious freedom may come into conflict with the right of parents to ensure education and teaching consistently with their convictions. Freedom of religion could conflict with parental rights to educate their children in the religious sphere, only if Art. 10 were to protect also the possibility of imposing one's religion on others. However, freedom of religion certainly does not cover this activity, that remains outside the scope of application of Art. 10 of the Charter. On the contrary, the imposition of a religious faith is the denial, even a cause of infringement, of the freedom of religion and conscience, this being understood as the freedom to choose if and to which confession to belong.[63] If that persuades, the parental right referred to above must be interpreted as a corollary, if not as a real completion, of the freedom of religion and, as such, cannot conflict with the latter.

Following the same assumptions, the conflict between wearing a religious symbol, albeit in an educational context, and educating one's children freely would not occur if the teacher attempted to educate the children about her faith either, since such behaviour would simply not be protected by the freedom of religion, plainly resulting in unlawful conduct.

This latest example concerning the selection of the terms subject to the balancing shows, once more, how ambiguous the attitude of the Court of Justice is in the application of the principle of proportionality.

The *WABE* case leads us to highlight a further critical profile, already mentioned above: the application of the proportionality principle in case of conflict between fundamental rights enshrined in the Charter.

It is for the Charter itself to identify the principle under discussion as the main criterion to adjudicate on the limitations to rights and freedoms listed therein. Indeed, Art. 52.1 of the Charter reads: "[a]ny limitation on the exercise of the rights and freedoms recognised by this Charter must be provided for by law and respect the essence of those rights and freedoms. Subject to the principle of proportionality, limitations may be made only if they are necessary and genuinely meet objectives of general interest recognised by the Union or the need to protect the rights and freedoms of others". In theory, it precisely corresponds to the principle of proportionality, which requires balancing of comparable, in nature, but conflicting, in the factual situation, rights and interests. However, several norms envisage inherent restrictions of specific rights and freedoms, expressed with formula, such as: "in accordance with Union law and national law and practices", or "may be regulated by law in so far as is necessary for the general interest". A

62 CJEU, C-804/18, 15 July 2021, *IX v WABE eV and MH Müller Handels GmbH v MJ*, 84. For how clear is the layout of the balancing proposed, the Court does not indulge in applying the proportionality principle, as its purpose was merely to suggest to the national legislator how to determine a more favourable provision within the meaning of Art. 8.1, Directive 2000/78, Frosecchi 2022.

63 Della Torre 2008.

distinction that may suggest a hierarchy of fundamental rights, where only rights without an inherent limitation can be limited as long as they comply with other comparable Charter rights, while rights inherently limited can be restricted on the ground of any general interest, obviously in so far as such limitation is provided by law. According to this view, only certain rights are guaranteed at equal level and therefore can be subject to balancing, through mutual maximisation.[64]

Not only is the principle of proportionality enshrined in Art. 52.1, but also the principle (although not expressed in terms of "principle") of the essential content of rights and freedoms: "the essence of rights and freedoms" must be respected even in case of limitation of such rights and freedoms. The operative application of the essential content approach at EU level is as complex as it is at national level and it is controversial whether it has a functional autonomy or it is, rather, linked to, or even dependent upon, the application of the principle of proportionality.[65]

Going back to the question articulated at the outset of this section (*i.e.* which is the content of the proportionality principle applied in the EU context?), the *Fedesa* judgment, even without being one of the most recent rulings, contributes to drawing a conclusive reflection and providing a tentative answer. In *Fedesa*, the Court summarises the content of the principle of proportionality, which constitutes "one of the general principles of Community law. By virtue of that principle, the lawfulness of the prohibition of an economic activity is subject to the condition that the prohibitory measures are appropriate and necessary in order to achieve the objectives legitimately pursued by the legislation in question; when there is a choice between several appropriate measures recourse must be had to the least onerous, and the disadvantages caused must not be disproportionate to the aims pursued".[66] Nevertheless, in the same judgment the Court clarifies that the discretion left to the EU legislator in the specific field of EU law under evaluation conditions the judicial review, which can be limited, in case of wide legislative discretion, "to examining whether the measure in question is vitiated by a manifest error or misuse of powers and that the authority concerned has not manifestly exceeded the limits of discretion".[67]

The quoted paragraphs of *Fedesa* confirm the understanding of the principle of proportionality in the EU context as a pliable (and opportunistic?) tool, that

64 Schiek 2017, 628 ff.

65 Surely, its endorsement in Art. 52 is influenced by the experience of the Member States that are familiar with it, as already present in the respective national traditions. Profile addressed, *inter alia*, by Brkan 2018, who, drawing on national constitutional case law, ECtHR case law and CJEU case law attempts to conceptualise "essence". On the essential content of fundamental rights, see Chapter 1, para. 4.

66 CJEU, C-331/88, 13 November 1990, *The Queen v Minister of Agriculture, Fisheries and Food and Secretary of State for Health, ex parte: Fedesa and others*, 13. Harbo 2010, 159, observes that the principle of proportionality in EU law is defined "general" to mark a distinction from the principles of law, as the principle of proportionality applies to innumerous and varied cases. In other terms, and in many national legal systems, it may be called a "general clause".

67 CJEU, C-331/88, 9.

provides some reference points for the CJEU to construct the legal reasoning, but it is far from constituting a stringent argumentative technique that assures rationality and predictability of judicial decision making.[68] We are far from the rigour envisioned by Alexy's theory and its proponents. Similarly, the CJEU approach is still distant from the consistency sought by the national constitutional courts and strongly claimed by national communities.[69]

2.3.2 *The ECtHR way of balancing: a labour reading*

The role of the European Court of Human Rights in the multilevel system of rights protection is well-known.[70] Although the ECHR does not explicitly refer to the proportionality principle as an hermeneutic criterion applicable to the interpretation of the rights guaranteed by the Convention, the Strasbourg Court consistently relies on a proportionality test, which noticeably echoes the adjudication techniques reviewed above.[71]

Also in this case, the structure of the scrutiny based on the proportionality principle absorbs the peculiarities of both the Court and the overall system in which it is enshrined, which is far, in nature and functioning, from national legal systems as well as from the European Union.[72]

The factors subject to balancing before the ECtHR are the national public interests pursued by the contested national measure and the fundamental rights enshrined in the ECHR. Not only, "[I]n various situations [...] the conflict we are facing is between a Convention right and an interest recognised an important weight under international or domestic law, but which does not have the status of a fundamental right guaranteed under the Convention".[73]

68 Similar conclusions are reached by De Búrca 1993, 111 and Harbo 2010, who grounds his thesis on a comprehensive assessment of relevant CJEU judgments. While Sauter 2013, 464–466, believes that the lack of a strict proportionality is a feature and, to some extent, an advantage for the EU integration process, rather than a flaw.

69 A thought provoking and well-informed reflection on the differences between national constitutional courts and the Court of Justice's adjudication methods, in Scaccia 2019, 24–31.

70 For a review of the ECtHR role in the employment law sphere see Dorssemont et al. 2013 and Perulli Sychenko 2018.

71 The Council of Europe documents still reflect the outdated division between first and second generation rights: ECHR for civil and political rights and ESC for social and economic rights. As a result of a similar dichotomy, only the rights enshrined in the ECHR are enforced by the European Court of Human Rights and by its binding decisions, while the conclusions of the European Committee of Social Rights, *i.e.* the body deemed to interpret the ESC and assess violations by national laws remain confined to the soft law sphere. See the relevance of a distinction as such in ICC, Judgment 194/2018, discussed in Chapters 3 and 4.

72 The European Convention on Human Rights, that the Court is called upon to enforce, does not create a proper *legal system*, but it rather represents a concise bill of rights that a number of states decided to undersign in 1970 to guarantee that joining states would never violate a minimum level of civil and political standards, Pirker 2013, 189.

73 De Schutter Tulkens 2008, 175.

The Convention's provision of outstanding significance for labour law is Art. 11, titled "Freedom of Assembly and Association", which has been repeatedly enforced by the ECtHR to protect trade union rights, including the right to collective bargaining and the right to strike.[74] As it occurs in most of the provisions of the ECHR, a specific limitation clause is provided in paragraph 2 of Art. 11, so that restrictions to "the right to freedom of peaceful assembly and to freedom of association with others, including the right to form and to join trade unions" are admitted, as long as they are prescribed by law and are necessary.

Association of Academics v Iceland, which provides an overview of the Court's case law on Art. 11 ECHR, reviews the adjudication technique applied in Strasbourg consistently with the second paragraph. It emerges that interference with the rights protected under Art. 11.1 ECHR must be "prescribed by law", "pursue a legitimate aim" and be "necessary in a democratic society" to achieve those aims. More precisely, the interference must correspond "to a 'pressing social need'"[75] and must be "proportionate to the legitimate aim pursued". Moreover, "[R]egard must be had to the fair balance to be struck between the competing interest of the individual and of the community as a whole".[76]

Not less remarkable is the weight attached to the proofs national authorities must provide to justify the contested act under all the mentioned profiles, which must be "relevant and sufficient".[77]

Last, the Strasbourg Court appreciates an element not new to our discourse, *i.e.* the discretion of the contracting state, which is articulated in terms of "margin of appreciation" and which exercise is evaluated by the ECtHR on the grounds of a number of factors that include: "the nature and extent of the restriction on the trade union right at issue, the object pursued by the contested restriction and the competing rights and interests of other individuals in society who are liable to suffer as a result of the unrestricted exercise of that right".[78]

A last profile, peculiar to a system such as that of the European Convention on Human Rights, is the relevance recognised, in principle, not just to the "apposite

74 On the right to collective bargaining see, *inter alia*, ECtHR, *Demir and Baykara v Turkey*, 2008, commented on by Ewing Hendy 2010, and *National Union of Rail, Maritime and Transport Workers v the United Kingdom*, 2014. On the right to strike, see *e.g.* ECtHR, *Association of Academics v Iceland*, 2018; as well as ECtHR, *National Union of Rail, Maritime and Transport Workers v the United Kingdom*, 2014. Cf. Mantouvalou 2013; Sagan 2018.

75 A condition that, for instance, was not met in another judgment concerning disciplinary measures against public sector workers who had participated in a one-day national strike: ECtHR, *Enerji Yapı-Yol Sen v Turkey*, 2009.

76 ECtHR, *Association of Academics v Iceland*, 25.

77 A glaring example is offered by ECtHR, *Ognevenko v Russia*, 2018, 73: "even assuming that railway transport was an essential service, serious restrictions such as a complete ban on the right to strike in respect of certain categories of railway workers would still require *solid evidence* from the State to justify their necessity", 73, italics added.

78 ECtHR, *Association of Academics v Iceland*, 25.

international instruments",[79] but also to the "degree of common ground between member States of the Council of Europe in relation to the issue arising".[80]

The three-prong test, thus, recurs, with the assessment of suitability, necessity and proportionality in a strict sense of the contested measure. However, it is evidently enriched with characteristic elements, such as the "pressing social need", or the attention paid to the democratic feature of a society.[81]

The incessant and dialectic relationship with national courts, mostly highest national courts, that is found in the ECtHR judgments is the result of the subsidiary role of the Court that leaves to national authorities the primary responsibility for implementing fundamental rights enshrined in the Conventions. The principle of subsidiarity, in conjunction with the "margin of appreciation", may be read as the inherent cause for the limited scope of action the Strasbourg judges retain to review compliance with fundamental rights.[82] Beyond any doubt, it is telling of the specificity of the ECHR system, as compared to national legal systems or, even, to the EU.

2.3.3 On reasonableness

As repeatedly stated, balancing is a method to adjudicate conflict between constitutional rights and interests. In order to be applied by courts, a technique, which normally takes the form of a hermeneutic principle, is necessary.[83] The large diffusion of the principle of proportionality in the jurisprudence of courts all over the world and the impressive success it has achieved among legal scholars have partially eclipsed the role that the principle of reasonableness still plays.[84]

In several legal systems, reasonableness has been slowly replaced by proportionality and, by now, is certainly less widespread. Understandably, given its more circumscribed relevance, it is also less discussed by the international literature. And, due to the peculiarities of the national legal systems in which it is embedded

79 Emblematic are ECtHR, *Al-Jedda v United Kingdom* (2011) and ECtHR, *Al-Dulimi and Montana Management Inc. v Switzerland* (2012) where the Court decided mostly on the grounds of UN principles, Palombella 2015, 15 ff.

80 ECtHR, *Association of Academics v Iceland*, 25.

81 For a discussion on the principle of proportionality in the ECtHR jurisprudence see, among the vast literature, McBride 1999; De Schutter Tulkens 2008; Pirker 2013, 187–234; Scaccia 2019; Gerards 2013.

82 Borowski 2021, 141 ff.

83 *A contrario*, Contiades Fotiadou 2012, 675–676, seem to understand "proportionality, balancing and reasonableness" as interrelated methods, without rigorously distinguishing between methods and techniques. Even though, at a later stage, they consider only "proportionality" and "reasonableness" as comparable tools, *i.e.* techniques. On "balancing" as a technique, or rather as a "logic", and "proportionality" as an "argumentative tool", see also Pino 2008, 97 ff.

84 It is emblematic the disagreement between Barak 2012 and Young 2017 on the criterion invoked by the South African Court. While the first identifies South Africa as one of the countries that have borrowed proportionality, according to Young the South African Constitutional Court argues in terms of reasonableness.

and invoked, the components of reasonableness can be hardly determined in general terms.[85]

As regards the principle of reasonableness, the differences are even more appreciable than for the principle of proportionality, which, at least at theoretical level, has gained a notable consent. This is, perhaps, also the reason why "[T]he conventional wisdom is that reasonableness is determined on a case-by-case basis, in accordance with each case's special circumstances".[86]

Notwithstanding that, Barak maintains that proportionality and reasonableness are "identical" in their function of balancing conflicting constitutional rights and/or interests.[87] By endorsing Robert Alexy's thesis, he argues that since the main component of reasonableness is "the balancing between competing principles" and, similarly, the main step of the proportionality test is balancing in the strict sense, there is an operative convergence among the two principles.[88]

However, the ease by which he reaches his conclusions suggests a bias against the principle of reasonableness, probably justified by a partial understanding of it, due to a limited access to non-English or non-German speaking legal systems where the principle of reasonableness is applied.

Indeed, even if the author conceptually values the differences in the definition of reasonableness that exist in the diverse legal systems and high courts' jurisprudence, he refers concisely and incidentally to the UK,[89] Canada and New Zealand (which, however, apply the principle of proportionality) to then briefly reflect on the relationship between proportionality and reasonableness on the basis of the Israeli definition of reasonableness, that is, what he calls, "reasonableness 'in the strong sense'".[90]

To the contrary, in *Smith and Grady v UK*,[91] the European Court of Human Rights seems to appreciate a relevant difference between proportionality adjudication and reasonableness. The UK Court judged the contested policy of the

85 Adinolfi 2009, 383.
86 Barak 2012, 373.
87 Barak 2012, 378.
88 Barak 2012, 378, drawing on Alexy 2009.
89 Where, it has been argued, instead, that "[T]he reasonableness principle, however unfashionable to commentators, is more pervasive, multifaceted and deep-rooted. And it still has a central place in public law" Hickman 2004, 198. The principle of reasonableness, also in its relationship with proportionality in UK case law is discussed by Hickman, who considers several relevant judgments in administrative and tort law, above all, the renowned negative formulation in *Wednesbury*: "[U]reasonableness rests to a large extent on unarticulated and underdeveloped values and lacks the same degree of structure and sophistication analysis [of the principle of proportionality]".
90 Barak 2012, 371–378. "Reasonableness", in its various nuances, can also be found in constitutional judgments adjudicating fundamental social rights of other legal systems, such as in South Africa and India, see Contiades Fotiadou 2012, 678 ff. and Bilchitz 2014, both discussing the renowned case *Grootboom v Government of the Republic of South Africa*, 2001. More specifically on the South African case, see Young 2017. For a charming reading on the flexible character of reasonableness, Gluckman 1963, 178–206.
91 ECtHR, *Smith and Grady v UK*, 2000.

Ministry of Defence in compliance with the principle of reasonableness, in as much as it "could not be said to be beyond the range of responses open to a reasonable decision-maker and, accordingly, could not be considered to be 'irrational'".[92]

The ECtHR subverted the national conclusions, in the application of the principle of proportionality, as it stated that "the threshold at which the High Court and the Court of Appeal could find the Ministry of Defence policy irrational [hence, under UK law, "unreasonable"] was placed so high that it effectively excluded any consideration by the domestic courts of the question of whether the interference with the applicants' rights answered a pressing social need or was proportionate to the national security and public order aims pursued".[93] In other words, the reasonableness criterion, as understood in the UK context, was insufficient to satisfy the standards of assessment required by the Strasbourg Court, *i.e.* the principle of proportionality.[94]

At EU level, the principle of reasonableness may be considered absorbed by the principle of proportionality, as in the case law of the Court of Justice, explicit reference to reasonableness can be hardly found and where the Court invokes "reasonableness", a convergence with the suitability test may be identified. However, the lack of a systematic application by the Court hampers the articulation of a proper content of the principle of reasonableness in EU law, and in the respective case law.[95] Unless we accept an interchangeability with the principle of proportionality, which is, as seen above, the hermeneutic principle chosen by the Luxemburg Court.

A later section in this chapter reviews the main features of the principle of reasonableness in the Italian jurisprudence, since it represents the key principle applied by the Italian Constitutional Court to adjudicate constitutional rights. While the international literature has only marginally discussed this principle, the Italian academic production is extensive and meaningful[96] and provides further informed insights for the discussion on reasonableness and its relationship with proportionality.

2.3.4 Around values, balancing and proportionality in supranational courts

The axiological perspective that has guided the first section on theoretical justifications of the balancing of conflicting rights and interests needs to be resumed

92 ECtHR, *Smith and Grady v UK*, 2000, 137.

93 ECtHR, *Smith and Grady v UK*, 2000, 138.

94 Craig 2013, 37, 38, who defines proportionality as a "more searching" criterion, than the reasonableness applied by UK courts. On the difficulties of British domestic courts in applying proportionality following ECtHR case law, Rivers 2014.

95 On reasonableness in EC law, see Adinolfi 2009 and Tesauro 2012.

96 It is no coincidence that one of the most significant volumes published on the topic in the latest decades has been edited by three Italian authors, see Bongiovanni et al. 2009.

to reflect on the constitutional character of the systems in which the CJEU and the ECtHR are entrenched.

Whether the EU is founded upon values is not under discussion,[97] considering that it originates from the encounter of constitutional national states, anchored to several values, which have represented the breeding ground for the CJEU, since the 1970s, to construct the EU legal order.[98] Not only relevant values are now listed in the Treaty on the European Union: human dignity; freedom; democracy; equality; the rule of law; the respect for human rights; the rights of persons belonging to minorities; pluralism; non-discrimination; tolerance; justice; solidarity; equality between women and men.[99]

The meaningful question is whether the EU has been able to fully and effectively turn those shared values into norms, or, better, if the EU has made a selection of the values that deserved to achieve a mandatory strength in the EU legal order. The answer given to these questions depends on the understanding of the European Union as a proper constitutional system, or, *vice versa*, as a legal system not (yet?) fully constitutionalised that has borrowed the proportionality adjudication technique for contingency reasons, despite lacking the necessary dogmatic assumptions.

In the literature, there is an attempt to justify the constitutional dimension of EU law.

According to Wolf Sauter, the European Economic Community (EEC) Treaty was already a proper constitutional Charter of the Community. The rule of law and the primacy of EEC law over the law of the Member States represented the pillars of such a constitutional system, which was further enriched with the introduction of legal principles, required to complete the more complex and open picture designed by the successive EU Treaties. The European Court of Justice has offered the main contribution to the enrichment of the constitutional character of the EU treaties, by constitutionalising its case law. Under this view, such a judicial process of construction of a constitutional system has been possible precisely because of the application of the proportionality principle.[100] Therefore, the author seems to overturn the nexus: the proportionality principle and, hence, balancing have allowed the construction of a constitutional system, and it is not the existence of a constitutional system that allows the application of the proportionality principle and, more generally speaking, of judicial balancing (as it is instead argued in this book).

97 A question asked by Fontana 2022, 85.

98 For a reflection on the European Union's values in the context of the economic crisis, see Martín y Pérez de Nanclares 2019.

99 Art. 2 TEU.

100 Sauter 2013; surely in the development of EU legal principles by the Court of Justice, the principle of proportionality stands out, Weiler Lockhart 1995.

Moreover, the recognition by Art. 6 TEU of the fundamental rights provided for by the Charter as legal principles is one of the key factors that, in Sauter's view, has contributed to the demise of the ordoliberal economic Constitution.[101]

This thesis doesn't completely solve the aporia, since it envisages a constitutional system without a whole-encompassing inclusion of fundamental rights. Indeed, even if fundamental rights are, to some extent, enforced by the Court of Justice[102] and, above all, guaranteed by the Charter, which now has the same legal value as the Treaties, the legislative competence is not admitted with respect to all of them, as the legislative competence derives from the norms of Treaties, not from the norms of the Charter. The nature of the fundamental rights in the EU legal order is that of a constraining tool of the discretion of legislators, whether European or national, acting in fields covered by EU law.[103] Therefore, the dogmatic paradox is that a law that implements a fundamental right or freedom guaranteed by the Treaty may be imposing limits upon a fundamental right guaranteed by the Charter, which has the same legal status as the Treaties, but does

101 Sauter 2013, 444. A reflection on the reasons that justify the application of proportionality by the CJEU is developed by Priker 2013, 246 ff. A positive stand towards a form of Euroconstitutionalism is taken also by Gerstenberg 2019.

102 Especially fundamental *social* rights remain recessive. A conclusion that is not disconfirmed by Gerstenberg 2020, who argues that the Court's jurisprudence has recently "'constitutionalized' directives by combining them with substantive CFREU" (203), hence providing fundamental rights with horizontal direct effect, as, in fact, fundamental social rights have never prevailed. The direct horizontal applicability of rights and freedoms of the Charter has been for long a controversial issue, partially solved by the Court in CJEU, C-414/16, 17 April 2018, *Vera Egenberger v Evangelisches Werk für Diakonie und Entwicklung eV*, 76: "that prohibition, which is laid down in Article 21(1) of the Charter, is sufficient in itself to confer on individuals a right which they may rely on as such in disputes between them in a field covered by EU law". On the mentioned judgment see Lourenço 2019. On the debate, see the relevant contributions in a recent book edited by Izquierdo-Sans, Martínez-Capdevila and Nogueira-Guastavino 2021. Gerstenberg 2020 also suggests that the Court has introduced a dignitarian conception of the Charter, by increasing the relevance of the Charter's provisions, both in the social and economic sphere, as in CJEU, C-201/15, 21 December 2016, *Anonymi Geniki Etairia Tsimenton Iraklis (AGET Iraklis) v Ypourgos Ergasias, Koinonikis Asfalisis kai Koinonikis Allilengyis*, thus implementing the idea of a social market economy introduced by Art. 3.3 TEU. On social rights in the Charter see also Barnard 2020.

103 "[T]he classification of a right as fundamental indicates that Community legal order grants to that right at least a minimum of weight and consequently increases the burden on public authorities to justify restrictions upon it", Tridimas 2006, 310. This includes when the EU institutions "act outside the EU legal framework", hence also in the context of the ESM Treaty, see CJEU, C-8/15, 20 September 2016, *Ledra Advertising Ltd and Others v European Commission and European Central Bank (ECB)*, 67. Although the same cannot be said for Member States, see CJEU, C-370/12, 27 November 2012, *Thomas Pringle v Government of Ireland and Others*, 178–181. On the controversial ruling in *Pringle*, see De Witte Beukers 2013. On Labour rights as fundamental rights in the EU, see also Dukes 2014, 173–193; Sciarra 2005, who reflects on the impact of the Open Method of Coordination on fundamental labour rights; and, with an eye on the 2008 crisis, Sciarra 2018.

not equally bind the legislator; on the other hand, the norms of the Charter are suitable to constrain the enforcement of – even – national constitutional rights.[104]

This view can convince only if there is an agreement about the assumption that for a value to become a positive norm, in a given legal system, that norm has to represent not just a limit to the legislator's action, but also a binding reference for the direction the legislative power shall take, by providing for a specific legislative competence, ultimately deemed to enforce the relevant value.

To the contrary, the EU legal system seems to offer three coexisting options of *postivizzazione*. First, the Treaty provisions that set the four economic freedoms, which constitute the very foundation of the internal market. Second, the Treaty provisions that confer competence on the EU legislator, such as Art. 153 TFEU, as regards the social policy sphere. Third, the articles of the Charter, which traditionally (at least from a constitutional system perspective) would be the ideal destination for provisions that confer normative relevance to founding values. Nevertheless, they lack the power to provide legislative competences, in the terms seen above.[105]

Finally, when the conflict occurs between rights or freedoms provided for by the Charter and freedoms provided for by the Treaty, judicial balancing, especially the third test of proportionality adjudication, *i.e.*, balancing in the strict sense, unavoidably takes the form of an "unequal balancing".[106]

In practice, the EU court finds itself weighing against each other two norms with a different nature, although both primary norms. In the end, that the pendulum swings towards the norm expressing both a fundamental freedom and a legislative competence cannot be surprising (which is coherent with the activism of the CJEU in the field of anti-discrimination law[107]).[108]

104 See CJEU, C-399/11, 26 February 2013, *Stefano Melloni c. Ministerio Fiscal*, 59, 60: "It is settled case-law that, by virtue of the principle of primacy of EU law, which is an essential feature of the EU legal order [...], rules of national law, even of a constitutional order, cannot be allowed to undermine the effectiveness of EU law on the territory of that State [...]. It is true that Article 53 of the Charter confirms that, where an EU legal act calls for national implementing measures, national authorities and courts remain free to apply national standards of protection of fundamental rights, provided that the level of protection provided for by the Charter, as interpreted by the Court, and the *primacy, unity and effectiveness* of EU law are not thereby compromised"; similarly, CJEU, C-617/10, 7 May 2013, *Åklagaren V Hans Åkerberg Fransson*.

105 Critical on this latest profile also Laforgia 2018, 50–52.

106 In the terms expressed by Luciani 1995. On this profile, see Chapter 2, par. 6.4.

107 See the exemplary comparison made by Camardi 2017, 1138, between the right not to be discriminated and the right of information and consultation at work (particularly, CJEU, C-176/12, 15 January 2014, *Association de médiation sociale v. Union locale des syndicats CGT and others*, 54: "It is therefore clear from the wording of Article 27 of the Charter that, for this article to be fully effective, it must be given more specific expression in European Union or national law").

108 Neither after 2006, the Court of Justice has turned into a "Court of rights", since the relevance of fundamental rights in its case-law has remained limited and circumscribed, Bin 2018, 83–84.

Admitting that a legal system that does not provide an all-encompassing protection of fundamental rights, not being bound to enforce them – in the sense of adopting secondary norms aimed to implement them – to the same degree[109] – not to mention the democratic gap[110] – is a constitutional system may represent an inacceptable step back in the historical process that led to modern social constitutions, even more in continental Europe.[111] The claim for "primacy, unity and effectiveness of EU law",[112] which can even go to the detriment of national constitutional rights, exacerbates the concern that the EU legal order, in its present political and legal structure, may be conceived as a proper constitutional model.

These points are raised with the aim to problematise a scenario which, at present, can hardly be defined, at least with the categories traditionally employed to label national legal systems.[113] As a consequence, the dogmatic arguments that support judicial balancing as the ideal adjudication method of fundamental – social – rights cannot be adopted to underpin judicial balancing by the Court of Justice. The incontestable fact that the Court invokes the proportionality principle exclusively demonstrates the malleability of the three-prong test and its adaptability to the contingency, but fails to justify such a pervasive role given to the Luxemburg Court and, consequently, the authority it exercises on the national legislator (the *Laval* case is again emblematic in this respect).

Without arguing that an EU *constitutional* system can never be achieved,[114] the view can be shared that "the social compromises found at national levels deserve protection until such time as a European level compromise has been established".[115]

109 The reference here is to the competencies provided by the Treaties in domains covered also by the Charter's norms, especially to Art. 153 TFEU, which establishes the EU competence over a number of matters of social, including labour, matters, one for all: information and consultation rights at work, enshrined in both Art. 27 of the Charter and Art. 153.1.e) TFEU. On the Charter from a labour rights perspective: Dorssemont et al. 2019. The EU commitment to social rights has been reiterated in the European Pillar of Social Rights, which is critically discussed by Rogowski 2019.

110 Grimm 2019, who highlights the contractual nature of the EU Treaties and the absence of a self-determination process of EU citizens. Bin 2018, 76, properly observes that the democratic deficit within the EU is not an unfortunate causality, but a structural feature of the EU legal order, which is rather based upon market integration.

111 In this respect, it is shared the view that the process initiated by the historic breakthrough represented by the overcoming of liberal constitutions in favour of a social state able to defuse the social conflict has been blocked by the institution of the European Economic Community, Bin 2018, 77.

112 Gutiérrez-Fons 2021, 239.

113 And many other profiles would need to be considered, such as the interaction of all this with the principle of subsidiarity.

114 The EU Constitution, an ambitious project abandoned after the negative results of the French and Dutch referenda – a result that has surprised many, but not all, see the analysis by Startin Krouwel 2013 – may have shifted the paradigm, Korda Schoukens 2006. For a reading of the Charter from the (national) labour law perspective, cf. Ballestrero 2000.

115 Schiek 2017, 616–617. The author, by speculation, develops the theory of the "constitutionally conditioned Internal Market". He derives from the Charter a set of hermeneutic

Such a critical profile is not equally problematic in the context of the European Court of Human Rights' case law, since the impact of the latter on the national constitutional equilibria is milder and mediated by the national legislator. Less controversial also is the nature of the European Convention on Human Rights, a human rights text adopted at regional level, which can be hardly conceived as a constitutional system, mostly in view of the subsidiary role of the ECtHR. Doubts may be also raised when it comes to the parameters (rights, freedoms and interests) subject to the judicial balancing applied by the European Court of Human Rights, but the main controversial profile lies in the – not irrelevant – fact that the ECtHR decides by balancing norms implementing national public interests, which are likely implementing constitutional norms, against rights provided by a regional convention. The subsidiary role of the Strasbourg Court and a lower propensity in positioning itself on a par with national constitutional courts, together with the structural feature of the ECHR and the ductile character of the proportionality test, raise less concern as regards possible incursions of the ECtHR in national constitutional equilibria and, consequently, in the enforcement of fundamental labour rights.

2.4 A reappraisal of constitutional balancing in Italy and Spain

The present section draws attention to two national perspectives of balancing, namely Italian and Spanish, with a focus on, respectively, the principle of reasonableness and the principle of proportionality, which is necessary to introduce the analysis of the constitutional case law on post-crisis measures in Italy and Spain, that follows.

This is done by carefully contextualising balancing in the respective legal systems, so as to avoid approximations and identify the criteria respectively used, their content and the national judicial practice to which they belong.

The necessity to approach the theoretical studies on judicial balancing in precise legal contexts is a direct consequence of the plastic content of these criteria, which are inextricably linked to their legal and judicial terrain, composed by legal sources, judicial tradition and academic literature,[116] where, anyway, the different national perspectives mutually influence each other.

principles, mostly based on the principle of proportionality, through which he proposes a speculative revisitation of the *Laval* quartet and *AGET Iraklis*, showing how, by applying a bi-directional proportionality test, social and labour rights can be treated not as restrictions to the Internal Market, but rather as conditions "under which the Internal Market can function", 639.

116 Following the global success of balancing and principle of proportionality, the academic literature has often addressed these concepts extrapolating them from their national legal context. See, for instance, the confusing international approach in Young 2017, who reflects on proportionality, reasonableness and economic and social rights.

The first and paramount reason for the Italian and Spanish Constitutional Courts to apply the balancing method stems from the absence of an abstract and predetermined hierarchy of constitutional rights and principles.[117] Where the creation of an absolute hierarchy would be in contrast with the pluralist character of a constitutional system.[118] The pluralist system *per se* rejects a crystallisation of the social structure and a rigid approach to the relationship between social interests. Indeed, all comparable constitutional interests have to be confronted on equal terms, and a system where certain interests are structurally defeated by others cannot be conceived.[119] In other words, balancing can be conducted only "among equals".[120]

Nevertheless, in relation to a concrete case, one principle can prevail over another.[121] In fact, it is in the occasion of a concrete judicial case, and in relation to factual assumptions,[122] that the "balancing, reconciliation, composition of and among different principles" takes place, without this resulting in a hierarchy of constitutional principles.[123]

117 See, for all, Cartabia 2013; Cheli 1999; Mengoni 1993 who suggests the elaboration of a system that may give more certainty to the judicial decisions, without renouncing the absence of an absolute hierarchy.

118 The ductile character "makes the Constitution particularly suitable to become sustainable projects of coexistence", Preciado Domènech 2016, 79, my translation.

119 Scaccia 2000, 3964. *A contrario*, Andreoni 2006, 116–134, who makes a distinction between rights (and hence values) differently and equally graduated, where in the first case certain rights surely prevail, at least in their essential content.

120 Luciani 1995, 569, my translation. A thesis that emerges again recently in Luciani 2016, 13, where the author makes clear that balancing between social rights and financial reasons would be *unequal* in the sense that the economic efficiency should inevitably surrender, although proportionally. This view is sharply criticised by Bin, who finds Luciani's assumption "strange", in the sense that "in order to address equal things it is enough to count them; while only unequal things can be weighted", and hence, balanced: Bin 2018, 39, my translation. However, this argument apparently fails to take into account that these "things" are equal, and absolute, only in abstract terms, while they have to be balanced in the concrete case, inasmuch as it is in relation to the concrete case that these "things" may acquire a different weight, but they still remain equal in abstract terms. While, according to Messineo, the necessity to conduct the "unequal balancing", introduced by Luciani, between economic and social interests, is imposed by the Italian Constitution itself, because of its structure and content: Messineo 2010, 112.

121 The lack of a fixed hierarchy necessarily implies a "balancing on a case-by-case basis" (Italian Constitutional Court, Judgment 104/1986), Prieto Sanchis 2000, 442, 443. On the prevalence of one principle against another in circumstantial and concrete cases, as well as on the various understandings of the term "*ponderacion*", see also Prieto Sanchis 2001 and 2003. Conversely, Andreoni 2006, 117, suggests that a balancing exclusively conducted on a case-by-case basis may lead to the "tyranny of the judge".

122 English expression used by Bin 1992, 35.

123 Modugno 2008, 247–250, the author marks the difference between an absolute hierarchy of values and the tendency of the Court to give prevalence to specific principles, which therefore acquire and progressively strengthen their supreme character. Of the same view, Bin: "the balancing of principles shall take place in relation to specific situations": Bin 1992,

2.4.1 Balancing in the Italian constitutional case law

What is generally called *giudizio di bilanciamento* has long been practiced by the Italian Constitutional Court.[124] The first step of the balancing reasoning is the identification of interests and rights in conflict, that is the terms to be balanced, which entails the Court looking for the *rationale* of the challenged norm, in order to identify which interest is pursued and to what extent.[125] Secondly, that extent has to be confronted with the extent of protection of the interest allegedly violated, which must be a comparable interest to that pursued by the challenged norm.[126] The Court shall understand whether the interest protected by the norm under scrutiny can justify a limitation of the constitutional right affected. If that is the case, the Court shall decide whether the sacrifice of the latter right is excessive. In order to provide an answer to this crucial question, the Italian Court has not elaborated a specific test.[127]

The Italian scholarship identifies constitutional balancing as a form of *sindacato esterno* (external scrutiny), that is the process, which retraces the justifications underpinning a legislative act, and, hence, refers to ethical issues, implying value judgments and regards the "foundation of the premises",[128] so that the Court addresses interests, values and principles overlapping the legislator's evaluations.[129]

In the Italian experience, constitutional balancing is operationalised through a specific criterion, which is widely identified in the principle of reasonableness

---

39, my translation. Romboli 1992, 215, refers to a "mobile hierarchy" of constitutional principles. Also, Scaccia 2000, 3953–3954.

124 *Inter alia*, Cartabia 2013, 8; Bin 1992.

125 A phase identified as "topography of the conflict" by Bin 1992, 62; on the same line Andreoni 2006, 110.

126 Morrone 2001, 286. It may occur that the Italian Constitution itself recognises a hierarchy of values and principles, by including limitation clauses in a constitutional norm. For instance, Art. 42 IC recognises and guarantees private property, but it also provides for its limitations, which derive from the duty to ensure its "social function and make it accessible to everyone". In that case, the Constitution establishes a so-called "garanzia d'istituto", by which it (pre-)creates an order of preference between potential conflicting interests, Morrone 2001, 287, my translation. The expression "garanzia d'istituto" is from Baldassarre 1898, *ad vocem*. If the interests have already been placed by the constitutional provisions on a different hierarchical level, they cannot be considered qualitatively homogeneous and the prevailing interest is set by the constitutional law, Scaccia 2000, 3957, 3958.

127 Scaccia 2000, 3962. For a review of key cases where the Court adopts similar legal reasoning, see Bin 1992, 81–88.

128 Bin 1992, 142, my translation. The author makes the following distinction: the internal justification addresses the logical process of the lawmaker; the external justification determines the point of equilibrium between conflicting interests, and hence determines the premise, therefore this is where balancing of interests belongs: Bin 1992, 143.

129 Bin 1992, 143. As opposed to *sindacato interno* (internal scrutiny) the process that assesses the norm directly and in relation to the whole legal system. See also Moscarini 1996 and Zagrebelsky 1998, 149 ff.

(*ragionevolezza*)[130] and is supposed to grant what is generally called a "reasonable balancing".[131]

2.4.1.1 *The principle of reasonableness and its genesis*

Albeit the principle of reasonableness is well established in the Italian legal system,[132] it is not expressly provided for by the constitutional text. Indeed, the principle of reasonableness has become one of the key criteria to judge upon the legitimacy of the legislative choices because of a consistent case law, which has developed its content on the basis of the principle of equality that finds expressed constitutional recognition in Art. 3 IC.[133]

During the first phase, the Constitutional Court has interpreted the principle of equality restrictively, focusing on the prohibition of discrimination expressed in Art. 3.1 IC.[134] In the second phase, it has interpreted the content of Art. 3.1 IC not just as a mere prohibition of discrimination and has admitted that a violation of the principle of equality could occur also beyond a difference in treatment based on one of the seven grounds listed in section one (sex, race, language, religion, political opinion, personal and social conditions).[135] Particularly, in Judgment 53/1958 the Italian Court overcomes the concern to interfere with the legislator's discretional power, in those cases in which situations, which are deemed to be different by the legal system, are treated in an analogous manner by the contested provision.[136] Therefore, during the first decade of its activity, the Court has progressively included in the judicial scrutiny the reasons justifying the adoption of a given norm,[137] and the principle of equality has been invoked with a view to ensuring the systemic coherence of the legal system.

The reasonableness criterion first appeared in Judgment 15/1960, where the Court holds that the principle of equality is violated even if the same situations are

130 The paramount role of reasonableness in the Italian constitutional jurisprudence has been explained on the grounds of the axiological character of the Italian Constitution, Baldaassarre 1991, 655. The contributions on the principle of reasonableness in the Italian system are countless, among them, see Cerri 2016; Modugno 2008; Morrone 2001; Moscarini 1996; Sandulli 1975.

131 Cartabia 2013, 8; Cheli 1999, 94.

132 On the principle of reasonableness in Labour Law, see Perulli 2005.

133 Art. 3 IC reads "1. All citizens have equal social dignity and are equal before the law, without distinction of sex, race, language, religion, political opinion, personal and social conditions. 2. It is the duty of the Republic to remove those obstacles of an economic or social nature which constrain the freedom and equality of citizens, thereby impeding the full development of the human person and the effective participation of all workers in the political, economic and social organisation of the country". Official translation available at: https://www.senato.it/documenti/repository/istituzione/costituzione_inglese.pdf

134 In this sense, *inter alia*, Modugno 2007, 11.

135 Barberis 2013, 193.

136 This judgment is considered a turning point by Modugno 2007, 11.

137 Cheli 1999, 88, 89.

treated differently, without a *reasonable justification.*[138] Consistently, the Court has then admitted a different treatment based upon one of the seven grounds listed by Art. 3.1 IC if "reasonably justified", eventually deducing from Art. 3 IC the unconstitutionality of unreasonable norms.[139]

The principle of reasonableness has gained now complete autonomy from the principle of equality.[140]

2.4.1.2 Reasonableness and proportionality

The principle of reasonableness, by simplifying, can be regarded as a hermeneutic criterion, which is unexpressed in the written sources of law, but stems from the interpretation of a constitutional norm (enshrined in Art. 3 IC) and is the result of a "process of generalization".[141]

Mostly because of the interpretative origins of the principle of reasonableness, a static and univocal definition can be hardly given.[142] However, the scholarship has extensively reflected upon its content and structure and has provided crucial contributions to its understanding, mainly on the grounds of the constitutional case law.[143]

138 "*Il principio di eguaglianza è violato anche quando la legge, senza un ragionevole motivo, faccia un trattamento diverso ai cittadini che si trovino in eguali situazioni*", Barberis 2013, 193; Modugno 2007, 12.

139 Cheli 1999, 90. The same author also emphasises that the constitutional case law has, thus, overcome Art. 28, Law 87/1953, which aimed to exclude that the Court may conduct any evaluation over the merit and purposes of the Law. Sandulli mentions also Judgments 108/1963 and 166/193 among the first cases in which the Court extends its understanding of Art. 3 IC: Sandulli 1975, 668.

140 The reasonableness scrutiny is now used in order to "detect the objective irrationalities of the law, independently from subjective prerogatives and, hence, independently from trilateral schemes" Modugno 2007, 12, my translation. See Barile 1994, also quoted by Moscarini 1996, 98; as well as Barberis 2013, 195. To be noted that the Court, on some occasions, still expressly refers to the principle of reasonableness as enshrined in Art. 3 Italian Constitution, *e.g.* Judgment 113/2015.

141 See Loi 2016, 171, on the grounds of the distinction developed by Guastini 2010. Although I agree with Bin's claim that balancing and interpretation must be distinguished, since the two techniques are parallel legal reasoning, given that the latter concerns the text of the law, while balancing mostly does not, Bin 1992, 143. In a similar way, Mengoni 1996a argues that the constitutional balancing is "a different technique (albeit not always easily distinguishable) from interpretation", 124–125. Modugno 2007, 252, emphasises that reasonableness is an interpretative criterion, rather than a proper and autonomous constitutional principle.

142 It is, indeed, "the complex content", Cerri 2016, 625 ff.

143 Romboli 2000, 89, states: "many things have been said and written about the reasonableness and often also quite different among themselves, but if we want to look for a common element among those who have addressed this topic, I think we may identify it in the argument the notion of reasonableness has pretty nuanced and elusive characters, which make it difficult to provide a real definition", my translation.

The principle of reasonableness has become an "all-encompassing and comprehensive criterion",[144] to the point that it does not represent one possible way to conduct the constitutional scrutiny, but the constitutional judgment "is completely permeated, is characterized by, the reasonableness method: *it is a reasonableness scrutiny*".[145]

It has been observed that "reasonableness is exactly the logic of values" and its purpose is to evaluate to what extent the ordinary norm is consistent with the constitutional values, mainly expressed in principles,[146] so that the application of this criterion "has the function of obstructing the infiltration in the legal system of any kind of fundamentalism, ethical, political or economic".[147]

Scaccia defines the constitutional scrutiny *per se* as the judgment over the existence of the minimum amount of "suitability, congruence, proportionality in respect of the fact (in a world, reasonableness)" of the legislative act.[148] While, according to Modugno, the principle of reasonableness allows the assessment of the internal "plausibility or persuasiveness".[149]

In 1975, Sandulli developed one of the first systematisations of the principle of reasonableness. The author has identified three sub-criteria, which shall compose the reasonableness judgment. According to the scholar, the unreasonableness of a norm can be identified by its *incoerenza* (lack of coherence) and the constitutional incoherence can take the form of *contradditorietà*, *impertinenza* or *inadeguatezza*.[150] These criteria emphasise the relationship between the norm, its *rationale*, its aim and the relevant legal context.[151]

Twenty years later, Moscarini has added the sub-criterion of *incongruenza* (inconsistency), which is grounded upon a reflection of the constitutional judge on the *ratio legis* and the values expressed by both the contested norm and the legal system as a whole, where it is also a matter of *incongruenza* if the means are

144 Scaccia 2000, 388, my translation.

145 In this way Modugno 2007, 50, my translation, drawing on Sciacca's thesis. Others are less thrilled by reasonableness, one for all Paladin who provocatively wrote, in 1992, that a "principle of reasonableness does not exist" in substance, but it is only a verbal expression. Paladin 1992, 163 ff., as reported by Modugno 2007, 52. See also Rossano 1994, 169 ff.

146 Modugno 2007, 46 ff.; in a similar way Morrone reminds us that the fact that the reasonableness criterion entails value-oriented choices is a clear element to distinguish this approach from the a-positivistic one, that would aim at an objective and value-unrelated solution: Morrone 2001, 387.

147 Mengoni, 1996a, 120, my translation; "it is therefore necessary that the norm is openly in contrast with the reasonableness criterion, that is it constitutes, in practice, the expression of a dysfunctional use of the dicretionality, so evident to be a clear symptom of an 'abuse of power [...]'" (Judgment 313/1995, as emphasised by Romboli 2000, 88, my translation).

148 Scaccia 2000, 387.

149 Modugno 2007, 10.

150 Sandulli 1975, 673 ff. An approach analogous, to some extent, to that of Maccormick 1978.

151 Also Cerri 2016, 638, emphasises the relationship between the rationale of the norm, in terms of congruence and coherence.

deemed excessive to achieve the aim pursued.[152] Last, *incoerenza* even allows one to judge the syntax of the norm, since it focuses on its linguistic incoherence.[153]

A different taxonomy is offered by Zagrebelsky, who divides reasonableness into three sub-criteria, namely: rationality, equality and justice, where *rationality* refers to the logic coherence of the norm with regard to the whole legal system.[154]

The relationship between reasonableness and rationality can also be understood in the sense that reasonableness simply reflects the *rationality* of a norm, understood as *coherence* and *non-inconsistency* of the provision.[155]

However, possible doubts over the relationship between reasonableness and rationality seem to be solved by the Constitutional Court, which, in Judgment 172/1992, has made a distinction between *razionalità pratica* (practical rationality), which is expressed by the principle of reasonableness, and *razionalità formale* (formal rationality), understood as a logic principle of non-contradiction (a distinction recently reiterated in Judgment 113/2015).[156]

Notwithstanding the numerous ways of interpreting reasonableness, it is uncontroversial that the Italian constitutional hermeneutic criterion entails a "dialectic way of developing a legal argument, not connected by deductive chains and definite procedural rules"[157] and none of the sub-criteria identified – or developed – by the academic literature, including those introduced above, has been consistently invoked by the Court.

The way of structuring the judicial reasoning is often considered the keystone to understanding the operational difference between reasonableness and proportionality.

The distinction between the principle of reasonableness and proportionality represents a controversial issue for the Italian scholarship and the constitutional case law does not provide clear answers, either.[158] Indeed, differently from other supreme courts, the Italian Constitutional Court makes use of various terms that

152 Moscarini 1996, 115–118, to be noted that according to Moscarini the *incongruenza* corresponds to the lack of suitability of the proportionality test.

153 Moscarini 1996, 119.

154 Zagrebelsky 1994.

155 Moscarini 1996, 88 ff. Also in Scaccia's opinion rationality represents an aspect of reasonableness, Scaccia 2000.

156 Rivera 2016; Cartabia 2013, 16; on the role of reasonableness and proportionality in labour law and other branches of law, see Perulli 2005 and Loi 2016.

157 Mengoni 1996a, 124. In favour of an increase in the structuration of the use of this principle, or even for the strict application of the test is Cartabia 2013, 6, 7; see also Pino 2014 and Cheli 1999, 97, and Cheli 2011, 33, who suggests that the tendency to interfere with the political discretion may be inextricably linked with the principle of reasonableness. Equally supporting a formalised approach to the application of the principle of reasonableness or proportionality: Luciani 1994 and Paladin 1992, who advocates the introduction of a rigid proportionality test in order to give content and strength to the balancing reasoning of the Court.

158 This research does not investigate the principle of proportionality as enshrined in Art. 36 of the Italian Constitution and related to the proportionality of remuneration. The principle of proportionality is here intended with regard to the legal technique used by the Court.

refer, more or less directly, to the concept of proportionality and reasonableness, *e.g. razionalità, adeguatezza, non arbitrarietà, congruenza* and many others. The terms are also often used as synonymous in the same judgment, or they seem to be overlapping.[159]

Drawing on the Italian academic literature, Piera Loi has systematised the plurality of academic views on this topic.[160] On the one hand, a number of constitutional law scholars argue that the connection between reasonableness and proportionality is so strict that they either coincide completely or, at least, proportionality is a sub-category of reasonableness.[161] Others reject an assimilation of the two concepts and hold that the feeble, not to say null, formalisation of the legal reasoning founded upon the principle of reasonableness does not allow any connection between them.[162] Yet, there are those who understand "reasonableness" as the principle applied to evaluate the coherence of the norm with the legal and economic system, while "proportionality" is the criterion used to measure the interference on the fundamental rights affected, in relation to the aim of the contested norms.[163]

According to Cartabia, "the Italian Constitutional Court does not make any distinction, neither explicit nor implicit, between the principle of reasonableness and the principle of proportionality, which are often used in a completely fungible way, so that a disproportionate provision is unreasonable and vice versa".[164] Under this view, proportionality and reasonableness appear synonymous and they express the guiding hermeneutic principle, which in the Italian Constitutional Court is applied in a similar way as in other highest national courts, at least in the merit (*an*), although it has not been formalised and systematised in a progressive fashion, yet (thus stressing a difference from the other judicial constitutional traditions, in terms of *quomodo*).

Authoratitative voices have, therefore, provided different understandings of the use made by the Italian Court of reasonableness and proportionality. As a matter of fact, in the latest years the Constitutional Court has increasingly referred – at least nominally – to the principle of proportionality especially when the infringement of social rights has been at stake, but it is beyond any doubts that it still strongly relies on *reasonableness* and refrains from applying the principle of

159 Cartabia 2013, 2.

160 Loi 2016.

161 Anzon 1990; Di Gregorio 2002, 237 ff., who concludes that the principle of reasonableness is an autonomous principle in the Italian legal system and structurally corresponds to the principle of proportionality applied in the German legal system.

162 See, *inter alia*, Morrone 2002, 285 ff., who argues for a complete difference in the nature of the two concepts; see also the review by Piera Loi 2016, 81 ff.

163 Sandulli 1975; about the scrutiny of the aim, see Chapter 2.3.1.

164 Cartabia 2013, my translation. According to Cartabia (Judge of the Italian Constitutional Court from 2011 to 2020), the Constitutional Court regularly uses the so called "*giudizio di ragionevolezza*" and "*giudizio di proporzionalità*", literally "reasonableness judgment" and "proportionality judgment", whether explicitly or implicitly: Cartabia 2013, 1. See also Loi 2016, 5.

proportionality by means of a structured method, as it is the case in, for instance, the German constitutional case law.

2.4.2 *Applied balancing in the Spanish constitutional case law and the principle of proportionality*

A constraint imposed upon a fundamental right is admitted only if justified "*por la necesidad de proteger o preservar [...] otros derechos constitucionales [...] u otros bienes constitucionalmente protegidos*".[165] Such interests (*bienes*), to be enough to justify a similar constraint, must be the expression of constitutional values, whose priority must result from the constitutional text.[166]

To adjudicate fundamental rights, the Spanish Constitutional Court relies on the principle of proportionality. It is quite uncontroversial that the Spanish Court has invoked the proportionality principle in an intuitive and informal way since the very beginning of its activity.[167] Indeed, the opinion that the principle of proportionality is embedded in the constitutional system and is structural of the Spanish legal system is widespread, especially because of the European Convention on Human Rights and Fundamental Freedoms and the case law of the respective court (ECtHR), which has remarkably influenced the Spanish Court.[168] However, the actual application of the principle of proportionality, by the Spanish Constitutional Court, is the outcome of a process started decades ago.

From the 1980s to 2015, 494 judgments using, either explicitly or implicitly, the principle of proportionality have been identified. Although the constitutional case law must be considered as a continuum, it can be systematised in

165 SCC, Judgment 2/1982.

166 Goig Martínez 2016, 152, quoting SCC, Judgment 22/1984.

167 Although the precise advent of the principle of proportionality in the Spanish constitutional case law is controversial, Gonzalez 2003 refers to 1981, when the principle of proportionality has entered the judicial discourse with expressions such as "natural balancing of values" and "balanced rationality". The author offers a very critical perspective over the use of constitutional balancing. His criticism is mainly based upon the argument that *balancing* constitutes an argumentative path, rather than an interpretative technique, which takes several names, as *razonabilidad*, *adecuación*, *proporcionalidad*, *ponderación*, and has gained a central role without being founded upon any legal basis. Differently, Bernal Pulido 2005 argues that a first use of the principle of proportionality can be detected already before the entrance into force of the Spanish Constitution in 1978.

168 González Beilfuss 2015, Barnes 1998a; Medina Guerrero 1998. However, the appropriateness of the application of the principle of proportionality in the Spanish constitutional case law is not uncontroversial: a different perspective, mostly critical towards the balancing approach and the use of terms such as "reasonable" and "adequate" is offered by Gonzalez 2003, where the author argues for the absence of a legal justification, in both the Spanish Constitution and the case law of the Spanish Constitutional Court, for the adoption of such an approach (see further in this chapter). On the value of the ECHR see Perello Domenech 1997, 70; the author also agrees on the progressive, but uncontroversial, incorporation of the principle of proportionality in the Spanish case law.

three main phases of application.[169] In a first phase, ending in the mid-1990s, the Constitutional Court initiated employing the proportionality principle, while progressively increasing its formal application.[170] It can be observed that, albeit the Spanish Constitution does not expressly provide for the principle of proportionality, this concept has appeared already in an early phase of the Constitutional Court's activity as an "argumentative formula semantically vague", mostly influenced by the ECtHR case law on the principle of equal treatment.[171] Although initially applied also at national level to adjudicate the principle of equality, the principle of proportionality was slowly extended to many other fundamental rights, such as the right to a fair trial, the trade union freedom and the right to property.[172]

At first, its use was "informal and intuitive". Nevertheless, various elements of the proportionality test were already present in the Spanish Constitutional case law, although still disconnected and mostly unstructured. Overall, two main elements were an explicit justification for the fundamental right's restriction and the proportionate character of the same restriction. Moreover, the concept of "adequate provision", as well as that of the "necessity" of the measure subject to constitutional scrutiny, the evaluation of the concrete proportionality of the challenged measure and the aim pursued appeared in the judicial discourse. At this stage, the judgments were mostly concluding in favour of the proportionality of the contested provision at issue: the case law was, in González Beilfuss's words, "*respetuosa con el legislator*".[173]

In a second phase, starting in the mid-1990s, the Constitutional Court introduced the so-called German test of proportionality, grounded upon three criteria: suitability (***idoneidad***), necessity (***necessidad***) and proportionality in the strict sense (***proprtionalidad en sentido estricto***), concepts only vaguely mentioned at an earlier stage.[174] Since Judgment 66/1995,[175] the Court expressly referred to the "proportionality judgment" and used the three requirements in a tidy and structured manner, thus formalising the principle of proportionality, analogously to the German Court, without, however, expressly referring to the German origins of this technique.[176]

169 A distinction proposed by González Beilfuss 2015.

170 On the fragmented use of this principle in the first years of activity of the Spanish Constitutional Court, see also Medina Guerrero 1998.

171 González Beilfuss 2015, 21.

172 González Beilfuss 2015. One of the uncontroversial features of the principle of proportionality is its paramount application in relation to fundamental rights; see Perello Domenech 1997, 73.

173 González Beilfuss 2015, 40.

174 González Beilfuss 2015, 16.

175 González Beilfuss 2015; Prieto Sanchís 2001. The turning point is identified also by Perello Domenech 1997, 72 ff., in Judgment 66/1995; on the gradually more systematic approach of the Spanish Court, since the mid-1990s, see also Villaverde 2008.

176 González Beilfuss 2015, 42. See also Preciado Domènech 2016, 141, and Stone Sweet Mathews, 2008, 161, who argue that the German tradition has strongly influenced the

In 1996, the Spanish Court clarified that the proportionality principle is based upon constitutional norms, especially those providing for fundamental rights, which are also its main scope of application[177] and, in 1999, by expressly referring to the ECHR,[178] it reiterated that the principle of proportionality is a "general principle, which can be derived from various constitutional provisions" and stems "from the value of justice [...], the principle of *Estado de Derecho* [...], the prohibition of arbitrariness of public powers [...] and the human dignity".[179]

Judgment 136/1999, where the Court, entirely and expressly applying the proportionality test, for the first time concluded for the violation of the proportionality principle, is regarded as a turning moment in the evolution of the constitutional case law,[180] notwithstanding the non-unanimous consensus among the judges.[181]

In the latest decades, the Constitutional Court has referred, more or less explicitly, to the "principle of proportionality" in several judgments, but since 2000 it has applied the proportionality test in a milder and inhomogeneous way and only in isolated cases the judges applied the proportionality test extensively and rigorously, thus assessing whether the norm was *idonea*, *necessaria* and *proporcionada*.[182] Indeed, at the beginning of the century the alleged third phase of the principle of proportionality in the Spanish constitutional case law began. Exemplary is Judgment 98/2000, where the Court used the German test criteria without explicitly mentioning them and in an unstructured fashion, while a few months later, with the same judge rapporteur, in Judgment 186/2000, the German test was again applied in a structured way.

The misuse of the principle of proportionality may be one of the causes of the strong criticism that certain authors advance as regards its application by the Spanish Constitutional Court.[183]

It has been argued that the informal application of the principle of proportionality is giving rise to both its "deconstitutionalisation" and the development of questionable lines of reasoning on fundamental rights and their normative content. The lack of a dogmatic approach risks making this principle nothing but an

adoption of the proportionality adjudication by European Constitutional Courts.

177 SCC, Judgment 55/1996, see González Beilfuss 2015, 43.

178 As discussed in Pereira 2004, 1048.

179 SCC, Judgment 49/1999, my translation; See also Perello Domenech 1997, 73.

180 These and other first cases in which the principle of proportionality was applied concerned issues of criminal law. *E.g.* of non-structured application of the test: SCC, Judgment 76/1996; SCC, Judgment 107/1996; structured application: SCC, Judgment 207/1996; SCC, Judgment 161/1997; SCC, Judgment 37/1998; SCC, Judgment 49/1999. Cf. also Preciado Domènech 2016.

181 Gonzalez 2003, 20; Pereira 2004, 1048.

182 *I.e.* suitable, necessary and proportionate. A structured application can be found again in *e.g.* SCC, Judgment 48/2005, SCC, Judgment 11/2006, SCC, Judgment 60/2010.

183 Beyond Gonzalez 2003; see also Pereira 2004, 1060, who criticises the application of the principle of proportionality by the Court, because of its partiality.

"empty category" used to justify decisions taken on extra-legal grounds, as well as hampering any predictability over further decisions.[184] The judgments that we are going to assess in the next chapter provide emblematic examples of this tendency.

2.4.2.1 Principle of proportionality and its content from the Spanish perspective

The structured application of the proportionality principle in the Spanish legal system is, at least theoretically, consistent with other judicial traditions. Indeed, a proper application of the proportionality principle by the Spanish Constitutional Court should entail a first assessment of whether the provision is able to achieve the aim pursued, that is its *suitability*. Second, the Court shall focus on the *necessity* of the norm, in the sense that a more moderate provision, equally achieving the aim, is not feasible. In the third phase, the Court shall evaluate whether the provision is *proportionate in the strict sense*, *i.e.* if it results in more advantages to the general interest, than prejudices to other interests or values. The added value of such a structured proportionality test is the possibility for the Court to assess beforehand the aim of the provision under scrutiny, giving relevance to the means-purpose relation, so that a provision pursuing an aim prohibited by the constitution would be rejected at hand. It is worthwhile to underline that, according to the Spanish Court, the aim pursued, to be legitimate, does not need to be expressly phrased in the constitution, but it is enough that it is allowed by the constitutional norms.[185]

In the development of the Spanish constitutional case law the introduction of the so-called German test[186] has helped to clarify the already existing principle of proportionality, introducing an – at least apparent – rationality. It has provided what in the words of Stone Mathews is an "argumentative framework" or "analytical procedure", and in Bernal Pulido's view a "methodological criterion",[187] which "clearly indicates to litigating parties the type and sequence of arguments that can and must be made, and the path through which judges will reason to come to a decision".[188] Under this view, the German test increases, first of all, certainty and transparency of the decision.

184 González Beilfuss 2015. Also Pereira Sáez 2004, 1049–1051, who discusses the case law since 2000, albeit with a different analytical method, emphasises that the Court mostly applies the principle of proportionality without mentioning and strictly following the proportionality test and while, in some cases, proportionality appears related to the essential content, in other judgments it seems to be coinciding with the necessity scrutiny, or composed by the three sub-requirements: suitability, necessity and proportionality in the strict sense, as in SCC, Judgment 14/2003.

185 González Beilfuss 2015, 42–56; Roca Trias 2013.

186 See Chapter 1.

187 Bernal Pulido 2005, 77, my translation. The author, writing in 2005, was arguing that this "*criterio metodologico*" is consolidated in the Spanish constitutional case law.

188 Stone Sweet Mathews 2008, 76–89.

The literature that describes the normative content of the principle of proportionality in the Spanish legal system draws extensively on the relevant German studies, first and foremost Alexy's theory.[189]

While the three requirements of suitability, necessity and proportionality in the strict sense are acknowledged unanimously by the literature, there is some inconsistency over the phase or phases that can be considered preparatory to the (so-called) proportionality test.[190]

One of the leading Spanish scholars, while assessing the principle of proportionality in the Spanish legal system, as well as in other legal systems, has identified five steps that characterise, in his view, the application of the principle of proportionality. The first two represent the precondition and the second three the proper application of the proportionality principle. On this view, first comes the identification of the fundamental right concerned and its embedment in a fundamental right's provision. Second, the judge has to verify whether the ordinary norm examined is related to the relevant fundamental right's provision.[191]

Whereas Prieto Sanchis breaks down the application of the proportionality principle into four phases, each of them based upon different elements to be evaluated by the judge. First, and as a precondition for the following three steps, the interference in the domain of a fundamental right must pursue a constitutionally legitimate aim, otherwise the balancing cannot take place, inasmuch as a main element is missing, that is the term of comparison.[192]

The theories, only slightly different, are consistent with the constitutional case law, which often addresses, as a first step, the constitutional legitimacy of the aim pursued.[193]

Proportionality entails the establishment of an order of preference related to the concrete case and it does not always provide a valid answer. Therefore, the result of the application of the principle of proportionality is a "mobile hierarchy, which does not lead to the declaration of invalidity of one of the interests or values in conflict, nor to the permanent demotion of one face to the other".[194]

The relationship between the proportionality test and the more general concept of *ponderacion* can be read in the sense that the "law of balancing", a "peculiar exercise of rationality",[195] precisely comes into play in the latest stage of application of the proportionality principle: the assessment of the proportionality

189 To the point that Gonzalez 2003 argues that the principle of proportionality has been completely borrowed by other legal systems and does not belong to the Spanish constitutional tradition at all; Pereira 2004 also refers to Latin American studies to introduce, from a theoretical perspective, the principle of proportionality in the Spanish Constitutional Court.

190 While in the literature discussing the application of the proportionality principle by the CJEU the use of the expression "test" is widespread, only some Spanish scholars use this wording, among them: González Beilfuss 2015 and Perez 2014.

191 Bernal Pulido 2005, 131.

192 Prieto Sanchís 2000, 445.

193 *E.g.* see SCC, Judgment 169/2001, 9.

194 Prieto Sanchís 2001, 216–217, my translation.

195 Prieto Sanchís 2000, 450.

in the strict sense, which is the key step to solve the conflict between the, inevitably, conflicting interests in a neo-constitutional state.[196]

Although a number of authors have argued that, so far, the Constitutional Court has failed to clarify the exact role of these criteria,[197] it is worthwhile acknowledging that, even if in 1992 the Court had stated that the principle of proportionality was just one of the ways in which the balancing judgment (*juicio de ponderacion*) could be carried out (SCC, Judgment 219/1992), in subsequent and consistent case law the Court reiterated that the balancing mandate is an integral part of the principle of proportionality; in particular it relates to the proportionality in the strict sense.[198]

Compared to the Italian experience, the principle of reasonableness *per se* has played a notably minor role in the Spanish constitutional case law, where it has been applied accidentally and inconsistently.[199] In some judgments it is linked to the principle of proportionality with expressions such as "reasonable proportionality",[200] while in others, it apparently corresponds to the suitability test,[201] as in Judgment 22/1981, where the Court has applied both the principle of reasonableness and the principle of proportionality, in the sense that the Court has invoked the reasonableness criterion "which implies that the distinction shall pursue a legitimate aim, as well as that the mean shall be suitable to achieve the aim".[202]

Drawing on Judgment 214/1999, Perez holds that the reasonableness scrutiny is based upon the formal coherence of the measure assessed, together with the absence of evident unreasonableness.[203] According to the scholar, the "reasonableness judgment" coincides with the content of the constitutional scrutiny, but it also constitutes its limitation, inasmuch as only what is reasonable is consti-

196 Prieto Sanchís 2001 understands neo-constitutionalism as an idea of state organisation, which combines strong normative content and a key role for judicial control, and represents a formula for the concretisation of the rule of law.

197 González Beilfuss 2003; Sánchez Gonzalez 2003; Sánchez Gonzalez 2015, 84; Barnes 1998a; Rodríguez Ruiz 1999.

198 *E.g.* SCC, Judgments 50/1995, 66/1995, 161/1997 and 53/2002, as reported to by Gonzales 2003, 19.

199 However, according to González Beilfuss 2015, 83, although in the proportionality adjudication, reasonableness corresponds to the assessment of the suitability of the law examined, hence to the first stage, it also constitutes an autonomous parameter; Roca Trias 2013. For an analysis of the constitutional case law over the principle of equal treatment and the legal reasoning and methods used, that is also the principle of proportionality, see Barnes 1998b, 337–343.

200 *E.g.* SCC, Judgment 178/1985.

201 Perello Domenech 1997, 71, my translation. On the Spanish constitutional case law on the principle of equality up to 1994, see Carmona Cuenca 1994; also Prieto Sanchís 2000, 75.

202 Perello Domenech 1997, 71, my translation.

203 Perez 2014; also in this respect, the use of the reasonableness principle, Gonzalez 2003, 22, is critical, in the sense that in his opinion this concept is too vague to constitute a valuable criterion for the constitutional case law. Cf. also Roca Trias 2013, who reflects on reinforced reasonableness.

tutional and the Court can validly conclude for the constitutional legitimacy of a norm, only if it is cleared of any arbitrariness. However, the author is aware of the indeterminacy of the legal concept of reasonableness and, by quoting a judgment from 2002 he argues that, in order to provide reasonableness with a content, it is necessary to start from the assumption that "the validity of a reasoning is, from a purely logical perspective, independent from the truthfulness or falseness of its premises and conclusions".[204] In other words, what the reasonableness scrutiny investigates is just the coherence of the norm.[205]

2.4.3 *Financial and economic factors in the Constitutional Courts' case law*

The precise focus of the following chapters on the case law delivered by the Italian and Spanish courts on measures adopted to manage the 2008 crisis requires one to linger on the place economic and financial elements have in constitutional legal reasoning and, more precisely, in constitutional balancing. Namely, the interest turns to the principle of balanced budget and the economic crisis argument.

I propose to distinguish three orders of arguments: first, the public budget restraints to which the Italian and Spanish legal systems were subject before the reforms promoted by the EU; second, the *principle of balanced budget* introduced in the Italian and Spanish Constitutions, respectively in 2012 and 2011, to comply with international commitments; third, the *economic (and financial) crisis*, described with a variety of expressions, such as economic emergency, or emergency context.

While the original constitutional provisions on public spending now belong to history (although a recent one), the second and third elements are matters of everyday discourse and profoundly interlinked. In fact, the principle of balanced budget lately introduced in the Italian and Spanish Constitutions is not disconnected from the economic crisis argument, as the constitutional amendments have been justified chiefly on the grounds of the 2008 economic and financial crisis. Therefore, referring to Art. 81 IC or Art. 135 SC means also indirectly calling into question the economic and financial crisis.

As a further element of distinction, allow me to add the economic and social *impact* of constitutional rulings, which may be affected in various manners by the way in which the court decides to introduce and deploy in the legal reasoning the factors listed above.

The Spanish constitutional post-crisis case law dealt with in the following chapters directly concerns exclusively the economic crisis argument, while the relevant Italian judgments relate to both the latter and the principle of balanced budget.

204 SCC, Judgment 164/2002, my translation.
205 Perez 2014, 9–10, my translation.

Since the 1980s, the public budget discourse has been pivotal in the Italian constitutional case law and in the respective literature. Following the mid-1970s oil crisis, the Italian government has initiated raising the public budget issue, in terms of necessity to constrain public spending,[206] referring to Art. 81 IC (still in its original version).

Fundamental social security rights (such as pension rights, which are fundamental labour rights, as they are understood for the purpose of this work) are immediately concerned by this political change, since they are strictly dependent upon the – discretional – legislative action, which cannot avoid taking into account organisational and financial resources,[207] while having to guarantee redistributive justice, in compliance with the principle of solidarity.[208]

It has been argued that the previous Art. 81.4 IC, now Art. 81.3 IC, which reads "[A]ny other law involving new or increased spending shall detail the means therefor" (official translation), is not directly applicable to the Constitutional Court decisions, since it pertained to the legislative power.[209] However, albeit the Court was not bound to include in its legal reasoning Art. 81.4 IC, it had to consider the general principle of *equilibrio finanziario* that derived from the constitutional provision.[210] This approach that takes into account financial constraints is coherent with the balancing technique and the subsequent application of the principle of reasonableness, which entails a comprehensive evaluation of "all constitutional principles and values involved in the controversy".[211]

As a matter of fact, since the mid-1970s, the approach of the Italian Court with respect to Art. 81 IC has fluctuated over the years, with phases where such a

206 Sorace 1984; Salazar 2013, 6; Pinardi 2019, 308.

207 It has even been argued that the legislative acts implementing *diritti di prestazione* enjoy a sort of presumption of legitimacy. As a consequence, these acts can be questioned by the court only if they make the exercise of the right at stake "excessively difficult" or "its content is frustrated", Modugno 2007, 42, my translation. On the point, cf. also Duarte 2018. De la Quadra-Salcedo Janini 2020, 66, 67, denies fundamental social security rights as even an essential content, since their concrete enjoyment depends upon the legislator's choice and, linked to that, the concrete budget possibilities; even though he does not recognise them as having a purely programmatic character, nor does he admit an uncontrolled freedom of the legislator in regulating them. While Ciolli 2012c, 101–104, distinguishes "essential nucleus" from "essential levels", precisely because, in her view, the latter criterion is used to combine the respect for financial constraints and social instances, in the enforcement of conditioned social rights.

208 D'Onghia 2019.

209 Romboli 1993 stresses that the same argument is advocated by Onida 1993 and Zagrebelsky 1993. Moreover, also the Court had always rejected the applicability of this norm to the constitutional judgments.

210 However, Romboli 1993 points out that the Court has never expressly referred to Art. 81 IC in its decisions, even in those cases in which it has applied the principle of balanced budget. The author hazards that the Court seems to have a sort of "fear" in making the use of Art. 81 IC explicit and it rather leaves the financial argument in the background: Romboli 1993, 194 (quoting Mortati 1970).

211 Romboli 1993, 187.

profile has been predominant in terms of necessity to recover the public budget; others, such as in the early 1990s, in which the focus was only indirectly on the constitutional norm and the argument expressly employed by the court was the economic crisis, to the point that certain legal reasoning appeared set on economic rules, rather than on legal arguments, while in the second half of the 1990s the public budget crisis acquired a rather ancillary position.[212]

Following the explicit inclusion of the principle of balanced budget in the Italian and Spanish Constitutions, with the reforms of Art. 81 IC[213] and Art. 135 SC,[214] a number of authors have observed a change in paradigm even in the Constitutional Court's case law and a tightening in the scope of application of the respective constitutional norms on public spending. This is true not only as regards Italy, as demonstrated also by the case law assessed in the next chapters, but also in relation to Spain and with reference to a number of fundamental social rights.[215]

Article 81 IC, particularly pertinent to the Italian case law assessed in the next chapters, has been reformed by adding the rule of equilibrium between available revenues and expenditures decided by the legislator, without resorting to indebtedness.[216]

ICC, Judgment 10/2015, where Art. 81 IC has been predominantly integrated into the legal reasoning, represents a "turning point", since it has conveyed the full binding character of the norms introduced by Constitutional Law 1/2012, even though the subsequent jurisprudence has not consistently corroborated the approach taken therein.[217]

212 For an attentive review, Benvenuti 2012. In a similar way, on "waving" case law on public budget, see Morrone 2015b, 582.

213 Reformed together with Articles 97, 117 e 119 IC, to introduce the principle of balanced budget, see Morrone 2013.

214 The reformed Art. 135 SC sets a rather flexible aim of "balance stability" for the state and the autonomous communities, while it provides for the rule of balanced budget ("equilibrio presupuestario") only for local authorities, besides introducing further rigidities; for an assessment of Art. 135 SC reform, see also Álvarez Conde, Suoto Galván 2012.

215 About Italy, Benvenuti 2012, 389 ff.; Guazarotti 2018 59 ff., who identifies mostly two occasions, not exemplary in his view, in which the Italian Court has "resisted": ICC, Judgment 70/2015, assessed in the next chapters, and ICC, Judgment 275/2016, often quoted by the Italian literature for having stated that is "*la garanzia dei diritti incomprimibili ad incidere sul bilancio, e non l'equilibrio di questo a condizionarne la doverosa erogazione*". About Spain, see, *inter alia*, Aparicio Wilhelmi 2019; Medina Guerrero 2012; Baylos Grau 2015, 26; Goig Martínez 2016. Preciado Domènech, acknowledging the economic constraints imposed by the reformed Art. 135 SC, advances a proposal, which is an open criticism of the political and social direction the EU has taken, as he denounces the absence of a mechanism suitable to ascertain the responsibility of the state that fails to fulfil a minimum level of enforcement of economic, social and cultural rights, while, instead, Member States have to respond to the EU institutions as to the implementation of the balanced budget principle, Preciado Domènech 2016, 107–119.

216 *Inter alia*, Morrone 2013, 366; Salazar 2013, 6; Chessa 2016.

217 Morrone 2015b, 591 ff. In ICC, Judgment 10/2015, released few weeks before Judgment 70/2015, the Court declared the unconstitutionality of the so called Robin Tax, that is

The constitutionalisation of the balanced budget principle may induce the Constitutional Judge to pay particular attention to the arguments in favour of the public finance equilibrium, which "carries the risk to compromise the possibility to achieve effective protection of social rights, both at national and local level".[218] However, not even after the adoption of Constitutional Law 1/2012 is the Constitutional Court "neither formally nor directly bound to respect Art. 81 IC [principle of balanced budget] and, therefore, as regards its judgments it can never discuss the issue of the quantification of financial expenditures in a strict sense".[219] This argument is effectively supported by a textual explanation: Art. 81 IC, also in its renovated version, assigns to "the law" the duty to provide for its fiscal coverage. Indeed, even if the Court cannot completely disregard the consequences of its decisions on the public budget it is not the Constitutional Court's duty to indicate the economic means, which are necessary to achieve the aim.[220]

Romboli suggested three possible methods for the Court to include the public budget in its legal reasoning. First, the contextual economic situation of the country could constitute a guideline. Second, the Court could decide the weight of the principle of balanced budget in each specific case on the grounds of the principles allegedly violated. As a tendency, the result may be that the principle of balanced budget would be predominant if only the general principle of equality is concerned, while it would be recessive if other constitutional principles also come into play. Third, in the case of *sentenze additive*,[221] a feasible criterion is the consideration of the economic burden upon the state, stemming from the constitutional ruling.[222]

Certainly, the international and European intervention in the aftermath of the financial and economic crisis has proved the complexity of such context, as well

a special tax put on oil companies. The Court made a careful consideration of the consequences on the public budget that a full declaration of unconstitutionality of the measure would have caused and, for that reason, it has regulated the effects of its judgment in such a way to avoid the reimbursement of the amounts already paid. Indeed, thanks to this temporal modulation, the judgment was effective starting from the day after its publication; see, among the several authors commenting on Judgment 10/2015, Pin Longo 2015, Veronesi 2015.

218 D'Onghia 2013, 132, my translation. The author develops an attentive assessment of the Italian constitutional case law on the "delicate balancing between social security rights and financial equilibrium", with an extensive focus on the concept of "adequacy" of social security benefits, provided by Art. 38.2 Italian Constitution: D'Onghia 2013, 133–256.

219 D'Onghia 2013, 131, my translation. Partially different are the conclusions reached by Caredda 2019, who recently discussed the relationship between constitutional judgments and financial requirements in the Italian legal system, with a focus on the rulings released after the reform of Art. 81 IC; in particular, on the nature of the reformed Art. 81 IC, Caredda 2019, 7–82.

220 D'Onghia 2013, 92–98.

221 A decision by which the Court declares the unconstitutionality of a norm "for the part in which it does not provide for…".

222 Romboli 1993,190.

as the potential that choices of political economy may have on the effective implementation of fundamental social rights, precisely in their – apparent – authority to guide the national legislator's choices.[223]

That the principle of balanced budget and the 2008 crisis are intertwined emerges bluntly from the case law, not just as concerns the constitutional norms recently introduced, but also due to the fact that if an economic and/or financial crisis occurs the public revenues equally suffer, inducing the Courts to deploy what has been called "the paradigm of scarcity".[224]

Since 2010, the crisis argument has acquired a different and more prominent place in the constitutional legal reasoning of both the Italian and the Spanish Courts, nevertheless it "remains external to the same balancing technique, even though it allows the constitutional judge to identify that dynamic and evolutionary point of intersection, by reason of circumstances – indeed, the crisis – endorsed as facts (and not as legal sources) of its reasoning".[225]

The latest economic crisis has, therefore, significantly impacted the way the constitutional courts develop their legal reasoning with paradigmatic effects on the fundamental labour rights concerned,[226] as well as on other fundamental social rights, such as the right to health, impaired by a reduction in the public revenues devoted to the public health system.[227]

It is virtually impossible to expect a constitutional court not to take into account the economic downturns and the principle of balanced budget, but what is still open for discussion is the nature and, therefore, the weight, attached by the legal reasoning to those unconventional parameters. The issue becomes even trickier when the social and economic impact, also called "consequences" or "costs" by the literature, is brought into play. In fact, most likely the court considers the principle of balanced budget and the economic crisis, with the intent of acknowledging the consequences of its ruling.

Economic and social consequences of a decision of unconstitutionality are traditionally – although with rare exceptions – taken into consideration by both

223 Luciani 2016 suggests that the reformed Art. 81 IC does not pose in itself specific and new problems to the fundamental social rights adjudication; the case is different as regards European constraints, "but here the problem gets political", 13, my translation.

224 Chessa 2018, 280.

225 Benvenuti 2012, 399, my translation. The judgments published since 2011 by the Spanish Court have recognised a prominent role to the economic crisis, and since then all fundamental labour rights, hence not only conditioned social rights, have been subject to "a double constitutional scrutiny: first, an ordinary one; second, an extraordinary one, activated in a situation of economic crisis", Goig Martínez 2016, 141 (see further in Chapter 4), the author, coherently with the Spanish legal dogmatics, identifies the ultimate limits that not even the second scrutiny can alter in the essential content of fundamental rights, where only the accessory content of such right can be adapted to the economic crisis.

226 See Chapters 3 and 4.

227 De la Quadra-Salcedo Janini 2020, 69.

the Italian and the Spanish Courts,[228] which does not entail them to ground the structure of the legal reasoning upon the probable impact of the ruling, but it calls upon the judges to find a legal and/or procedural tool to alleviate such consequences, if both necessary and feasible, without jeopardising the points in law and the legal arguments that have led to the decision of unconstitutionality.[229]

Two main underlying reasons justify a careful consideration of the consequences: the pursuit of an ethic of responsibility and the need to rationalise the constitutional judgment. However, an evaluation of the social consequences of the judgment cannot always prevail over other elements: "[T]he balancing model cannot be confined to a purely consequentialist way of thinking, especially when fundamental rights are at stake. However, the justice principle has to be always interpreted in such a way to highlight also the collective interests (*interessi della collettività generale*) and the duty to preserve the common good".[230]

The consequences do not constitute a legal argument. Indeed, as a general rule, they are discussed in order to either complement or reinforce the *ratio decidendi* resulting from an evaluation of the ordinary norm in light of the constitutional principles or solve persisting doubts. From this perspective, the role of the social consequences criterion seems to be downsized and placed in an ancillary dimension of the constitutional judgment, not because the social consequences are an ancillary element *per se*, but because they do not pertain to the constitutional legal reasoning strictly speaking, inasmuch as they do not constitute a legal argument.

Mengoni, who is in favour of the use of the social consequences argument which, he argues, allows one to underscore the practical effects that are simultaneous to the legal effects, emphasises some crucial shortcomings of a similar approach. First and foremost, the consequences to be considered cannot be unlimited, but they should be restricted. Yet, the scholar fails to indicate a possible method to identify these limits, which raises a doubt about the feasibility of such an identification. The need to identify the boundaries to the social consequences' argument, in the opinion of whom is writing, would further complicate the constitutional proceeding, inasmuch as the judge should engage in an in-depth assessment in the sphere of the norm's "practical effects", hardly conceivable, especially considering a further problematic element, that is the impossibility of relying on a "law of evidence" for the constitutional judgment.[231]

228 Goig Martínez 2016, 147; see also Mengoni 1996a, 136, my translation; as well as Mengoni 1996b, 99–102.

229 The Courts have developed innovative decision-making techniques in order to contain the costs that may derive from its judgments. The Italian Court has for long promoted a graduality in the application of fundamental rights, Scagliarini 2019; or it had modulated the temporal effects of its decisions. The modulation of the temporal effects serves the purpose to prevent a dysfunctional effect over the public budget, Silvestri 1993, 81; Modugno 2007. See also Caredda 2019, 184.

230 Mengoni 1996a, 134, my translation.

231 Mengoni 1996a, 133–139; Nogler 2006.

It is incontestable that the court retains a political responsibility, being institutionally committed to consolidating the constitution, that entails the duty to take into account the possible consequences of its judgments, which are both applicable *erga omnes* and not open to appeal;[232] the centrality such costs may acquire in the legal reasoning is less uncontroversial.[233]

Indeed, conversely, it cannot mis-consider the difference between facts and legal sources, "objective information and reliable data are, therefore, relevant when kept in the background of Constitutional courts' judgments".[234]

What is, then, the boundary line for the court between losing the law in the *ratio decidendi* and failing to fulfil its share of political responsibility? I argue that it lies in keeping the constitutional balancing anchored not only to the written norm, but also to the axiological nature of principles and rights. Every factor, therefore, finds its collocation in the constitutional ruling, but even though the enforcement of fundamental labour rights impacts on the public budget, the legitimacy is not decided on the grounds of the constraints imposed by a contingent choice of political economy, nor is the undermining of such rights admitted as an instrument to overcome an economic crisis.[235]

The principle of balanced budget and the economic crisis lay underneath the balancing. Besides the assumption of legal dogmatics adopted in this book, a practical argument supports such a conclusion: to include those factors in the balancing, the court should have access to all available resources, in order to evaluate if they have been employed for achieving aims that tolerate the restriction of fundamental labour rights; similarly, to recognise the centrality of the costs possibly stemming from its judgments it should engage in an unrealistic evaluation of the economic, legal and social context.[236] We risk, thereby, falling into the *paradox of necessity*, which entails the court scrutinising a profile (the necessity of a norm) that it is ontologically unable to truly discern.

Still, the "scarcer are the available resources, the more stringent the constitutional control has to be"[237] and the legislator is therefore called upon to cautiously illustrate the reasons that have led to a reduction in the effectiveness of a fundamental labour right, which cannot simply lie in the economic crisis, but requires an accurate identification of the constitutional interests – *i.e.* values – pursued with the ordinary norm that has the effect of constraining the scope of a

232 Pinardi 2019, 312, 313.

233 Still Pinardi 2019, *e.g.* 317, appears to recognise to the evaluation of the possible judgment's costs a pivotal role, which may even determine the legitimisation of the court.

234 Sciarra 2018, 137. Ciolli 2012c, 95, goes as far as to advocate that the "financial-economic emergency" does not have any legal significance, but it ends up being, instead, a psychological element that invades and conditions constitutional balancing.

235 As, otherwise, the economic crisis argument may have "unexpected consequences" on the effectiveness of social principles; see the dissenting opinion to SCC, Judgment 8/2015, by Judge Valdés Dal-Ré. *A contrario*, Morrone 2015b, 598.

236 As it conversely suggests Pinardi 2019, 329.

237 Giubboni 2015a, 529, my translation.

fundamental labour right. Maintaining the ultimate focus on the social state and on its axiological articulation does not entail denying the possibility for the content of fundamental labour rights to adapt to the changing social and economic context,[238] but it rather means assuring that, notwithstanding the changing social and economic context, the founding pillars of the social contract embedded in the constitutional text endure.[239]

It would be, furthermore, misleading to use the argument of the court's political responsibility to alleviate the legislator's responsibility.[240] This responsibility does not occur exclusively in the phase of developing the norm's justification, but also following a ruling of unconstitutionality of the Constitutional Court.

The empirical consequences of a constitutional judgment cannot be avoided, as empirical consequences are the ultimate result of any process that occurs at legislative level, including the constitutional revision of legislative norms; however, such consequences must be mediated by the legislative action that follows the judgment. The legislator retains the political power and the definitive role in establishing the material equilibria of the pluralist society in compliance with the social state, the principle of equality and fundamental labour rights, given that a financial and/or economic crisis is not necessarily the outcome of an excessive social state spending, but it may well be caused by an absent or low growth caused by other variables, such as poor industrial policies, a widespread tax-evasion or financial variables.[241]

Fundamental rights are not born limited by financial requirements and it is up to the legislator to conduct a transparent balance to select the resources to be invested in the enforcement of these rights.[242]

In fulfilling its responsibility, which requires giving attention to the social and economic context and the respective possible consequences of its decisions, the judge has to face a twofold challenge, which lies, first, in the duty not to mistake the economic and financial contingency (facts) with the law, second, in the prudence not to replace the legislator in the implementation of norms of economic policy, such as Art. 81 IC and Art. 135 SC. A delicate equilibrium is to be reached, which tests the courts every time a fundamental labour right is at risk, as while the second profile engages social security rights, the first may have

238 Goig Martínez 2016, 147 ff.

239 The option advanced by De la Quadra-Salcedo Janini 2020 is intriguing. The scholar suggests adopting the principle of relative irreversibility of the social conquest, which would contrast regressive measures in the social sphere, 68–70, even though it risks becoming a boomerang for all those social norms that are not easily referrable to a social struggle.

240 Which cannot be disregarded by the legislator in the application of the solidarity principle, either; see D'Onghia 2019, 299.

241 Elements upon which national legislators and/or the European Union have the faculty to intervene, Luciani 2011, 67; Chessa 2016, 476; it is emblematic the renunciation of EU public powers to design a binding policy for finance, Ciolli 2012c, 88; see also Thompson 2009.

242 D'Onghia 2015.

a remarkable impact on other fundamental labour rights, which do not directly require public spending.

The challenge is outstanding, considering that economic and financial elements have the capacity to creep in the balancing technique applied by the Constitutional Courts in an ambiguous fashion, mingling with hermeneutic criteria and constitutional principles, in an attempt to achieve the status of decisive factors of the constitutional ruling. A status that is often granted by the legislator who seeks the most rapid tool to positively impact on the public budget and on the short-term economic growth.

2.5 Conclusions

Constitutional balancing is a complex, articulated and multifaced notion. The impressive expansion of the principle of proportionality, in its countless variants, has not eradicated all remaining balancing techniques, but, admittedly, it has an ascendancy on constitutional and supranational courts worldwide.

It is inappropriate and nonsensical to refer to the balancing techniques reviewed above in terms of better and worse. Every national constitutional court constructs and applies the hermeneutic principles it considers most suitable to respond to the legal structure and necessity of the respective legal systems. Equally, interpretative criteria are destined to evolve. An extent of flexibility, which must not degenerate into uncertainty and inconsistent fluctuations, needs to be preserved, not only because it is in the very nature of hermeneutic principles, but also because it guarantees an honest openness of the constitutional rulings to the dialogue with the legislative power, the scholarship and the civil society as a whole.

Most of all, constitutional rulings must be contestable for the democratic character of a society to express itself at its best. A mathematic understanding of the principle of proportionality must, therefore, be avoided, since it is neither apt to read the reality of a pluralist system made of compromises between conflicting forces, that are constantly in question, nor able to guarantee the development of a collective dialectic around a constitutional ruling.

Without claiming to be exhaustive, this chapter has turned the attention to some of the main features of the balancing techniques applied worldwide, particularly by the Court of Justice and the European Court of Human Rights – which, being in constant dialogue with national constitutional courts, are likely to have a direct or indirect ascendance on their adjudicating methods and argumentative techniques – as well as by the Italian and Spanish Constitutional Courts.[243]

243 Not to mention the interaction between the ECtHR and the CJEU, which finds one of its main demonstrations in the fact that most of the norms of the Charter are based upon the ECHR and the ESC provisions and, at the same time, they are inspired by the case law of the Court of Justice, which is in turn inspired by the case law of the European Court of Human Rights (Gutiérrez-Fons 2021, 232, 233). But, most of all, it is notable the commitment of the EU to accede to the ECHR, provided in Art. 6.3 TEU; Paul Jacqué 2011, for a critical consideration Lock 2020.

Among the balancing techniques, an evident predominance of the principle of proportionality of German origins cannot go unnoticed. However, the view that is "reductive and unilluminating" to identify "proportionality as the one-size-fits-all solution to judicial management of social rights challenges in times of crisis" is to be welcomed. "There are real differences in approach between courts in relating the economic crisis with fundamental rights. Each court decides which constitutional provisions are engaged, takes a specific position on how fundamental rights apply in times of economic 'emergency' and develops distinctive analyses of proportionality".[244]

Indeed, even though it cannot be underestimated that the remarkable reliance on the proportionality test by the European Court of Human Rights and the Court of Justice of the EU is likely to have an influence on the interested national courts, and a glaring example is provided by the experience of the Spanish Constitutional Court, the operative diffusion of proportionality adjudication is not enough to exclude the possibility for constitutional courts to adopt other techniques, as demonstrated by the Italian experience that relies on the principle of reasonableness, and still reaches coherent and effective constitutional rulings.

Besides those authors who challenge the existence of a balancing procedure and/or the use of balancing as a valid and effective way for deciding disputes over conflicting rights and interests, others have recently contested the assumption that we are in an "age of balancing", a theory developed since the end of the 1980s that observes a sort of globalisation of constitutional balancing.[245] The authors who embrace this thesis tend to emphasise the points of convergence of the case law of various national and supranational legal systems, even though they do acknowledge that some differences exist.[246]

Those who dissent from this reading of the constitutional judicial dynamics call into question the "global age of balancing",[247] and argue that, although "basic similarities" cannot be denied, "crucial differences" still exist in the way in which the courts balance conflicting interests and rights, starting from, and especially because of, the differences in the "language of balancing".[248]

The Italian and Spanish experiences do not intend to provide a decisive example in support of the assumption that "we are not in a global age of balancing", but the consistent differences cannot be underestimated, both in the merit and in the so-called "language of balancing".

244 Kilpatrick 2015, 10, reflecting from the perspective of EU bailout states.

245 See the critique by Aleinikoff 1987.

246 One for all, the idea that "We all live in the age of constitutional balancing" has been reiterated by Gardbaum 2010.

247 That Bomhoff 2013, 15, defines as "an age in which even those wanting to emphasize differences between legal systems find themselves having to rely on this unifying language to make their point".

248 Bomhoff, the author draws his theory upon the Bundesverfassungsgericht and the US Supreme Court's case law.

Even though the theory in favour of an overlapping of the two concepts seems quite accredited, especially in the Italian literature, it would be contrived and reductive to attempt to find a perfect correspondence between the reasonableness criterion and the principle of proportionality. While the proportionality test is clearly – at least formally – composed by the suitability test, the necessity test and balancing in a strict sense, *reasonableness*, by simplifying, serves the purpose to assess the internal coherence of the norm, that is evaluating the relationship means-aim (which may be only theoretically compared to the suitability test), and the coherence with the overall legal system, especially in relation to fundamental rights and principles (which may only superficially seem to correspond to the necessity test)[249] and permeates the legal reasoning in all its phases in a discursive manner.[250]

Nevertheless, albeit the criteria applied do not precisely coincide, courts review the balance of conflicting rights and interests in such a way to establish, or validate, an order of preference, which is not absolute, but is pertinent only to the concrete case under scrutiny.

As discussed above, the necessity to conduct judicial balancing stems precisely from the structure of the two constitutions, which provide for fundamental rights and principles, which are absolute, in the sense that they are not hierarchically ordered, but limited, in the sense that their enforcement cannot infringe upon other rights and principles equally granted by the constitution. This feature of fundamental rights and the evolving economic and social context leads to assessing the legislative acts in a dynamic way, as is the case with a balancing technique, which determines the recessive and the predominant constitutional value, and hence principle, on a case-by-case basis. Indeed, an absolute hierarchy would be in contradiction with the pluralist character of the constitutional systems under assessment and would cause a "tyranny" of one value over another.[251]

The reliability of constitutional balancing fades away if the conflicting terms do not express comparable values, and therefore, it is arguable whether they can be addressed through such argumentative technique. For that reason, the choice of the elements eligible for a proper balancing, that is those that are in *real conflict* with each other is likely the most sensitive moment of the constitutional reasoning.[252]

Everything that belongs to facts, such as social and economic contingencies, as well as principles that do not conform to the original design of the constitutional system and, hence, do not express founding values cannot become factors

249 Where reasonableness may be also understood as a parameter of rationality in relation to the values expressed by the constitution, see Baldassarre 1991, 655.

250 Modugno 2007.

251 The concept of "tyranny of values" was expressed first by Schmitt, in a lecture delivered in 1959, although with a slightly different connotation. Amongst those who have recently refreshed and discussed the concept, see Zagrebelsky 1992, 160, Andreoni 2006, 117, Perulli 2018, 688, Speziale 2022, 139.

252 In this way, also Andreoni 2006, 116.

of constitutional balancing, since they lack the axiological nature that justifies the application of the balancing method.

That fundamental labour rights may be conditioned – also – by the above mentioned factors is, however, unquestionable. Constitutional courts retain a role of guardians of last instance of the constitutional systems that confer them a responsibility to both consider the material dynamics of the relevant society and, conversely, avoid getting overwhelmed by the latter, in the exercise of a margin of discretion, which inevitably derives from responsibility. This means not providing contingent facts and/or contingent constitutional reforms with an axiological dignity they do not possess and maintaining the focus on the protection of fundamental rights (also, fundamental labour rights), not with the aim to replace the legislator in their implementation, but rather to guide the governing bodies to select policies that, ultimately, allow a full guarantee of the constitution and its fundamental rights.[253]

The analysis conducted in the following chapters builds on the reflections developed in both Chapter 1 and Chapter 2, which, besides providing the essential notions to assess the constitutional case law under the balancing perspective, have identified the most sensitive aspects of this process. This allows a better understanding of what elements of the case law selected need to be investigated and provides a guideline for approaching the units of analysis.

The strong similarities in the constitutional setting of the Italian and Spanish Courts enable us to address the way in which the two national courts have approached constitutional balancing in the case law on post-crisis measures in a parallel fashion. On the other hand, the criteria of *proporcionalidad* and *ragionevolezza* are not strictly comparable, especially because of their application in the legal reasoning of the courts: the – not always consistent – application of a rigid test in the first case and a more dialectic approach in the second.

The assessment of exemplary and recent constitutional judgments on labour and social security norms adopted on the wave of the 2008 crisis, with a strong focus on the balancing perspective, has the purpose to contribute both – and mainly – to define the status of the constitutional conflict of fundamental labour rights, with other interests of an economic nature in national legal systems strongly influenced by specific EU economic policies geared towards favouring primarily financial necessities, and to reflect over the latest developments in the use of the balancing method in the respective legal arguments.

253 On the guiding responsibility of the constitutional court and its relationship with the discretional power of the legislator see also Caredda 2019, 93 ff.

3 Italian and Spanish post-crisis case law and "its" fundamental labour rights

3.1 Introduction

The broad investigation on the application of the balancing techniques and the hermeneutic principles invoked in the Italian and Spanish constitutional case law, conducted in the previous chapter, is functional to the evaluation of a number of judgments of the respective Constitutional Courts, which are representative of the Italian and Spanish constitutional post-crisis case law on labour rights, that is some of the constitutional rulings that have decided upon legislative measures, whose adoption has been triggered by the 2008 crisis and its consequences on the economic context of the Eurozone.

They constitute the post-crisis judgments precisely because, with them, the courts have answered questions of constitutionality concerning reforms adopted not only in a context of financial constraints and economic downturns, that have followed the latest financial and economic crisis, but with the aim to regulate and/or manage the subsequent – actual or potential – negative consequences.

The relevant Italian case law refers to the economic crisis context, as well as to public budget constraints deriving from the 2012 constitutional amendments, whereas the Spanish judgments do not scrutinise reforms immediately pertaining to the principle of balanced budget and primarily concentrate on the economic crisis, coupled with the rising unemployment levels. Both clusters of judgments are evidently, intrinsically, concerned with economic and financial issues raised after the 2008 crisis.

The Italian judgments of interest concern the reduction of public employees' wages, the reduction of the revaluation of retirement benefits and the mechanism to calculate the compensation for unjustified dismissal introduced in 2015. Judgment 223/2012, Judgment 310/2013, the extensive legal reasoning of Judgment 178/2015 and Judgment 124/2017 belong to the first cluster; while the controversial Judgment 70/2015 and the subsequent and consistent Judgments 173/2016 and 250/2017 concern the pension system;[1] and, last, Judgment 194/2018 addresses compensation for unjustified dismissal.

1 ICC, Judgment 10/2015, which is often included in the reflections around the post-crisis case law, is not addressed since it does not concern fundamental labour rights. For a brief review

DOI: 10.4324/9781003155362-4

Most of these rulings have been widely discussed by the academic literature from various perspectives, but a detailed and comprehensive analysis of the balancing conducted by the Court and its effects on the fundamental labour rights concerned has not yet been developed, even though a number of scholars have provided remarkable insights.

For the purpose of this analysis, only two Spanish judgments are relevant. They are, however, ample and extensive, as well as consistent with each other. Overall, the hermeneutic principles are applied in a way that raises doubts of a possible strategic use of the legal reasoning. Indeed, both in Judgment 119/2014 and in Judgment 8/2015, the Spanish Constitutional Court has ruled in favour of the constitutionality of the challenged legal provisions, to the point that its approach has been defined as "maybe close to the government"[2] and surely very cautious.

The academic literature has focused, first, on the relevance of the economic crisis and unemployment as crucial arguments to justify the contested norms of Law 3/2012. Second, it has emphasised and criticised the high discretional power recognised as held by the legislator, which seems to undermine not only the role of constitutional labour rights and collective actors, but also that of the Spanish Constitutional Court itself. Third, the use in the court's legal reasoning of articles traditionally not pertaining at all to the interpretation of labour rights has been highlighted.

Both the Italian and the Spanish judgments may be addressed under various profiles; however, the following pages circumscribe the analysis to the elements that are significant to evaluate the constitutional balancing and its effects on the relevant fundamental labour rights, leaving aside the other, significant and anyway controversial, aspects.

The analysis is based upon the social state theory and, therefore, upon the assumption that the Italian and Spanish Constitutions are social constitutions that guarantee full enforcement of social rights to realise substantial equality among citizens. In particular, the focus of this work is on fundamental labour rights, which are understood as rights aimed at protecting workers, either during their working life or after retirement.

Clearly, the constitutional case law of the two countries is far richer than the cases discussed in this book. Indeed, this section does not claim to systematise in an absolute and all-encompassing manner the Constitutional Courts' approaches, it rather aims to highlight some elements common to the most recent judgments on fundamental labour rights, in order to trace constitutional trends in the application of the balancing technique and identify the status of the relationship

of the constitutional judgments on social rights, which can be included in the post-crisis case law, see Fontana 2015, 151–159; Faraguna 2016; for analysis and comments on Judgment 10/2015 cf., *inter alia*, the commentaries by Romboli 2015; Pugiotto 2015; Ruggeri 2015. In a different way, Anzon Demming 2015.

2 Fontana 2015, 147.

between fundamental labour rights and other interests of an economic character in the context of an economic crisis.

The present chapter, first, reviews the relevant factual and normative circumstances of the judgments selected and, second, focuses on the fundamental labour rights concerned, to discover the content and the level of protection guaranteed in the face of pressing economic and financial requirements. The judgments' outcomes are examined with an integrated reading of the Italian and Spanish legal reasonings that, without conducting a systematic comparison, reflects on the post-crisis case law of the two countries highlighting common or, rather, discordant trends.[3]

3.2 The relevant Italian post-crisis case law

3.2.1 Public employees' wage reduction before the Court

Each of the cases selected for the purpose of this analysis relates to a "particular category of workers".[4]

What has been identified as the first – in a chronological order – judgment on post-crisis measures, that is Judgment 223/2012, scrutinises a norm that had the effect of suspending the automatic adjustment mechanism of the judges' salaries and reducing progressively indemnities that are peculiar to the judiciary members. In other words, the provision at stake, provided for by subsections 21 and 22 of Art. 9, Decree Law 78/2012 of 31 May 2010 on "Urgent measures for the financial stabilisation and the economic competitiveness", converted into Law 122/210, of 30 July 2012, was freezing given items of the judiciary's salary for an overall period of five years, from 2011 to 2015. The Court observes that the legal mechanism affected by the norm under scrutiny provides for the salary of judges to be automatically adjusted every three years, according to a percentage calculated by the General Statistics Office (*Istituto Centrale di Statistica*) and approved by Prime Minister Decree[5] and concludes that the principle of independence of the judiciary (Art. 104 IC) has been sacrificed in an unreasonable way, by the blocking of wage rises.[6] Once released, this has been considered the leading case of the Italian post-crisis case law; nevertheless it has been mostly commented jointly with other subsequent judgments, that are equally relevant: Judgment 310/2013 and Judgment 304/2013.[7]

3 The Italian judgments' quotations are my translation, but for ICC, Judgments 70 /2015, 178/2015, 194/2018 have been officially translated in English, by the Italian Constitutional Court. The Spanish judgments' quotations are my translation.

4 Lo Faro 2014a, 66.

5 ICC, Judgment 223/2012, 11.2.

6 Bonardi 2012 discusses the judgment with a focus on the relevant case law and reflects on the possible effects of this judgment on the legal system as a whole; in this respect see also Mancini 2013.

7 Fontana 2015, 151; Lo Faro 2014b emphasises the inconsistencies among the first and second rulings.

In Judgment 310/2013 – which strongly reiterates the conclusions of Judgment 304/2013 on the wage block for the diplomatic staff – the Court addresses the constitutionality of Art. 9.2 and Art. 9.21 of Decree Law 78/2010, which had provided for a block of wage rises and deactivated service seniority for university lecturers and researchers for the years 2011, 2012 and 2013.[8] In a concise judgment, the Court rules in favour of the constitutional legitimacy of the challenged norms, which, although representing a sacrifice for the employees concerned, cannot be considered unreasonable, not even for the employees subject to the heaviest sacrifice, such as the researchers, because of three main reasons: the limited temporal scope; the necessity to contain public spending; and the general character of the sacrifice imposed. This is one of the first occasions in which the Court, in order to justify the length of the block and its reasonableness, emphasises the need to respect the principle of balanced budget and enforce the reformed Art. 81 IC, as well as Directive 2011/85/EU, which has imposed a medium-term approach to economic policies (sources not mentioned at all in Judgment 223/2012).

The further relevant step, Judgment 178/2015, concerns the right to collective bargaining and the necessary temporary character of its limitation. The *Tribunale di Roma* and the *Tribunale di Ravenna*, respectively in November 2013 and in March 2014, referred to a question of constitutionality concerning certain measures provided for by reforms aimed at urgently addressing the economic and financial situation; these measures were adopted by Decree Law in 2010 and 2011, the effects of which were partially extended by the Stability Laws for 2014 and 2015. A number of parties, including trade unions, intervened in the proceeding. In particular, the employees of the Ministry of Justice and the CONFSAL-UNSA brought the reasonableness and proportionality arguments to the forefront. They argued that the further extension of the block of collective bargaining (for the economic part) by the Stability Law for 2015 had violated a number of constitutional norms, and, in particular, it had balanced in an unreasonable and disproportionate way Articles 35.1, 36.1, 39.1 IC, with the aim of achieving economic recovery, and in particular, with the principle of balanced budget enshrined in Art. 81 IC. Although in Judgment 178/2015, the Court had the occasion to discuss a number of provisions and elaborate on the right to a fair remuneration (Art. 36.1 IC) as well,[9] this analysis focuses on the legal reasoning concerning the freezing of the bargaining procedures for the economic part and the right to collective bargaining provided for by Art. 39 IC. Eventually, the Court concluded that subsequent provisions limiting the right to collective bargaining in the public sector for an overall period of five years cause an infringement of Art. 39.1 IC, which protects trade

8 Considering the referral requests presented by various regional courts the constitutionality of the measure has been challenged on the grounds of Articles 2, 3, 9, 33, 34, 36, 37, 42, 53, 77 and 97 IC. On ICC, Judgment 310/2013, see Miriello 2014.

9 *Inter alia*, Orlandini 2018.

union freedom and, hence, the right to accede bargaining procedures. In particular, the constitutional legitimacy of the restriction imposed by Art. 9 of D.L. 78/2010, which had already been scrutinised in previous Judgments from 2013 and 2014, are reiterated and the Court briefly recalls the legal grounds used in its case law to conclude in favour of the reasonableness of this norm. Subsequently, the Court assesses the legitimacy of Art. 16.1.b), D.L. 98/2011, which authorised the adoption of a regulation providing for the extension until 31 December 2014 of the provisions limiting the increase of financial remuneration. Already at a very first stage of its argumentation, the Court points out that, in order to decide upon the constitutionality of the contested provision, the latter has to be read in conjunction with the Stability Law for 2014 (because of an "inseparable link" between them) (Art. 1.453, Law 147/2013) for the part that provides for the suspension of the bargaining procedure on the economic aspects for 2013 and 2014. In other words, these norms have the effect of suspending for an additional two years the collective negotiation in the public sector.[10] After having concluded for the non-unreasonable sacrifice of Art. 36.1 IC, that is the principle of proportionate remuneration, and, consequently, having dismissed the claims for damages,[11] the Court finds "a clear violation of the trade union freedom", based on the fact that the suspension of collective bargaining was "so prolonged over time".[12] This conclusion is supported by the evaluation of another provision that further prolonged the block of collective bargaining up until the end of 2015: the Stability Law for 2015 (Art. 1.254, Law 190/2014).

Eventually, the Court rules that, although a partial suspension of collective negotiation in the public sector may be justified by the contingent economic context, such a prolonged block – interpreted as evidence of the intention of the legislator to give structural effect to the constraint – is unreasonable, since it causes an unbearable sacrifice of the right to collective bargaining. The same conclusions are reached as far as the block of the non-renewal indemnity is concerned.[13]

In 2017, the reduction of public employees' wages was discussed again by the Constitutional Court. Even though Judgment 124/2017 has not equally attracted the attention of the academic literature, it needs to be briefly addressed, since the judicial reasoning makes use of certain elements that are recurrent in the case law under assessment, namely the use of the principle of reasonableness, the supervision over a proper balancing of different constitutional principles, the relevance of the economic context and the general character of the measure under scrutiny, as well as the discretional power of the legislator. The first measure discussed in Judgment 124/2017 provides for an all-encompassing maximum limit for the economic treatment of any person working for the public administration, whether employed or self-employed, which shall not

10 ICC, Judgments 178/2015, 13.
11 See ICC, Judgments 178/2015, 14.1, 14.2.
12 ICC, Judgments 178/2015, 15.
13 For a commentary, cf. Fiorillo 2015.

exceed the economic treatment perceived by the First President of the Supreme Court (*Corte di Cassazione*), at that time set at 240,000 euros (Art. 23-ter D.L. 201/2011, converted by Law 214/2011 and Art. 13.1 D.L. 66/2014, converted by Law 89/2014). The second provision assessed (Art. 1.489 of Law 147/2013, *Stability Law for 2014*) prevents public bodies from paying the remuneration to those who already receive a retirement benefit, in a way that the total amount received, by summing up remuneration and retirement benefit (including annuities), exceeds the limit of 240,000 euros per annum. Both norms have passed the test of constitutionality and have been found reasonable beyond any doubt.

3.2.2 Retirement benefits revaluation and the modulation of the Court

The extremely controversial Judgment 70/2015 scrutinises the constitutional legitimacy of a norm providing for a limit to the revaluation of pensions by 100%, for the years 2012 and 2013, exclusively for pensions worth an overall amount of up to three times the minimum INPS (National Institute of Social Security) pension, namely Art. 24.25 of Decree Law 201/2011, of 6 December 2011 (Urgent provisions on growth, equity and the consolidation of the public accounts), converted with amendments into Art. 1.1, Law 214/2011 (known as "Salva Italia").[14] The Court discusses the questions of unconstitutionality on the grounds of Art. 36.1 IC (providing for the right to a fair remuneration) and Art. 38.2 IC (on the adequacy of social security benefits), read in light of Art. 3.2 IC (on the right to substantial equal treatment). Eventually, the block of the revaluation of pensions is declared in violation of all constitutional norms invoked.[15]

In Judgment 173/2016, the Court evaluates the legitimacy of two norms of the Stability Law for 2014: Art. 1.483 and Art. 1.486 of Law 147/2013. Both provisions have passed the judicial scrutiny and have been declared consistent with the constitutional sources. The first measure addressed provided for a new modulation of the retirement benefits revaluation, which concerned all pensions, for the years 2014–2018. The legal reasoning of the judge, which declared the claim of unconstitutionality against this norm unfounded, widely refers to

14 For an early commentary cf. Cinelli 2015b; for a summary in English of the judgment see Bergonzini 2016; On follow-up to the judgment cf. Giubboni 2015a, 532–535; Morelli 2015, 709–710; D'Onghia 2015, 349–352.

15 A number of authors, mainly constitutional lawyers, have addressed Judgment 70/2015 in comparison with Judgment 10/2015, released a few weeks before Judgment 70/2015, where the Court declared the unconstitutionality of the so called Robin Tax, that is a special tax put on oil companies. The Court in this decision has made a careful consideration of the consequences on the public budget that a full declaration of unconstitutionality of the measure would have caused and, for that reason, it has regulated the effects of its judgment in such a way as to avoid the reimbursement of the amounts already paid. Indeed, thanks to this temporal modulation, the judgment was effective starting from the day after its publication. On the comparison between the two rulings, *inter alia*, Pin Longo 2015, Bergonzini 2016. Profoundly critical towards ICC, Judgment 70/2015 Morrone 2015a.

Judgment 70/2015.[16] Indeed, the Court does not develop a proper legal reasoning around this norm, but it reiterates the crucial distinction between a block and a modulation in the revaluation of pensions, to conclude by declaring Art. 1.483 legitimate. Therefore, the analysis of this judgment focuses on the legal reasoning developed as regards the second norm assessed by the Court, Art. 1.486, that provided for a solidarity contribution to be detracted from the highest retirement benefits (15–30 times higher than the minimum INPS pension), for a three-year period (2014–2016). The contested provision is found reasonable, "albeit to the limit" and, therefore, consistent with the right to adequate retirement benefits (Art. 38 IC). Overall, the line of thought of the judge is brief and at times hasty, but it offers interesting elements to be added to the general reflection on the constitutional post-crisis case law.

One of the latest episodes of a case law in search of some coherence is represented by Judgment 250/2017, released in December 2017, which responds to 15 questions of unconstitutionality raised by several ordinary courts and assesses the legitimacy of three norms concerning the automatic revaluation of pensions. One of them, namely the question referring to Art. 1.483, has been solved mostly on the grounds of the relevant case law. Therefore, this section focuses on the other two norms and the elaborated legal reasoning that have declared their constitutionality. Art. 24.25 and Art. 24.25-bis of D.L. 201/2011, as substituted by Art. 1.1)-1) of D.L. 65/2015, have been adopted with the explicit aim of implementing Judgment 70/2015 and amending the regulation on the automatic revaluation of pensions censured by that judgment, in compliance with the principle of balanced budget and the public finance targets. In particular, paragraph 25 rules out any automatic revaluation for retirement benefits six times as high as the minimum INPS benefit and provides for a revaluation based upon decreasing percentages for retirement benefits between three and six times the INPS minimum, for the years 2012–2013. Paragraph 25-bis has to do with the so-called *trascinamento*: the norm regulates the percentage of the revaluation for the years 2012–2013 recognised in order to determine the automatic revaluation for the years 2014, 2015 (20%) and 2016 (50%). Both provisions are declared legitimate because they do not affect the adequacy of the retirement benefits, precisely due to the application of the progressivity criterion, which ensures conservation of the purchasing power and resistance to erosion.

3.2.3 On compensation for unjustified dismissal

Most recently, the Italian Constitutional Court has released a series of judgments that have assessed the legitimacy of certain dismissal reforms adopted with either Law 92/2012, also known as *Riforma Fornero*,[17] or Legislative Decree 23/2015,

16 Thus creating a continuity between the two decisions, Guiglia 2016, 18; see, also, Pedullà 2016, 4, Sandulli 2016, 688.

17 For a review in English of Law 92/2012, see Biasi 2014.

part of the so-called JOBS Act (JA) – which name was inspired by the Obama reforms and stands for Jumpstart Our Business Startups Act – that is a series of reforms approved in 2014 and 2015 by the Renzi Government.[18] In Judgment 194/2018, the first of the saga, the Court ruled on the legitimacy of a norm enshrined in Legislative Decree 23/2015, acting on authorisation of Art. 1.7(c) of Law no. 183 of 2014, for the stated "purpose of enhancing opportunities for entry into the workplace by persons seeking employment";[19] nonetheless, the Court has assessed only Art. 3, para. 1, since such a norm was the sole applicable to the proceedings before the lower court. The measure provided for an inflexible and automatic mechanism to be applied by the courts for calculating the compensation due to workers hired after 7 March 2015 and dismissed without justified objective or subjective reasons, or in the absence of good cause, that is in case of unjustified dismissal. The same provision also envisaged – and still does – a minimum and maximum threshold within which it was possible to set the compensation payable to a worker unfairly dismissed, namely between four (minimum limit) and 24 (maximum limit) months' salary. But what is challenged by the lower court is precisely the automatic mechanism and not the provision of minimum and maximum limits.[20]

Eventually, the Constitutional Judges upheld the complaint against Art. 3, para.1, Legislative Decree 23/2015 on the grounds of the inflexible character of the compensation which derives from the quantification mechanism provided by the contested norm, based exclusively on the parameter of the length of service and it declares Art. 3.1 unconstitutional, partially accepting the questions raised by the lower court, with regard to the phrase "in an amount equal to two times

18 Caruso has identified four academic approaches to the JA: (a) the position of constitutional and statutarian traditionalism identifies in the JA the end of the labour law history of the 20th century; (b) a softer variation of the first theory understands Renzi's reforms as the misapplication of the European flexicurity; (c) what the author names the "celebrative approach" praises the JA for being the concretisation of the law and economics theories, which finally breaks with the statutarian positions; (d) last, a branch of literature positively looks at the JOBS Act as a first step towards an innovation of the labour law paradigm, see Caruso 2016, 266. For a general reflection on the matter, Pizzoferrato 2015, 197 ff.

19 Legislative Decree no. 23 of 4 March 2015, by implementing Law no. 183 of 10 December 2014, has introduced the so-called *Contratto di lavoro a tempo indeterminato a tutele crescenti*. Nevertheless, whether an "increasing protection" had been effectively introduced has always been disputed. See, *inter alia*, Giubboni 2015b, 12, who talks of a "spectacular backing down of guarantees in case of unjustified dismissal", my translation; a number of criticisms have also been raised by Perulli 2015, Carinci 2015. For an attentive assessment of unjustified dismissal, also from a case law perspective, see Bolego 2016; Nogler 2015. In support of the reform was, instead, Ichino 2015; while Caruso Del Punta 2016 encourage one to assess carefully every aspect of the new type of contract together with the Fornero reform of Art. 18 of Law 300/1970.

20 Which is also the reason why the amendment made by Decree Law no. 87 of 12 July 2018, converted with amendments into Law no. 96 of 9 August 2018, which has increased those limits, from four to six times and from 24 to 36 times did not impinge upon the proceedings, given that the contested mechanism has not been altered (ICC, Judgment 194/2018, 3).

the last qualifying monthly salary for the purposes of calculating the TFR for each year of service", which violates a number of constitutional norms: "Articles 3 (in relation both to the principle of equality, in terms of the unjustified treatment as identical of different situations, and the principle of reasonableness), 4(1), 35(1), 76 and 117(1) of the Constitution (the last two Articles in relation to Article 24 of the European Social Charter)".[21]

The judgments dealing with dismissal provisions subsequently released by the Italian Court, *i.e.* Judgments 150/2020, 59/2021, 120/2022 and 183/2022, which come in the wake of Judgment 194/2018, are not comprehensively assessed here. Indeed, even if they may partially fit into this study, the analysis of Judgment 194/2018 is sufficient for the purposes of this work, since, being a landmark case, it provides all necessary elements to identify the impact on the right to work of the Italian post-crisis case law from the constitutional balancing perspective.[22]

3.3 The relevant Spanish post-crisis case law

The Spanish constitutional case law on post-crisis measures discussed in this chapter deals with several norms of a unique – but comprehensive and significant – Act: Royal Decree Law (RDL) 3/2012 of 10 February, converted into Law 3/2012 of 6 July, on "Urgent measures to reform the labour market".

In Judgments 119/2014 and 8/2015, the applicants advocated the infringement of a number of constitutional provisions: Art. 14 SC (equality before the law), Art. 23.2 SC (equality in participation of citizens in public affairs), Art. 24.1 SC (right to effective judicial protection), Art. 28.1 SC (trade union freedom), Art. 35.1 SC (right and duty to work), Art. 37.1 SC (right to collective bargaining) and Art. 103.3 SC (civil servants status).

The following sections focus on the right to work and right to collective bargaining, mostly because the claims concerning the other constitutional articles have been dismissed rather hastily. The claimants raised a substantial number of issues. Most of them concerned the lack of proportionality of the measures adopted; indeed the principle of proportionality was, in several cases, already invoked by the claimants.

3.3.1 *The first and comprehensive judgment on the 2012 labour reform*

Judgment 119/2014 was initiated by a question of constitutionality submitted by the *Parlamento de Navarra* in October 2012. According to the claimant,

21 Judgment 194/2018 has had a remarkable academic echo; just to mention some contributions: Carinci 2018; Ichino 2018; Ballestrero 2019; Maresca 2019; Tosi 2019; Zoppoli 2019; Magnani 2019; Orlandini 2019; Maio 2022.

22 On the consistent approach of the Court in the first three rulings, see Perulli 2021; Ghera 2022.

Articles 4, 14.1, 14.2 and 14.3 and the fifth attached provision were infringing upon Art. 14 SC (principle of formal equality), Art. 24 SC (right to effective judicial protection), Art. 28 SC (trade union freedom and right to strike), Art. 35 SC (right to work) and Art. 37 SC (right to collective bargaining and the right to engage in industrial disputes). Nevertheless, the Spanish Court admits only the questions of constitutionality as regards Art. 4 and Art.14, paragraphs 1 and 3, of Law 3/2012.

In particular, the applicants argue that the contract of employment introduced by Art. 4.3 of Law 3/2012, which provides for an open-ended contract of employment with a probationary period of one year, known as the open-ended entrepreneur-support contract (*Contrato de Apoyo a los Emprendedores* (CAE)), infringes upon the right to work, granted by Art. 35.1 SC.[23] In their view, first, a norm as such, which does not foresee any possibility for the social partners to intervene, has the effect of undermining collective bargaining autonomy. Second, it creates a different regime for companies based on the quantitative criterion of 50 employees. Third, the possibility to dismiss the worker during the first year of employment, without indemnity and excluding the judicial review of the dismissal, infringes upon the right to equal treatment (Art. 14 SC), the right to work (Art. 35 SC) and the right to collective bargaining (Art. 37 SC). The Court ruled in favour of the constitutionality of Art. 4.3, Law 3/2012, since the norm was found to be in compliance with Art. 35.1 SC.

According to the Court, also Art. 14.1, Law 3/2012, which amends Art. 82.3 Workers' Statute and provides the *Comisión Consultiva Nacional de Convenios Colectivos*, and the respective bodies in the Autonomous Communities, with the power to allow the disapplication of terms and conditions agreed by workers' and employers' representatives in the generally binding collective agreements (regulated by Title III of the Workers' Statute), is consistent with the Spanish constitutional norms. Mostly because, albeit collective agreements in Spain have a binding effect, terms and conditions of collective agreements are not "petrified" and, hence, can be modified, also if technical or productive fluctuations arise, under the conditions established by law. Although the measure enshrined in Art. 14.1, Law 3/2012, represents an exception to the binding character of collective agreements, it pursues a legitimate aim (internal flexibility) and it carries enough limits to its application (as the rigid list of terms that can be modified) to be considered protected under Art. 35.1 SC, Art. 38 SC and Art. 40.1 SC and, therefore, justified. The challenged norm, thus, does not infringe upon Articles 37.1, 28.1 and 24.1 SC as advocated by the claimants.

Last, according to the claimants, Art. 14.3, Law 3/2012, which amends Art. 84.2 Workers' Statute and establishes the supremacy of company-level agreements

23 The *Contrato de Apoyo* has been ironically defined the "star" of Law 3/2012, see Moreno Vida 2013, 194 and Pérez Rey 2012. On the provision at issue, see also Garcia Blasco 2012 and Vicente Palacio 2012.

as regards certain matters, infringes upon both the trade union freedom (Art. 28.1 SC) and the right to collective bargaining (Art. 37.1 SC).[24]

Again, the Court stresses the legislator's discretional power over the articulation of collective bargaining and its levels, as well as over the margin of intervention of collective actors. In this case, the power of determining the structure of collective bargaining confers an absolute supremacy to the law, over the social partners' autonomy. Likewise, according to the Court, the norm aims at fostering productivity and sustainability of the companies, which are objectives protected under Art. 35.1 SC, Art. 38 SC and Art. 40.1 SC, and it does not hamper the social partners from negotiating at sectorial level.[25]

3.3.2 The second and consistent judgment, one year later

From a labour law perspective, the latest relevant constitutional post-crisis ruling is Judgment 8/2015. On 5 October 2012, 104 deputies of the Socialist Group in Parliament and 11 of the parliamentary group *Izquierda Plural* challenged the constitutionality of given norms enshrined in Law 3/2012. In particular, the present Chapter addresses the legal reasoning related to Articles 4.3, 12.1, 14.1 and 2, 18.3 and 8, which were deemed unconstitutional by the applicants because in violation of various Constitutional norms: Articles 14, 23.2, 24.1 (right to participate in public affairs), 28.1, 35.1, 37.1 and 103.3 (statute of civil servants). Some of the questions of constitutionality raised in this case had already been raised, discussed and solved in Judgment 119/2014. The Court points out, at a very first stage, that the legal reasoning on those norms reiterates the same arguments developed in Judgment 119/2014.[26] Subsequently, the Court devotes the first part of the judgment to dismiss a general claim against Law 3/2012, according to which the Law at issue "was born outside of the constitutional coordinates", in other words the applicants argue that Law 3/2012 ignores the structural and axiological framework of labour relations designed by the Spanish constitutional model.[27]

As to the norms already discussed in Judgment 119/2014, on Art. 4.3, Law 3/2012 (one-year probationary period in the CAE), the Court reiterates the arguments of its previous judgment, thus, in brief, it stresses that the norm is justified, reasonable and proportionate, since it aims at supporting the creation of stable employment in a context of economic crisis. Therefore, Articles 35.1, 37.1, 24.1 SC and Art. 14 SC are not violated.

24 The claimant also suggests that the norms at stake violate ILO Convention No. 158 and No. 98. For a reflection over the measures challenged before the Constitutional Court in the case at issue, see Senra Biedma 2014.

25 For an attentive review of Judgment 119/2014 see, *inter alia*, De Val Tena 2014 and Senra Biedma 2014; in a similar way Suarez Corujo 2015, 434. On Art. 14, Law 3/2012, see Navarro Nieto 2013 and Meilán Delgado 2016.

26 SCC, Judgment 8/2015, 1, c).

27 SCC, Judgment 8/2015, 2.

Also Art. 14.3, which prioritises collective negotiation at company level, was newly challenged in October 2014, for breaching Art. 37.1 SC, on the binding effect of collective agreements, and the freedom of association protected by Art. 28.1 SC. Apparently, the new issues raised by the claimants were not persuasive enough to induce the Court to rule for the unconstitutionality of the reform of Art. 84.2 Workers' Statute. Indeed, in order to strengthen its point, the Court puts forward more arguments on the legitimate aim of the reform and stresses that no restriction to negotiate for any trade union has been imposed. However, on this issue, the Court had elaborated more extensive arguments in Judgment 119/2014.

The claimants challenge the constitutionality of Art. 12.1, Law 3/2012, which amends Art. 41 Workers' Statute, paragraphs 4 and 5, and allows the employer to impose unilateral changes to working terms and conditions established in *extraestatutarios* collective agreements (not generally applicable), on the grounds of Art. 37.1 SC, Art. 28.1 SC, Art. 24.1 SC. This norm, according to the claimants, violates the constitutional provisions even more seriously than the reform providing for a "compulsory arbitration" (Art. 14.1, Law 3/2012), since, in this case, the unilateral power of the employer is unlimited. The claimants underline that every party to a collective agreement is bound by the *pacta sunt servanda* principle, which is guaranteed by Art. 37 SC – and indirectly by Art. 28.1 SC – and cannot be at the mercy of the legislator. Furthermore, it is advocated that, in practice, the extensive scope of the justificatory reasons makes the unilateral amendments always possible. Consequently, the broad liberty granted to the employer does not guarantee effective judicial protection, either (Art. 24.1 SC).

The Court admits that the mechanism introduced by Art. 12.1, Law 3/2012, affects the content of collective agreements, but it justifies this interference by first arguing that a system as such is not new to the Spanish legal system and the purposes of the norm are in compliance with the right to work (Art. 35.1 SC), the full employment policy (Art. 40.1 SC) as well as the business freedom and defence of productivity (Art. 38 SC). Second, it – apparently – applies the test of constitutional proportionality, which is eventually passed by the norms under scrutiny. The Court expressly mentions the three criteria: suitability (*idoneidad*), necessity (*necessidad*) and proportionality in the strict sense (*proprtionalidad en sentido estricto*). Eventually, the element that upholds the proportionate character of the reform lies in the aim of the norm, *i.e.* to tackle unemployment. Also in this case, the challenge of unconstitutionality on the grounds of Art. 24.1 SC is dismissed.

Art. 14.2, Law 3/2012, amending Art. 84.2 Workers' Statute, is deemed unconstitutional by the claimants on the grounds of Art. 37.1 SC and Art. 28.1 SC. The norm, by referring to the third paragraph of Art. 14, establishes an absolute priority of company-level agreements and the complete exclusion of social partners from any decision over the hierarchy of collective bargaining levels. This entails the possibility to disapply the sector-level agreement at any time, also in favour of company agreements concluded by workers' representatives not belonging to any union, as well as the ineffectiveness of the agreements reached by the social partners on the collective bargaining structure. According to the claimants, the violation of Art. 37.1 SC and Art. 28.1 SC is plain, given the exorbitant intervention by the legislator and the lack of objectivity, proportionality and necessity, inasmuch as in order to allow the establishment of terms and conditions of employment closely to the entrepreneurs' needs a different, and less detrimental, norm could have been adopted.

Given the substantial identity of effects between this norm and the subsequent paragraph, already addressed in the previous ruling, the Court reiterates its reasoning and the conclusions reached in Judgment 119/2014. Moreover, it adds that the new claims do not constitute solid grounds for concluding in favour of the violation of Art. 37.1 SC and Art. 28.1 SC.

The claimants also raise the unconstitutional legitimacy of the second paragraph of the final dispositions of Law 3/2012, which amends the 10th additional provision of the Workers' Statute. Once again, it is argued that the norm violates Art. 37.1 SC and Art. 28.1 SC since it substantially restricts the trade union autonomy in an unjustified and disproportionate way by declaring null the collective agreement's clause that provides for the termination of the employment contract once the retirement age is reached. The claimants also deny the existence of objective reasons for labour public order, which would justify this reform and advocate that the different treatment caused by the norm between public servants and the other workers violates Art. 14 SC and the right to equal treatment, as well as the right to access public employment (Art. 23.2 SC and Art. 103.3 SC).

Furthermore, two paragraphs of Art. 18, Law 3/2012 were challenged. Art. 18.3, Law 3/2012, which reforms Art. 51 Workers' Statute, titled "collective redundancy" and provides for the power of the employer to terminate the employment contracts, following a consultation period with the workers' representatives, if "economic, technical, organizational and productive causes" occur, is considered disrespectful of the relevance of the causal element of dismissal and of the role of the judicial review. As a consequence, it is deemed in violation of the right to work (Art. 35.1 SC) and the right to effective judicial protection (Art. 24.1 SC). According to the Court, Law 3/2012 does significantly modify the definition of technical, organisation and productive causes, while it does affect substantially the meaning of economic causes. Nevertheless, the Court does not observe the establishment of a hypothesis of an ***ad nutum*** and a-causal dismissal, nor the lack of effective judicial protection. Therefore, neither Art. 35.1 SC, nor Art. 24.1 SC, are deemed violated.

Art. 18.8, Law 3/2012 (and consequently Art. 23.1) amends Art. 56.2 WS and limits, in case of judicial declaration of illegitimate dismissal and reintegration of the worker, the payment of the *salario de tramitación*, that is the amount of salary the worker would have received if he/she had not been dismissed. This provision, according to the claimants, violates both the right to work (Art. 35.1 SC) and the right to equal treatment (Art. 14 SC). In this case, the Court extensively refers to *Auto* 43/2014, which had previously dismissed the unconstitutionality of the provision under certain conditions. However, it adds that the Court's duty is to evaluate whether the legislator's choice fulfils the limits imposed by Art.

35 SC, while it cannot assess the merit of the legislative decision and judge upon whether it is the more appropriate or the best possible option.

Last, the claimants challenge the constitutional legitimacy of the 3rd additional disposition of Law 3/2012, on the basis of Articles 14, 23 and 103.3 SC, in connection with Art. 35.1 SC. The reasons attached to this claim are, first, the inconsistency with the objectives of the reform, that is to grant the internal flexibility, and, second, the indirect support to collective redundancy, which remains the only procedure for the Public Administration to operate staff reduction, inasmuch as the latest is excluded from the application of Art. 47 Workers' Statute, and therefore from the possibility to reduce working hours and suspend employment contracts for economic, technical, organisational and productive reasons. The judges dismiss the claim of unconstitutionality on the grounds of the violation of the principle of equal treatment, since different situations cannot be treated equally. In a similarly offhandedly way, the Court dismisses the claims for unconstitutionality based on Art. 23 SC and Art. 103.3 SC.

Judgment 8/2015 is strongly in line with Judgment 119/2014 and it refers to the latter extensively, reiterating core arguments, to the point that it has been considered an "extended confirmation" of Judgment 119/2014.[28]

3.4 Fundamental labour rights in the balance

A focus on the fundamental labour rights discussed by the selected judgments recapitulates the status of the said rights at the latest interpretative (national) stage. Although none of the courts has conducted the so-called "definitional balancing",[29] the legal reasonings contribute to identifying the content of the relevant labour rights in the context of a pluralist legal system and in the face of pressing economic and financial constraints.

The fundamental labour rights addressed in the Italian constitutional post-crisis case law are the right to work (Art. 4.1 IC), alongside the "protection" for work "in all of its forms and applications" (Art. 35.1 IC); the right to a fair remuneration (Art. 36.1 IC), which is applied also to extend the scope of the principle of independence of the judiciary (Art. 104 IC); the right to an adequate pension (Art. 38.2 IC); the right to collective bargaining (Art. 39.1 IC).

28 Indeed, several authors have analysed and discussed the rulings together, see García Murcia 2015, 284; as well as García Murcia 2015; Cruz Villalón 2015; Diaz Aznarte 2015; Fernández López 2015.

29 One for all, Nimmer 1968, who used this expression to describe the creative activity of judges, who frame the rules limiting legislative power. "Definitional balancing", applied by the Italian Court on several occasions, especially in its first decades, still belongs to the domain of the interpretation, inasmuch as it serves the purpose to understand the content of the constitutional provisions which provide for fundamental rights, Bin 1992, 68. On the topic, also Cerri 2016, 655 ff, who differentiates between ***definitional balancing*** and ***balancing ad hoc***.

Moreover, Art. 3.2 IC retains a peculiar position, on the one hand, it intersects the analysis of all relevant fundamental labour rights, as it constitutes the legal basis for the reasonableness criterion, and, on the other, it has a pivotal value as regards Art. 36.1 IC and Art. 38.2 IC. In fact, the latter rights are identified by the Court as the proper concretisation of Art. 3.2 IC and the respective principle of substantial equality.

In the Spanish case law, the fundamental labour rights at issue are the right to work (Art. 35.1 SC) and the right to collective bargaining (Art. 37.1 SC). Overall, their content and protection hardly benefit from the legal reasoning addressed in this chapter and the Court's main concern seems to be underlying that the fundamental rights at stake are "limited" and "not absolute", although it recognises that the limitations must be justified and legitimate.

Both Courts have focused on the right to work and the right to collective bargaining. Yet, given that the factual cases that have triggered the constitutional rulings are unlike, the decisions of the two Courts are differently oriented also in the considerations over the fundamental labour rights at issue, as they emphasise the most relevant profiles of the said rights in relation to the contested measure.

3.4.1 The right to work

The right to work is defined for introductory purposes in a substantially analogous manner by the two Courts. It is uncontroversial that the employment stability it aims to enforce does not translate into an absolute right to remain at work, as it is "nothing other than a terminological synthesis of the limits on the power of dismissal, associated with a sanction of invalidity",[30] but it implies proper guarantees in case of dismissal, which are, first and foremost, enacted by the principle of justification as a necessary requirement for the legitimate exercise of the unilateral power of the employer to terminate the employment contract. Second, the right to work shall be guaranteed by an "appropriate reaction", or "adequate compensation", whose configuration is left to the discretion of the legislator.[31] As shown below, the Italian Court elaborates further on the principle of adequate redress, since the norm it is called upon to scrutinise directly concerns such profile.

To the contrary, the Spanish Court does not focus on the consequences for unfair dismissal, since it claims that the one-year probationary period introduced by the Spanish legislator, as a measure to improve employment (Art. 4.3, Law 3/2012), is not related in any way to a discussion on the cause for dismissal, nor to the reaction to the a-causal dismissal, given that the termination during the probationary period does not constitute a dismissal, but, rather, the "formalization, by a declaration of will, of the resolution, affirmative and arbitrary (*positiva y potestativa*), expressly accepted by the parties at the time the contract

30 ICC, Judgment, 268/1994, 5, *Conclusions on points of law*, as corroborated in ICC, Judgment 194/2018, 9.2.

31 ICC, Judgment 194/2018, 9.1 and SCC, Judgment 119/2014, 3, A b.

was signed".[32] Although it seems to suggest that the applicability of Art. 35.1 SC shall be excluded, it proceeds by recognising that the possibility to terminate the contract – during the probationary period – only upon declaration of will of one of the two parties implies that the probationary period as it is framed by the legislator "can act as a limitation to the right to employment stability" and, hence, Art. 4.3 must be examined in light of Art. 35.1 SC.

Eventually, both in Judgment 119/2014 and Judgment 8/2015, the one-year probationary period is declared legitimate and in compliance with Art. 35.1 SC, since "it provides a legitimate justification, it results reasonable and proportionate with respect to the aims pursued".[33] The legal grounds that justify the declaration of constitutionality of the contested norm are the context of serious economic crisis; the aim, that is to foster the conclusion of open-ended contracts, given the context and the serious situation of unemployment; the time-limited character of the norm, linked to the decrease in the unemployment rate; the limited subjective scope of application; fiscal benefits that the company can enjoy only if the employment relationship continues after the probationary period and the employment level is maintained; other related norms that moderate the negative effects of the measure, that is the legal context.[34] These "legal limits", to which the application of the one-year probationary period is subject, reduce the impact the contested provision has on the workers' right to employment stability, which, therefore, is not violated by the provision of a one-year probationary period.

The Spanish Court adds, among the arguments that shall justify the legitimacy of the contested norm, an apparent hierarchy between the fundamental rights covered by Art. 35 SC. Indeed, it claims that "both from a logic and a chronologic point of view", the right to access employment, which constitutes the "essential content" of the right to work, *ex* Art. 35.1 SC, comes before the right to a stable employment.[35] This phase of the legal reasoning apparently recognises an absolute hierarchy between the right, and hence the value, of a decent work above the right (and value?) of having a job. The Court seems to suggest that, in absolute terms, a decent employment does not have the same constitutional weight as being employed. The two rights are not, under this view, integrated into the social constitution, but they are hierarchically ordered. Paradoxically, the fundamental rights in conflict, that – apparently – need to be hierarchically ordered, are protected by the same constitutional disposition, which essential content is "the right to work", while, by exclusion, we can deduce that (although the Court does not explain this clearly) the right to a stable employment is not an expression of the essential content of the fundamental right to work.

In view of such a dull understanding of the right to work, apparently driven by economic and political contingencies, it is fairly reassuring the reference made by

32 SCC, Judgment 119/2014, 3, A, b).
33 As reiterated also in SCC, Judgment 8/2015, 3, b).
34 SCC, Judgment 119/2014, 3, A, f) and SCC, Judgment 8/2015, 3, b).
35 SCC, Judgment 119/2014, para. 3, A, f).

the Italian Court to the centrality of the individual in the employment contract, which distinguishes it from the rest of long-term contracts and requires the legislator to specifically protect the worker, thus enforcing Art. 4 IC and Art. 35 IC[36], which, together with Art. 1 IC, afford a particular significance to work as a mean to achieve the full development of the human personality.[37]

The "right to work" (Art. 4.1 IC) and the "protection" of work "in all of its forms and applications" (Art. 35.1 IC) assure that other fundamental rights guaranteed by the Constitution may be exercised in the workplace. A proper nexus is observed between rights linked to the employment relationship, as "in Judgment no. 63 of 1966, where it is asserted that 'the fear of termination, *i.e.* of dismissal, induces or may induce the worker to waive some of his or her rights'".[38]

As mentioned above, the right to work is addressed by the Italian Court, in relation to the compensation regime in case of unjustified dismissal. In this respect, the consolidated case law of the Court admits that the legislator (in the exercise of its discretional power) enforces the fundamental labour right at stake by envisaging a "protective mechanism involving only financial compensation (Judgment no. 303 of 2011), considering that the mechanism is structured in a manner that is compliant with the principle of reasonableness".[39]

In other words, even though a dismissal without good cause or justified reason remains an illegitimate act, compensation can be a sufficient form of remedy.

Nonetheless, compensation, which must comply with the principle of equality, cannot be uniform, inflexible or standardised and "irrespective of the specific circumstances of and differences between dismissals intimated by the employer", therefore cannot be based solely for instance – as in the case at stake – on the length of service having the status of a lump-sum legal settlement, where "the legislator has in effect clearly sought to set out in advance the full consequences of unlawful dismissal".[40]

Indeed, to comply with the principle of reasonableness, compensation must be "adequate", that is able to strike an "adequate balance between the interests in conflict".[41] In practice, it must both dissuade the employers "from any intention to dismiss a worker without a valid justification and to compromise the equilibrium of contractual obligations"[42] and provide adequate compensation for the detriment suffered by a worker who has been unfairly dismissed".[43] In brief, to

36 ICC, Judgment 194/2018, 9.1.
37 ICC, Judgment 163/1983, 6, *Conclusions on points of law*. Cf. Speziale 2022, 151.
38 ICC, Judgment 194/2018, 13.
39 ICC, Judgment 194/2018, 9.2.
40 ICC, Judgment 194/2018, 11. While the minimum and maximum threshold for compensation is judged in compliance with the requirement of adequacy, hence it is consistent with the right to work as defined above (ICC, Judgment 194/2018, 12.1).
41 ICC, Judgment 194/2018, 12.1.
42 ICC, Judgment 194/2018, 12.2.
43 ICC, Judgment 194/2018, 12.3.

comply with the right to work, interpreted through the reasonableness criterion, the compensation must constitute adequate deterrent and adequate redress.

The contested provision (Art. 3.1, d.lgs. 23/2015), insofar as it provides for compensation in an "amount equal to two times the last qualifying monthly salary for the purposes of calculating the TFR for each year of service", being a certain lump sum compensation, fails to comply with the constitutional provisions since it does not constitute an adequate deterrent for employers.[44]

The Italian jurisprudence is aligned with the content of Art. 24 of the Charter on the right to protection in case of termination of employment, which is equally grounded upon adequate compensation and appropriate relief. Therefore, the contested norm also violates Articles 76 e 117 Italian Constitution, on the ground of the Charter.[45]

3.4.2 The right to collective bargaining

Both the Italian and the Spanish Courts provide insights into the status of the fundamental right to engage in and conduct collective bargaining procedures (respectively recognised by Art. 39 IC and Art. 37.1 SC).

The Italian case is interesting especially as regards the content of the right to collective bargaining, in terms of objective scope of collective bargaining and legitimacy of limitations imposed by legislative acts. While the Spanish judgments contribute to a reflection on the subjective scope, the actors entitled to conduct the negotiation and the respective bargaining levels, as well as the role of public authorities in interfering in the content of collective negotiations.

Already at the first stage of the legal reasoning developed in Judgment 178/2015, on the grounds of the relevant case law, the Italian Court reiterates that a restriction of Art. 39.1 IC may be legitimate in "exceptional and eminently transitory situations, provided that the 'safeguarding of higher general interests' is at stake",[46] also in the public sector, which is entirely covered by the freedom to collective bargaining.[47]

As regards the specific case discussed in Judgment 178/2015, the Court underlines that the structural character of the block persists even though the collective negotiation on the normative part is not suspended, given that "the bargaining procedure must allow a comprehensive position to be stated regarding every aspect pertaining to the determination of employment conditions, which invariably also impinge upon the significant issue of financial aspects".[48] On this occasion, the Court provides additional elements to define the content of the right to collective bargaining, which is not exclusively functional to the determi-

44 ICC, Judgment 194/2018, 12.3.
45 Orlandini 2019; Ballestrero 2019; Frosecchi 2019.
46 ICC, Judgment 178/2015, 10.2.
47 As fully corroborated by ICC, Judgment 178/2015, Zoppoli 2017, 184.
48 ICC, Judgment 178/2015, 15.2.

nation of financial aspects, but is deemed to regulate the employment relationship comprehensively, thus including terms and conditions of employment in the widest sense. This argument is crucial to explain an infringement of Art. 39.1 IC by a legislative act, which is, instead, found in compliance with Art. 36.1 IC.[49]

The structural character of the block, holds the Court, "violates the principle of trade union freedom". The connection between the right to access collective bargaining procedures and the trade union freedom explicitly granted by Art. 39.1 IC and the fact that the bargaining autonomy is a "necessary complement" of, and functionally linked to, the trade union freedom can be derived not only from the national case law and scholarship, but also from the international sources that apply in the Italian legal order, such as the ILO Conventions[50] and the case law of the European Court of Human Rights (ECtHR),[51] deployed to corroborate the argument that the suspension of the bargaining and contractual provisions cannot be "extended at will", since the Strasbourg Court envisages in the time-limit a key element to determine whether a fair balance between fundamental rights of the individual and the general interest of the community is met.[52]

The Court also found direct support for the protection of the right to negotiate and conclude collective agreements in Art. 6 ESC and Art. 28 of the Charter. Last, the judgment contextualises and therefore upholds the right to collective bargaining in the EU by referring to another primary source, specifically Art. 152.1 TFEU, which aims to promote the dialogue between social partners without infringing on their autonomy.[53]

49 The causal relation between the violation of Art. 39 IC and the infringement of Art. 36 IC does not always occur, as in the case at stake. See Fiorillo 2015, who strongly agrees with the conclusions of the Court in this respect – and not only. Noticeably, the lack of violation of Art. 36 IC implies the exclusion of compensation, as also specified by the Court, Dalfino 2017, 178. On the profile at issues see also Mocchegiani 2015, Orlandini 2018, 11–14.

50 With regard to ILO sources, three ratified conventions were mentioned: Convention No. 151, which guarantees the right to organise and negotiate conditions of employment in the public sector; Convention No. 98, which protects the right to organise and to collective bargaining; and Convention No. 87, on freedom of association and the right to organise. ILO Convention No. 87 must be read in light of the interpretation provided by the Digest on Freedom of Association, which underpins the right to collective bargaining as an essential corollary to the freedom of association in both the Public and the private sector, Digest of Decisions and Principles of the Freedom of Association Committee of the Governing Body of the ILO, 5th ed. (Geneva: International Labour Office), especially paras. 880–1064.

51 ECtHR, *Demir and Baykara*, 2008, which establishes that trade union freedom, guaranteed by Art. 11 of the ECHR, also includes the right to collective bargaining for public workers.

52 ICC, Judgment 178/2015, 17. As rightly pointed out by Orlandini 2018, this interpretative choice, strongly oriented towards international sources, represents a remarkable new element in the Italian constitutional case law. The use of supranational sources has been emphasised also by Fiorillo 2015 and Occhino 2017, 9. For an early evaluation of this element of the legal reasoning, see Frosecchi 2016.

53 ICC, Judgment 178/2015, 16

Throughout its legal reasoning, the Court makes use of expressions such as a "repeated prolongment",[54] in order to convey that the temporal limit has been exceeded, which had the effect of unbalancing the relationship. Indeed, it is not the act of suspending collective bargaining in the public sector *per se* to be judged unconstitutional, but the "unreasonable" prolongation of the block. A conclusion is reached by the constitutional judges after a comprehensive evaluation of the norms that have been provided in this sense since 2010, up to 2015.[55] Furthermore, and still in light of its case law, the Court insists on the strict relationship between the three-year duration of the contractual rounds (collective bargaining) and the multi-year nature of budgetary policies.[56] This consideration contributes to identifying a further element of the content of the right to collective bargaining, that is the programmatic dimension of collective bargaining in relation to both the normative and the economic part.

In light of the generous legal reasoning developed, the Court concludes that what makes the sacrifice of the right to accede collective bargaining no more bearable is "[t]he now *structural nature* of this suspension",[57] which derives from an impact on the constitutional values at stake "anything but episodic".[58]

The right to collective bargaining is widely discussed by the Spanish Court, in nearly all rulings delivered, which contributes to the understanding of the constitutional features of the Spanish industrial relations system.[59]

Art. 37.1 SC does not frame an abstract and rigid model of industrial relations and/or collective bargaining, nor does it recognise exclusive prerogatives as regards collective bargaining. Notwithstanding that employers' and workers' organisations are recognised as having a "peculiar role" in the Spanish system, which is corroborated by Art. 7 SC that reads: "[T]rade unions and employers' associations contribute to the defence and promotion of the economic and social interests which they represent", thus including trade unions among the fundamental bodies of the society entrusted with the duty to defend, protect and promote collective interests of workers.[60]

54 ICC, Judgment 178/2015, 12.2.

55 Fiorillo 2015; Zoppoli 2017, 184, who argues that the temporal element is a decisive factor in the evaluation of the unconstitutional nature of the block, which cannot assume a structural character.

56 ICC, Judgment 178/2015, 12.1.

57 ICC, Judgment 178/2015, 17, italics added.

58 ICC, Judgment 178/2015, 15.1, 15.2.

59 It is argued that the Spanish post-crisis case law under discussion has mostly affected the right to collective bargaining and the collective autonomy. Particularly, Valdés Dal-Ré points out that, although a closed model of labour relations does not exist, the legislator lacks absolute discretional power as regards its regulation, especially because Art. 37.1 SC implies the promotion of collective negotiation, see Diaz Aznarte 2015, 200; Fernández López 2015, see 260–263; Cruz Villalón 2012a.

60 SCC, Judgment 8/2015, 2, b). The Court also quotes a number of constitutional judicial precedents that underline the relevance of this institution in the Spanish constitutional sys-

Indeed, the Spanish Constitution admits various legal solutions to regulate the industrial relations system,[61] consistently Art. 37.1 SC merely recognises the right to collective bargaining, "which protection is assigned to the legislator", and identifies the right holders, that is workers' and employers' representatives, and the legal effect of the collective bargaining outcome, *i.e.* the binding effect of collective agreements. As a consequence "[T]he legislator enjoys a wide margin of freedom in the elaboration of the right to collective bargaining, even though this freedom is not absolute".[62]

In theory, trade unions are considered constitutionally relevant, as they are entrusted with the specific responsibility "to determine the content of the employment relationship, together with the minimum regulation by the legislator", which the social partners fulfil by exercising their right to collective bargaining. Collective agreements are "sources of the employment relationship" with binding force and, as corroborated by the Spanish Court, collective bargaining improves the working conditions, as well as workers' lives, and, hence it is "an essential tool to manage the employment relationship".[63]

Nonetheless, although trade unions have a constitutional role as warrantors of workers' rights and interests, and collective negotiation is not only deemed relevant, but the main expression of the trade union action, as well as a crucial part of the essential content of the trade union freedom (Art. 28.1 SC), inasmuch as the collective negotiation is a "necessary mean for the exercise of the trade union activity",[64] "surely, the Constitution, by institutionalizing the labour collective rights (strike, collective negotiation and collective conflict) has not reserved their regulation exclusively to trade unions",[65] as demonstrated by the wording of Art. 37 SC. In other words, the right to collective negotiation is not a trade union prerogative, but it is recognised to workers' representatives in the widest sense, hence also to those organisations, which are workers' representatives, but are not covered by Art. 7 SC.[66]

The essential content of the right to collective bargaining includes the freedom to conduct collective negotiations and the freedom to conclude a collective agreement, understood as the faculty to select subjects and topics to be negotiated, but this freedom is not absolute and "for justified reasons, can be limited by the law".[67]

---

tem, *e.g.* SCC, Judgment 11/1981, 11 that defines trade unions "basic bodies of the political system".

61 SCC, Judgment 119/2014, 4, A).

62 SCC, Judgment 119/2014, 4, A).

63 SCC, Judgment 8/2015, 2, c). *Inter alia*, the Court quotes SCC, Judgment 151/1994, 2, and SCC, Judgment 208/1993. 4.

64 SCC, Judgment 119/2014, 4, A; SCC, Judgment 8/2015, 2, c).

65 Also as regards this point the Court makes wide use of its case law, see *inter alia*, SCC, Judgment 134/1994, 4; SCC, Judgment 95/1996, 3.

66 SCC, Judgment 8/2015, 2, d).

67 SCC, Judgment 119/2014, 3, C).

Indeed, Art. 37.1 SC entrusts the legislator with the responsibility to enforce the right to collective bargaining and the binding effect of collective agreements and cannot be read in such a way to interpret the freedom to conduct collective bargaining as a "sphere free from interference". The legislator has the duty to implement the right at issue, "without prejudice to the legislator's possibility to set restrictions to the binding effect of collective agreements in order to protect or preserve other rights, values or goods constitutionally protected or constitutional interests".[68] It can also "exclude given subjects from the collective negotiation and provide for imperative norms that cannot be deregulated by collective agreements". In addition, the principle of legal certainty is not violated even if the legislator amends terms and conditions set by collective agreements still in force when the relevant legislative act is implemented.[69]

The constitutional case law has specified that the limits to the right at stake are "beyond the social partners' control".[70] To corroborate its argument, the Court adds that Art. 53.1 SC provides for a general competence of the legislator to regulate the exercise of the rights and freedoms recognised in the section to which Art. 37 belongs.[71] Therefore, it concludes that it is constitutionally legitimate for the legislator to limit the scope of collective bargaining with regard to given aspects and subjects.[72]

In sum, trade unions are not the sole bodies entitled to the right to collective bargaining and the right to collective bargaining can be limited by the legislator.

The "principle of collective autonomy can be derogated from, only if its limitation is found justified".[73] Therefore, the Law, which is a hierarchically superior source of regulation,[74] "can limit the collective negotiation, and, on an exceptional basis, it can retain the regulation of certain subjects, by excluding them from the collective negotiation".[75]

So, for instance, according to the Court, Art. 4.3, Law 3/2012, does constitute a limitation to the right of collective bargaining.[76] Nevertheless, this restriction is justified on the grounds of the same arguments that validate the limitation to the right to the employment stability (Art. 35.1 SC), which support once again, the reasonable and proportionate character of the contested provision. The Court underlines: the "serious economic crisis context" and the "high unemployment rate"; it recalls the duty of public powers to adopt a policy oriented to

68 Here it expressly refers to SCC, Judgment 11/1981, 24.
69 SCC, Judgment 119/2014, 4, A). The reference is to: SCC, Judgment 58/1985, 3; SCC, Judgment 177/1988, 4; SCC, Judgment 210/1990, 2; SCC, Judgment 62/2001, 3.
70 In particular, the Court refers to SCC, Judgment 136/1987, 5; SCC, Judgment 208/1993, 3.
71 On Art. 53 SC in the context of the post-crisis case law, see De la Quadra-Salcedo Janini 2020, 63 ff.
72 SCC, Judgment 119/2014, 3, C, a).
73 SCC, Judgment 11/1981, 24.
74 Judgment 119/2014, para. 3, C, a).
75 SCC, Judgment 8/2015, 2, e).
76 SCC, Judgment 119/2014, 3, C, b).

the full employment (Art. 40.1 SC), which is an aim pursued by this measure; it stresses that the application of the contested provision is subject to certain legal constraints. As far as concerns particularly the rights protected by Art. 37 SC, the Court lists (but does not elaborate) two main reasons that corroborate the legitimacy of the contested norm. First, it aims to avoid that collective bargaining "may reduce or delete" the incentive to conclude open-ended contracts that the legislator has introduced; second, it contributes to preventing the collective autonomy from frustrating the legitimate objective of creation of stable employment.[77]

On the one hand, the Constitution recognises the role of trade unions as fundamental bodies, as well as bodies authorised to conduct collective bargaining and conclude collective agreements with *erga omnes* effect. Conversely, the Constitutional Court suggests that the collective autonomy must be constrained and the legislative prerogatives maintained, since the collective autonomy may hamper the creation of stable employment. In other words, social partners (and not just trade unions) are implicitly considered potential enemies of employment stability (and hence of the right to work under Art. 35 SC). However surprising this conclusion may sound, the Court's approach is not inconsistent with the rest of the judgment, to the contrary such a vision of the trade unions' role is coherent with the logic that places job creation at a higher level than stable jobs (see above, the reflection on the internal hierarchy of Art. 35 SC).

As far as concerns the binding force of collective agreements, the Court reiterates that Art. 37.1 SC provides for a legislator's duty to guarantee the right to collective bargaining and the binding force of the agreements, without, however, imposing the adoption of a precise option. In implementing this norm, argues the Court, the legislator has legitimately decided to recognise general binding effect to those agreements that have respected precise procedural and content rules (*estatutarios* collective agreements), while the agreements that do not apply the rules provided for by Title III Workers' Statute have a personal limited scope and follow the civil law norms (*extraestatutarios* collective agreements).[78] Both types are covered by Art. 37.1 SC. A possible "interference" with the fundamental collective labour right is not necessarily "unconstitutional", indeed, "it can be legitimate if it provides a reasonable justification, proportionate to the aim".[79] That is the case as regards Art. 14.1, Law 3/2012, which entrusts the *Comisión Consultiva Nacional de Convenios Colectivos* with the power to disapply terms and conditions set by collective agreements. The Court lists a number of reasons that justify the reform. First, in case the causes to justify the disapplication are met, the Commission will be able to adjust the final decisions in light of a general evaluation and it may also consider the disapplication of employment terms with "varying degrees of intensity". Second, the Court underlines that the Commission cannot decide for the disapplication of the whole agreement, but

77 SCC, Judgment 119/2014, 3, C, a).
78 SCC, Judgment 8/2015, 4, a).
79 SCC, Judgment 8/2015, 4, a).

only for given subjects listed at Art. 82.3, which, in sum, concern working time, including shifts, remuneration system productivity and tasks. The fact that these subjects are numerous and regard substantial aspects of the employment relationships, allowing for significant modifications, does not ring any bell with the Court as to the possible violations of workers' rights, that may arise from different points of view. Third, the Court emphasises that the Commission's decision is subject to a temporal limit. Either the decision itself sets a limit of effectiveness for the disapplication, or, in any case, the arbitral decision ceases its effects when a collective agreement applicable to the company comes into force. Fourth, the Court highlights the "subsidiary character" of the Commission's interventions, which steps in only after a consultation phase between the company and workers' representatives and only as *extrema ratio*, which shows, according to the Court, that "the contested provision gives priority to the collective autonomy to solve the conflict". Fifth, the Court includes, among the features that make the contested provision reasonable, the independency and impartiality of the Commission, demonstrated both by its composition (tripartite body) and by the decision-making procedures, which is taken "preferably by consensus", but if not possible, by absolute majority.[80] As a last element, the Court points out that the ordinary courts can exercise judicial control over the arbitral decision.[81]

The relationship between levels of collective agreements is also addressed. When discussing Art. 14.3, Law 3/2012, that amended Art. 84.2 Workers' Statute and gave priority to the application of company-level collective agreements as regards a number of subjects,[82] the Court offers some insights on the value of Art. 37.1 SC with respect to the possibility to decentralize collective bargaining, by means of legislative acts.[83] Art. 37.1 SC does not provide any indication as to the relationship between centralised and decentralised collective bargaining, nor it sets a priority between the two levels. Once again, the Court underlines that the right to collective bargaining *ex* Art. 37.1 SC is a "right of

80 This system should be a guarantee precisely because of the role of the public administration's representatives, as understood by the Court. Indeed, on the one hand, the administration cannot take decisions unilaterally, on the other hand, "there is no reason to suppose that the public administration representatives' vote would be in favour of the disapplication of the agreement". And that's because of a series of constitutional norms that the Administration has to comply with: "*La Administración pública debe servir con objetividad los intereses generales (Art. 103.1 CE), que evidentemente no están sólo integrados por la defensa de la productividad y la libertad de empresa (Art. 38 CE), sino también por el respeto a los demás derechos, bienes y principios constitucionales, como el derecho a la negociación colectiva (Art. 37.1 CE), el derecho al trabajo (Art. 35.1 CE), o la realización de una política orientada al pleno empleo (Art. 40.1 CE)*", SCC, Judgment 119/2014, 5, A, c).

81 SCC, Judgment 119/2014, 5, A, c).

82 RDL 32/2012 has recently excluded salary items from the matters that can be derogated from by company level agreements, Baylos Grau 2022.

83 According to Valdés Dal-Ré, the absolute priority of company level agreements, introduced with the amendment of Art. 84.2 Workers' Statute deprives the social partners of the possibility to come to an agreement as to the structure of collective bargaining.

legal configuration" and the legislator is entitled to restrict or extend the scope of intervention of the collective autonomy depending on the context, to the point that: "both a legislative policy that gives priority to collective agreements at sectorial level and a legislative policy that gives preference to the company level collective agreement are constitutionally legitimate".[84]

A further argument in favour of the constitutional legitimacy of the amended Art. 84.2 Workers' Statue, according to the Court, is the fact that "it does not hamper the negotiation of sector level collective agreements", hence it does not restrict the trade union freedom to determine collective bargaining levels, the contested norm only intervenes on the *relationship* between the levels.[85] Therefore, in other words, elements that contribute to guaranteeing the effectiveness of the right to collective bargaining are extraneous to the content of the right to collective bargaining, since as long as the parties are free to negotiate, Art. 37.1 SC is not violated, even if, in practice, they negotiate in vain.

The Court draws attention to the fact that "the contested provision does not exclude completely the intervention of collective bargaining in the establishment of the negotiation structure", since the inter-professional agreements can still regulate some aspects, as the rules to solve possible conflicts between collective agreements at different levels. In addition, Art. 84.2 Workers Statute does not oblige the social partners not to regulate certain subjects within the sector-level collective agreements. Indeed, in those companies where a company-level collective agreement does not exist the sector-level agreement applies.[86]

The Court then underlines that the company-level agreement, concluded later than the higher-level agreement, has priority only in relation to some of the labour terms and conditions. These subjects are listed in an imperative way, which should corroborate the conclusion that collective bargaining at higher levels is not hampered by the contested norm.[87] Under this view, recognising a priority to the company-level agreement does not mean that the collective negotiation conducted by trade unions is undermined. Indeed, it is true that at company level the collective negotiation can be conducted by bodies which represent workers, but are not trade unions, as the company committees. To support this argument the Court opportunistically refers to the ILO Committee on Freedom of Association, which states that "the determination of the bargaining level is essentially a matter to be left to the discretion of the parties", which shall demonstrate how a reform as the one at issue is consistent with the ILO indications, given that it does not tackle the social partners' autonomy in determining collective bargaining levels. However, this quotation disregards completely the context in which the sentence was placed.[88]

84 SCC, Judgment 119/2014, 6, a).
85 SCC, Judgment 119/2014, 6, b).
86 SCC, Judgment 119/2014, 6, c).
87 SCC, Judgment 119/2014, 6, d).
88 SCC, Judgment 119/2014, 6, b, the reference is to the ILO CFA Report, No. 371 of March 2014, para. 454. The whole para. 454 states: "The Committee further notes that article 14,

In sum, neither Art. 37.1 SC, nor any other constitutional provision establishes a rigid constitutional collective bargaining system. On the one hand, Art. 37.1 SC entrusts "the law" with the duty to guarantee the right to collective bargaining and the binding force of the agreements, considering that the right to collective bargaining is a "right of legal configuration".[89] On the other hand, as with any other right,[90] the right enshrined in Art. 37.1 SC is not absolute and can be subject to limitations, if justified.

3.4.3 *The right to a sufficient and proportionate remuneration and the principle of adequacy of pensions in the Italian case law*

The Italian case law selected covers a wider number of matters. Besides the right to work and the right to collective bargaining, the Italian Court has discussed the right to a fair remuneration (Art. 36.1 IC), also combined with the principle of independence of the judiciary (Art. 104 IC), when scrutinising reforms of public employees' wage, as well as the right to an adequate pension (Art. 38.2 IC) combined with the right to a fair remuneration, when dealing with measures affecting pension levels.

The principle of independence of the judiciary (Art. 104 IC) has been the focus of both Judgment 223/2012[91] and Judgment 124/2017, even if it is not a fundamental labour right, since it immediately pertains to the division of powers in a democratic legal system. However, its content, as elaborated by the Court in the first part of the legal reasoning, is connected to the domain of fundamental labour rights of judges, especially since it guarantees the enforcement of the right to a fair remuneration, given the impossibility of this group of public employees to access collective bargaining procedures (Art. 36.1 IC).[92]

A norm infringes upon Art. 104 IC, read in conjunction with Art. 36 IC, if it has the effect of creating "permanent effects of the block" of the automatic

paragraph 2, of Act 3/2012 introduces new rules for private sector collective bargaining and the structure thereof, including by giving enterprise collective agreements priority of application over higher level collective agreements on certain matters, which, as the Government points out, were not covered by the previous legislation. The Committee also notes that the complainant unions and other complainant organizations have clearly expressed their opposition to this new legislation and recalls its position that the determination of the bargaining level is essentially a matter to be left to the discretion of the parties" (ILO CFA Report, No. 371 of March 2014, para. 454).

89 See, *inter alia*, Judgment 8/2015, 6, a), on Art. 14.2, Law 3/2012.

90 De la Quadra-Salcedo Janini 2020, 63, finds this constitutional case law extremely disappointing, precisely because it turns social rights from fundamental principles to merely rhetorical precepts left at the disposal of the legislator.

91 Beyond any doubt, the relevance of the principle of autonomy and independence of the judiciary (Art. 101 ff.) is what makes this case substantially different from the following judgments (Fontana 2015).

92 The link between the two constitutional principles has been criticised by certain scholars, see Ricci 2014, 216–217.

adjustment mechanism exclusively for the salary of the members of the judiciary, while the legitimate time limit of the legislative emergency action that concerns the salary "freezing" for the generality of public employment is temporarily limited (2011–2013), and it has non-reversible effects, meaning that it lacks a transitory character, in the sense that the reform influences the amount of certain salary items for the future, as well. As a consequence, both the principle of equality (Art. 3 IC) and the various principles that protect the independence of the judiciary (Articles 100, 101, 104, 108 IC) are violated by the norm scrutinised in Judgment 223/2012, as it constitutes a source of "unreasonable discrimination", which damages only one category of public employees.[93]

Before returning to assess Art. 104 IC, the Italian Court published Judgment 310/2013, which deals with a reduction of wages of a different cluster of public employees (by means of freezing of the adjustment mechanisms) and the outcome is substantially different from its precedents.[94] The ruling on university lecturers' and researchers' wages mostly highlights that the consistency of an ordinary norm with Art. 36 IC cannot be assessed by looking at the "single elements of the economic treatment", but rather at the "overall remuneration". As a consequence, the contested provision, which does not tackle the overall structure of the university lecturers' and researchers' wages, cannot be deemed illegitimate.[95]

Coherently with the legal reasoning developed in Judgment 223/2012, in Judgment 124/2017, the violation of Art. 104 IC is excluded.[96] Indeed, in the case at stake, the general scope of the contested provision (read in a comprehensive way), together with the maximum limit set at the remuneration of the Supreme Court's President (a decent and fair wage) excludes the violation of the principle of independence of the judiciary. This conclusion strengthens the principle that the effective enforcement of a fundamental labour right (understanding, in this context, the principle of independence of the judiciary as a speci-

93 ICC, Judgment 223/2012, 11.7.

94 Judgments 223/2012, 304/2013, 310/2013 have given "rise to an irrational inequality among public employees, some of them having been 'saved' from the pay cuts and some of them not" and have been criticised for being incoherent, since "in the very same judgment proclaiming the unconstitutionality of the wage cuts the Court relied much more on the specific nature of the job performed by public employees at stake in that particular case, rather than on what I would call the general principles of the economic constitution seen in a fundamental social rights perspective", Lo Faro 2014a, 61. In particular, he emphasises that the conclusions have been reached without following a fundamental social rights logic, 62.

95 ICC, Judgment 310/2013, 13.9. It has been observed that the legal reasoning is excessively hurried for the status of the subjective rights under discussion. A more careful and attentive evaluation of the norm would have been required, as well as a deeper argumentation on the reasons leading to the conclusions, Ferrante 2014, 1. The inconsistency with Judgment 223/2012 and the different treatment to which university professors and researchers, compared to judges, are ultimately the subject is criticised by Lo Faro 2014, who emphasises notable incongruences between the rulings.

96 ICC, Judgment 124/2017, 8.5.

fication of the right to a fair remuneration under Art. 36 IC) depends also on the normative context, in the sense of the extent of generality of the sacrifice.

The constitutionality of the norm is furthermore supported by the fact that the limit is not only *general*, but also *foreseeable*.[97] At the same time, the sacrifice is reasonable because the professional levels are not damaged, which entails full compliance with the core of the right to work of the claimants (Art. 4 IC), and their dignity. Further on, the Court recalls that "the legislator is called upon to ensure a systematic, and not fragmented, protection of the constitutional values at stake", in the specific case it refers to the fulfilment of the principle of proportionality between remuneration and work performed (Art. 36 IC). The circumstance that the resources are limited again plays a crucial role and justifies the comprehensive predetermination of the payments the public administration can guarantee, as provided for by the norm under scrutiny, hence corroborating the relevance of a *foreseeable* limit.[98]

Art. 36.1 IC is again at the forefront in Judgment 70/2015, where it is deployed to interpret Art. 38.2 IC (on the *adequacy* of social security benefits). The Court underlines that Art. 36.1 IC (right to a fair remuneration) and Art. 38.2 IC (right to an adequate pension), read jointly, guarantee a full implementation of the principle of substantial equality (Art. 3.2 IC).[99] Therefore, the combination of these two constitutional principles represents a further elaboration – and concretisation – of the principle of substantial equality. In the case at stake, the Court identifies in Art. 36.1 IC and 38.2 IC, as development of Art. 3.2 IC, the fundamental rights that ground the automatic adjustment system for retirement benefits. Nonetheless, it admits that these principles can be partially sacrificed by a reform of the said automatic system.[100]

The contested provision is unreasonable since it violates Art. 36.1 IC and Art. 38.2 IC, by reaching what the judgment calls the "critical levels",[101] which in the case of retirement benefits, are represented by the "detriment of the purchasing power". Even though the Court does not mention the "essential content" of the fundamental labour right to adequate and proportionate pensions, this concept seems to find application in the case at stake and it is reflected precisely in the conservation of the purchasing power.

97 As can be understood from paragraph 8, in which the Court points out that the fact that the limit is steadily set at 240,000 euros per annum reveals the intention of the legislator to establish a foreseeable and general limit and high-level professionals are respected inasmuch as the maximum limit is set taking as parameter the remuneration of a high and prestigious office (of the Supreme Court's President) (ICC, Judgment 124/2017, 8.6).

98 In quantitative terms, the Court expressly refers, also in this case, to the point of reference taken to set the limit, that is the First President of the Supreme Court's salary, which implies that the right to a proportionate remuneration is not sacrificed in an illegitimate way (ICC, Judgment 124/2017, 9.2).

99 ICC, Judgment 70/2015, 8.

100 ICC, Judgment 70/2015, 8.

101 ICC, Judgment 70/2015, 10.

The "strict connection" between Art. 36.1 IC and Art. 38.2 IC is explained with the aim "to avoid the occurrence of 'an untenable mismatch' between pension increases and salary trends, the legislator cannot disregard the *limit of reasonableness*".[102]

All in all, the considerations of labour – but not only – lawyers are mostly in contrast with the dominant constitutional rhetoric.[103] Employment law scholars have assessed the ruling from the perspective of fundamental social rights, which, indeed, does not allow to ground the analysis on a systematic comparison with Judgment 10/2015, and have revealed the intrinsic value of this judgment, that is the "reaffirmation of the constitutional value of social rights", against the tendency to push for their deconstitutionalisation.[104] On this view, the Court has done nothing but fulfil its role as guardian of the constitutional fundamental rights, which is also its source of legitimacy.[105]

One year later, in Judgment 173/2016, the Court newly modulates the relationship between the principle of fair remuneration and that of adequateness of retirement benefits by arguing that Art. 38 IC is "coupled also to Art. 36 IC, but not in a constant and strictly proportional way".[106] The Court has confirmed the functional link between Art. 36 IC and Art. 38 IC set in Judgment 70/2015, by mitigating the scope of this connection. Nevertheless, in practice, the link seems to remain tight. It is emphasised that the Court applies the principle of sustainability of retirement benefits, in order to verify the compliance with the principle of proportionality and assess whether the benefits are proportionate to the pension contributions (Art. 36 IC) and not to the adequacy of the benefit itself (Art. 38 IC).[107]

The normative element subject to the constitutional balancing scrutinised in Judgment 173/2016 can be identified by assessing, especially, paragraph 11 of the judgment. The evaluation of the legislator's balancing, according to the Court, should be conducted bearing in mind the necessity to balance "the legitimate

102 ICC, Judgment 70/2015, 8, italics added; see ICC, Judgment 226/1993.

103 *E.g.*, Pin Longo 2015, 698 and Veronesi 2015, 695.

104 Giubboni 2015a, 529.

105 Cf. Cinelli 2015b, 443; D'Onghia briefly reviews the approaches of the Court towards the "spending judgments" since the 1980s, and notes that while in the 1980s the Court had conducted a proper judicial activism in favour of fundamental rights, in the 1990s its approach has shifted towards a self-restraint more keen to support economic arguments: D'Onghia 2015, 328–330; Cinelli 2015c emphasises that Judgment 70/2015 recognises the full constitutional value of social security rights, differently from the general judicial trend that rather leans towards a blind recognition of the absolute prevalence of the principle of balanced budget.

106 ICC, Judgment 173/2016, 11.1.

107 Persiani 2017, 286. The author reflects upon the missed opportunity of defining the meaning of "adequate means to life needs" and the controversial application of Art. 36 IC to measures regulating the retirement system, especially since the sole application of Art. 38 IC, in his view, would have led to the same conclusion; in this respect see also Giubboni 2015a, with regard to Judgment 70/2015.

expectation of legal certainty, with other values constitutionally protected".[108] What is meant by "legitimate expectation of legal certainty" becomes clearer in the following paragraph,[109] where it is argued that the principle of reasonableness, the principle of legitimate expectation and the principle of social security protection shall be applied jointly, in order to assess whether the solidarity contribution does not exceed the mandatory "limits". Indeed, the Court, while pointing at these three principles, only refers to Art. 3 IC and Art. 38 IC. Considering that Art. 3 IC provides for the reasonableness principle and Art. 38 IC for the principle of adequacy of the social system benefits, it may be deduced that the legitimate expectation, which constitutes one of the elements subject to the balancing exercise, is understood, for the purpose of this judgment, as the legitimate expectation to an adequate pension, which turns out to be an aspect of the right protected under Art. 38.2 IC.[110]

In addition, this is one of the rare occasions in which the Court clearly identifies the essential nucleus of the fundamental right concerned, by arguing that a contribution deducted from the pensions has a solidarity character and is reasonable, in the sense that it does not violate Art. 38 IC (and the linked Art. 36 IC), if it only affects the higher benefits, to be identified taking into consideration the "essential nucleus" of the pension rights, that is the minimum INPS retirement benefits.[111] Moreover, the norm "passes the 'strict' scrutiny of constitutionality" because it acts within the overall social security system, which is undergoing a crisis phase; it contributes, as other structural or occasional reforms adopted to manage this phase, to finance this troubled system, hence it pursues a strong solidarity goal,[112] is *exceptional*[113] and has a "temporary character".[114]

In the last episode of this case law in search of some coherence, Judgment 250/2017, Art. 36.1 IC and, especially, Art. 38.2 IC are again at the forefront of the balancing exercise. The Court legitimates the legislator's choice by "clarifying even better the nexus between Art. 36 and Art. 38 Constitution".[115] This ruling

108 ICC, Judgment 173/2016, 11.

109 For a reflection on the difference between "legitimate expectation" and "legal certainty" see Persiani 2017, 284–285.

110 ICC, Judgment 173/2016, 11.1.

111 ICC, Judgment 173/2016, 11.

112 It has been claimed that the Court has established, for the first time, a principle of solidarity and responsibility between generations, thus adopting an approach that understands rights and duties in a circular way, which is founded upon Art. 2 IC and Art. 38 IC, Pepe 2017; differently, on Judgment 173/2016, Procopio 2016; see, also, D'Onghia 2019, 297, 298. Eventually, Constitutional Judge Silvana Sciarra made clear that the matter of intergenerational solidarity cannot be addressed by the Court, which has a limited sphere of intervention that is not suited to address such far-reaching matters, Sciarra 2019 268–269. Lately on the inter-generational solidarity in the Italian legal system, Cinelli 2022.

113 ICC, Judgment 173/2016, 11.1.

114 ICC, Judgment 173/2016, 11.2. A profile anyway criticised under the assumption that "It seems ingenuous to think that the social security financial crisis is a temporary phenomenon", Sandulli 2016, 691, my translation.

115 D'Onghia 2017, 98, my translation.

makes clear that the nexus between the right to a proportionate remuneration (Art. 36 IC) and the right to adequate retirement benefits (Art. 38 IC) is indirect, even though the principle of adequateness is in any case informed also by meritocratic criteria.[116]

Indeed, also in this case, it is stressed that the right of pensioners can be sacrificed only in a partial and temporary way. This argument is supported by reasonable choices of the legislator, namely the fact that the revaluation of pensions is modulated according to a decreasing percentage in favour of the lower benefits, considering that the higher benefits have a stronger resistance to inflation.[117] The Court asserts that the negative impact of the contested provisions on the higher retirement benefits is not sufficient to affect their adequacy, which is safeguarded even if the automatic revaluation is temporarily suspended, as is the case for retirement benefits six times higher than the INPS minimum. Indeed, these pensions enjoy a higher margin of resistance to the erosion of the purchasing power caused by inflation.[118]

3.5 Conclusions

The heterogeneous character of the case law reviewed in this chapter, which scrutinises different types of norms, does not prevent addressing the judgments jointly, since, from our perspective – that of a case law scrutinising norms adopted with the aim to address a context of financial and economic constraints – the assessed judgments are all suitable to identify the impact of the constitutional case law on fundamental labour rights under a crisis.

This chapter has framed the elements relevant to identify the content and scope of the fundamental labour rights at issue that can be inferred by the Italian and Spanish post-crisis case law. However, pretending to frame such content and scope in general terms, exclusively relying on this case law, would be unreliable and reductive. An evaluation of the status of fundamental labour rights after the 2008 crisis in front of the constitutional courts, which is not the aim of this book, could not be based solely on the analysis of the post-crisis case law, but it would require an attentive analysis of each right, which would comprehensively take into account the evolution of its content and scope in light of the national constitutional case law, to eventually observe the relevant novelties, or confirms, of the post-crisis case law.

The reflection conducted so far on the fundamental labour rights concerned has a twofold purpose: first, it is essential to introduce and comprehend the analysis of the technique applied by the Courts provided in the next chapter; second, even without claims of exhaustiveness, it pinpoints the main features of the

116 D'Onghia 2017.
117 ICC, Judgment 250/2017, 6.5.2.
118 ICC, Judgment 250/2017, 6.5.3.1.

content of fundamental labour rights, as framed by the constitutional post-crisis case law.

From a methodological perspective, the essential content criterion, which in Spain constitutes a hermeneutic criterion expressly recognised by the Spanish Constitution, while in Italy is progressively being integrated by the Italian Court, has partially found its way in the assessed case law, although not in a systematic fashion.

Just by way of example, the Spanish Court, as far as concerns the right to collective bargaining, has apparently adopted the relative theory of the essential content, by including therein the freedom to conduct collective negotiations and the freedom to conclude a collective agreement, at the same time it has repeatedly stressed that this freedom "is not absolute, but, for justified reasons, can be limited by the law" (SCC, Judgment 119/2014). On the other hand, while the right to collective bargaining is understood as part of the essential content of the trade union freedom (Art. 28.1 SC, discussed only in relation to the overall assessment of the industrial relations system), trade unions are not the sole actors entitled to exercise this collective right. The use of this criterion is not methodologically consistent in the rest of the judgment, considering that in some cases it is not used at all, while with regard to the right to work is rather adopted to construct a sort of internal hierarchy between the right to a stable employment and a supposed and apparently implicit right to easily find a job.[119]

The Italian Court also deploys the notion of essential content in a single occasion, where it defines the essential content of the right to an adequate pension in an extensive way, by emphasising the real value of retirement benefits, instead of the nominal value. The essential content of Art. 38.2 IC, as read in conjunction with Art. 36.1 IC, is identified, first, in the conservation of the purchasing power of an acquired right (ICC, Judgment 70/2015) and, second, in the minimum state benefit (ICC, Judgment 173/2016). And, ultimately, the Court confirms that the essential content of the right to an adequate pension corresponds to the preservation of the purchasing power of retirement benefits (ICC, Judgment 250/2017). Nevertheless, the essential content has not been employed in a systematic fashion and with theoretical consistency, hence as a proper criterion, but rather as a notion functional to label, on a case-by-case basis, that portion of a fundamental labour right that cannot be touched for the norm to be constitutional, which is identified by applying the conventional techniques, such as the principle of reasonableness, and not on the grounds of a precise "essential content criterion".

To conclude, it is remarkable the different applications of supranational sources and the practical consequences on the definition of the right to collective bargaining. The Italian Court, in Judgment 178/2015, has widely used the supranational sources to define the constitutional right to collective bargaining

119 The misuse of the essential content criterion was criticised also in the dissenting opinion by Valdés Dal-Ré.

and strengthen its effectiveness in front of the economic arguments, whereas the Spanish Court has made a fragmented and strategic use of selected ILO tools, in order not to elaborate on the fundamental labour right concerned, but rather to validate its limitations (the same misuse of international sources by the Spanish Court could be raised as regards the legal reasoning on Art. 4.1, Law 3/2012).

4 Constitutional balancing in the Italian and Spanish post-crisis case law

4.1 Introduction

The assessment of the Italian and Spanish post-crisis case law proceeds with a focus on the elements of the legal reasonings that are characteristic of constitutional balancing, in order to shed a light on the main profiles of the constitutional judgments that influence the enforcement of fundamental labour rights by constitutional courts in times of economic and financial crisis, namely: first, the role of the courts, which is relevant to determine, on the one hand, the space of manoeuvre left to the court for the guarantee of fundamental labour rights and, on the other, the courts' recognition of the legislative prerogatives in this domain; second, the technique adopted to build the legal reasoning, which, by conditioning the structure of the *ratio decidendi*, burdens the adjudication of fundamental labour rights, both in terms of the profiles valorised by the court and of legal certainty, inasmuch as if the technique is inconsistent or indecipherable the judgment fails to provide clear guidance to the legislator and contribute to a constructive institutional dialogue on the enforcement of fundamental labour rights; third, the factors that have contributed to determine the adjudication of the fundamental labour rights at issue and what approach the two courts have adopted, respectively, that is whether such elements have been recognised as part of the constitutional balancing or have otherwise contributed to the legal reasoning.

Those factors are, for the Italian case law, the principle of balanced budget, the economic crisis argument and the freedom of enterprise; for the Spanish case law, the economic crisis argument, the public duty to conduct a policy of full employment and the freedom of enterprise. The choice to maintain the principle of balanced budget separated from the economic crisis, in sharing the results of this study, is due to the intention to emphasise the different nature of these factors, which are respectively a constitutional norm, expressing one possible choice of political economy, and an environmental fact that does not have normative, nor legal, character.

The three profiles addressed – role, technique, decisive factors – do not constitute tightly separated areas of analysis as they interlink and mesh in various scenarios, but they simply provide a systematic guideline to conduct the analysis

DOI: 10.4324/9781003155362-5

and organise the main findings. Common and recurrent elements are identified, even though the lines of thought of the various judgments are not consistent, nor technically comparable.

4.2 The role of the Courts

That Roberto Bin has recently felt the need to elaborate on the role of the court, with regard to constitutional balancing, is telling of the lack of clarity over this crucial element.[1] Indeed, this aspect is of paramount importance, since the less the court can be accused of overcoming the boundaries of its competence the more its authoritativeness is recognised and its conclusions accepted by the legislator and the civil society.[2]

The relationship the court establishes with the legislator demonstrates to what extent it acknowledges its discretional power. In several cases, the Mediterranean Courts have explicitly underlined the discretion of the legislator; as "*discrezionalità*", the Italian Court[3] and as "*libertad*", the Spanish Court.[4] In contrast, the legislative competence is recognised implicitly when the court establishes a dialogical relationship with the legislator by providing clear and direct indications as to the principles to be complied with by future reforms, like in some of the Italian judgments.[5]

Consistent also is the attempt to detect the intention of the legislator, which emerges in nearly all Italian judgments. For instance, in Judgment 223/2012, the Court carries out the legal reasoning by considering, first of all, the reasons why the legislator has originally put in place the automatic mechanism tackled by the norm under scrutiny. In a similar way, in Judgment 70/2015, the Court investigates the rationale of the overall legislation on the automatic revaluation of pensions in order to identify the aim pursued.[6] The assessment in light of the norm's rationale, and the respective case law, reflects the will of the Court not

1 Bin 2018; to the contrary, in favour of a balancing-court is, *inter alia*, Miani Canevari 2015.

2 For a reflection on the dangers of a political role of the court, one for all, Cheli 2011.

3 *E.g.* see the conclusions in ICC, Judgment 124/2017.

4 See the first section of SCC, Judgment 8/2015. Where labour lawyers have raised attention to this profile of the judgment – few and marginal cases, to be honest – the main argument was that the court has simplistically recognised in the legislator an almost unlimited discretion in regulating the content of the rights provided for by the constitutional norms. The judgments have resulted in a hymn to the law and its capacity to affect, especially, collective bargaining, see Fernández López 2015, 261; Suarez Corujo 2015, 434; Salcedo Beltrán 2014, 151. More recently, Giubboni Orlandini 2018 have argued that the role of the collective autonomy has been "mortified" in favour of the discretion of the legislator.

5 In particular, see ICC, Judgment 70/2015 and the consequent ICC, Judgment 250/2017.

6 But also ICC, Judgment 223/2012; ICC, Judgment 173/2016; ICC, Judgment 124/2017; ICC, Judgment 178/2015, as well as Judgment 194/2018, 9, where the Court holds that the balance between the values underlying Art. 4 IC and Art. 41 IC does not require a specific regime of protection because it is an area which is inevitably left to the discretion of the legislator.

to be the main character of the balancing process, but rather the supervisor of the consistency with the whole legal system of the new balancing of interests conducted by the legislator and expressed in the norm under scrutiny.[7] Indeed, the Court does not enter into the merit of the legislative choices, but it merely controls whether these choices are in compliance with the criteria of reasonableness and proportionality (in its widest sense). Eventually, it declares the full unconstitutionality of the block. By doing so, it does not overstep the boundaries of its institutional competence and does not reach beyond its role – as if it had concluded with a ruling of ***additivo di principio***. On this view, the decisive argument of the court is that the legislator has not made clear under which criteria it has balanced the constitutional interests at stake and it has only vaguely mentioned the "contingent financial situation", which does not allow a norm to pass the reasonableness scrutiny.[8] The constructive dialogue with the legislator, respectful of its discretional power, proceeds in Judgment 250/2017, where the Italian Court appreciates the efforts made by the legislator to implement Judgment 70/2015 and newly balance the values and constitutional interests at stake with norms that do not represent a "mere reproduction" of the provisions declared unconstitutional in 2015, but are characterised by "relevant novelties", alongside being adopted promptly.[9] A conclusion is reached also on the grounds of the technical reports explanatory of the legislative choices attached that "represent an instrument for the ***verification*** of the legislator's choices"[10] (although the reference to the technical documents carries along other criticalities, addressed in the next paragraph).

Among the Spanish rulings, a timid analysis of the rationale behind the legislative choices is conducted in Judgment 119/2014, where it is used to uphold the constitutionality of Art. 4.3 Law 3/2012, even if while on the one hand the Court states that is not its competence "to judge upon the opportunity and efficacy" of the contested norm, it upholds the state attorney argument, by arguing that "in a crisis context as the present one" such a probationary period allows one to understand if the working position is economically sustainable,[11] thus, in fact, judging upon the opportunity of the norm. Notwithstanding that, the

7 *A contrario*, on the role of the Court in Judgment 70/2015, Barbera 2015.

8 According to D'Onghia 2015, 340, the lack of indication by the lawmaker on the reasons underlying the balancing does not allow the judge to fulfil its task, that is to scrutinise the necessity of the norm, on the grounds of the impossibility to adopt other measures less harmful; cf. also Cinelli 2015b 442; Giubboni 2015a, 529, according to Giubboni, the Court has anyway conducted the scrutiny of reasonableness in a way which is somehow close to the structured proportionality test. According to Lieto 2015, 5, 6, the absence of any reference to Art. 81 IC is clear evidence of the fact that the Court has not directly applied the balancing technique, but it has rather assessed the balancing operated by the legislator; differently from the approach adopted in ICC, Judgment 10/2015, where the Court has being accused of acting as the main character of the balancing and not as a mere supervisor see Morelli 2015, 711.

9 ICC, Judgment 250/2017, 6.1, 6.2.

10 ICC, Judgment 250/2017, 6.5.1, italics added.

11 SCC, Judgment 119/2014, 3, A, e), in a similar way SCC, Judgment 119/2014, 6, e).

link between the phase of crisis of the country and the need to make use of a full year to understand whether the working position can be maintained is not elaborated. Nor does the Court seem to look for such a causal link in the words of the Law. Moreover, it expressly refuses to assess the contested norm considering the overall regulation of the probationary period, as regulated by Art. 14, Workers' Statute (*Ley del Estatuto de los Trabajadores*).[12]

In the following judgment, the Court clearly expresses the extent of its own margin of action, denying its competence to enter into the merit of the legislative choice. In particular, it argues that "it is not the Court's competence to establish if the solutions adopted by the contested Law are the most correct from a technical point of view, or if they constitute the most appropriate among possible alternatives, in order to achieve the aim pursued".[13] The sole aspect that, according to the Court, can be subject to its analysis is if a contested provision "complies with the mandates, rules and principles that the Constitution imposes upon the legislator". Indeed, by quoting previous judgments, the Court argues that "every legislative option [...] is admissible from a constitutional point of view if it complies with the constitutional rules".[14]

In other words, in this paragraph, where the scrutiny of the constitutionality of the contested norms has not yet begun, the Court denies the application of the proportionality test and justifies the Court's – limited – role, by underlining the wide scope of action of the legislator.

Also further on, the Court points out that it is not in its faculties to evaluate the "appropriateness or convenience of the legislator's choice",[15] but it only has to assess whether the option picked by the legislator "in the exercise of the competence attributed by the Constitution" is respectful of the "reasonable margin of freedom recognised by Art. 35 Constitution".[16]

In the legal reasoning on the Spanish industrial relations system and collective bargaining, the Court does not even dare to discuss the intention of the legislator, in line with the unconditional acceptance of the prerogatives of the latter. As a result, the discretional power of the legislator is an implicit leitmotiv in those cases where the Court has to evaluate the compliance with Art. 37.1 SC (right to collective bargaining and binding force of collective agreements), as when it states: "[T]he legislator enjoys a wide margin of freedom in the elaboration of the right to collective bargaining", in the first part of Judgment 8/2015, to answer the general claim according to which Law 3/2012 would be in contrast with the Spanish constitutional model. Indeed, the legislator enjoys enough freedom to

12 SCC, Judgment 119/2014, 3.

13 SCC, Judgment 8/2015, 2, g). To strengthen this argument, and hence its limited scope of action, it quotes a recent constitutional judgment, that excludes the possibility for the court to "examine the necessity of the legal provision to decide whether it is the most appropriate or the best among the possible options", SCC, Judgment 17/2013, 11.

14 SCC, Judgment 8/2015, 2, g), quoting SCC, Judgment 20/2013, 3.

15 The Court quotes SCC, Judgment 198/2012, 11.

16 SCC, Judgment 8/2015, 7, a).

choose among possible alternative options and realise its "legal concept", by taking into account "the economic circumstances" and the "social needs" that the legislator wants to address.[17]

The only relevant exception to a rigorous supervisory role is observed in Judgment 178/2015 of the Italian Constitutional Court, where the Italian Court has, in fact, actively balanced the conflicting elements: the right to conduct collective bargaining procedures and the general interest to a balanced public budget. Here, the Court declares the "supervening unconstitutionality" of the freeze of collective bargaining procedures, with effect from the day after the publication of the judgment.[18] Even though the Italian scholarship has discussed this ruling very critically,[19] the decision to postpone the judgment's effect on the grounds of a careful evaluation of the public financial situation (indeed it refers to "the particular seriousness of the economic and financial international context" and the "repercussions on the national economy"[20]) can be attached to a will of the Court to tackle the *intention* to give structural effect to the block, and its possible future crystallisation, rather than the norms *per se*, thus avoiding the risk of interfering with the legislator's discretional power.[21]

Besides the concluding moment in which it has released the ruling of supervening unconstitutionality, in Judgment 178/2015 the Court has also acted as a supervisor, as proved by the attentive analysis of the norms concerned, which has

17 SCC, Judgment 8/2015, 2, g). The margin of freedom left to the legislator in shaping the national labour relations system is mentioned often in these rulings. As in SCC, Judgment 8/2015 on Art. 18.8, when the Court simply states that the Court concludes that the norm is in compliance with Art. 35.1 SC, because the legislator has acted within the margin of freedom the Constitution guarantees as to the configuration of the labour relations (para. 8, a). In the same ruling, the Court stresses that it is up to the legislator to decide on the consequences of unfair dismissal "in view of the economic and social circumstances" (SCC, Judgment 8/2015, 8, a), see Fernández López 2015, 262 and Goig Martínez 2016, 143, 144; less critical is Gómez Garrido 2015, 114; for a deep reflection of the Court's legal reasoning in this respect, see García Murcia 2015, 287–290.

18 The ruling of supervening unconstitutionality implies that the judgment is effective from the day after its publication, which implies that the public spending is not tackled at all by the ruling, since the legislator does not have to reimburse the public employees deprived from their right to negotiate. Zoppoli 2017, 187, emphasises that the declaration of supervening unconstitutionality, hence effective from the day in which the judgment is released, is consistent with the Italian constitutional case law and in the case at stake it does not hamper workers' organisations from initiating a suspensive action against further unconstitutional conduct. See also Barbieri 2017, 167, 168.

19 For instance, severe is the criticism by Mocchegiani 2015.

20 ICC, Judgment 178/2015, 12.2.

21 This type of decision is not new to the Italian Court: in 1993, Silvestri was already arguing that there is a duty of the court to limit the retroactivity of the ruling's effect in order to prevent a dysfunctional effect over the public budget, which stems from the "active" – not "political" – role of the Constitutional Court, Silvestri 1993, 81; also Modugno 2007 and Zoppoli 2017 on the specific case.

been carried out in order to detect the intention of the legislator that represents a decisive element to understand whether the provision is reasonable.[22]

The assessment of whether the court directly conducts the balancing or rather supervises the balancing carried out by the legislator and remains a warrantor of last resort of fundamental labour rights can concretely contribute to understanding whether a constitutional court borders into an area which is beyond its competences. The political character of a constitutional judicial decision is avoided if the court acts as a supervisor and not as a direct balancer.[23] Indeed, addressing this profile first allows one to assess the proper legal reasoning without bias, which may affect also the analysis of the arguments developed by the court. One for all: if the court does not apply the proportionality test, it runs the risk of trespassing into the political role.

4.3 The technique applied to supervise the legislator's balancing

The assessment of the technique used by the court, and the respective criteria, has emphasised the peculiarities of each approach and has allowed us to identify the most sensitive moments of each legal reasoning. Moreover, while the Italian judgments are, at times, discontinuous, as far as concerns the structure of the argumentation, the Spanish judgments are consistent, in operational terms.

The technique traditionally applied by the Italian and Spanish Constitutional Courts to decide upon the constitutionality of ordinary norms is considerably different. In extremely synthetic terms, while the Spanish system has endorsed the German test of proportionality, even though the Spanish Constitution does not explicitly provide for such a method, the Italian Constitutional Court has developed the principle of reasonableness as the main hermeneutic criterion and it has applied it over the years.

The Italian post-crisis judgments are fairly coherent with the respective tradition, whereas the Spanish judgments confirm a recent trend, characterised by a lax application of the principle of proportionality. To the point that, in fact, in Judgment 119/2014 and in Judgment 8/2015 the test is not applied at all.

22 It has been argued that the crucial weakness of the provision challenged in Judgment 178/2015 – namely its prolonged character – and the consequent declaration of unconstitutionality has been caused by the inability of the legislator to achieve a reasonable balance between the right to collective bargaining and public budget constraints. See, one for all, Butturini 2016, 29, 30. Cf. also Occhino 2017, 9. Scagliarini 2015 argues that, differently from the legislator, the Court, in this judgment has achieved a "reasonable balance".

23 Over the decades, the alleged "political" power of the Constitutional Court and its connection with the hermeneutic criteria invoked has triggered wide debates, see, *inter alia*, Mezzanotte 2014; Mezzetti 2010; Modugno 1982. To the point that someone may even suggest that the court should refrain from deciding the most political cases, see Romboli 2000, 90–91.

4.3.1 The principle of reasonableness that permeates *the Italian constitutional post-crisis case law*

The Italian Court extensively refers to the principle of reasonableness, as the main criterion to determine the legitimacy of the challenged norms and to assess the violation of fundamental rights, which are infringed upon if the norm "does not achieve a balanced settlement between the interests in play" and, therefore, "it excessively impinges upon the interest of [in the case at stake in Judgment 194/2018] the worker".[24]

Also in the post-crisis Judgments, the principle of reasonableness is strictly linked with the fundamental labour rights at issue, to the point that the scrutiny over the violation of such rights would be impossible without applying the reasonableness criterion, that has the merit of moving the analysis beyond the mere "absence of arbitrariness" from the public powers. It is exemplary that the Constitutional Judge, when recognising the legislator's faculty to introduce a solidarity contribution on retirement benefits, stresses that a legislative intervention as such shall be supported by a "comprehensive degree of reasonableness" way higher than what is normally considered *lack of arbitrariness*. The message is clear, and it helps to further understand the content of the hermeneutic criterion applied by the court: it is not enough to detect the absence of arbitrariness in the legislator's choices, in order to declare a norm reasonable.[25]

Consistently, the Court expressly regards it as *principio di sistema* of the pension system, a cornerstone criterion to be applied by the legislator when dealing with the legal framework for retirement benefits.[26]

The sub-criteria that allow application of the reasonableness criterion vary. Some can be identified, such as *exceptionality*, *transitoriness*, *non-arbitrariness*, *suitability to achieve the aim* or if the norm responds to the *need to contain public spending*,[27] but it remains a non-exhaustive and non-binding list, whose applicability also depends on the type of norm under scrutiny.

The general character of the provision is also a relevant feature to declare the reasonableness of a norm suspending public employees' economic rights, as in Judgment 178/2015, where this general scope is coupled with the "particular seriousness of the economic and financial international context" and the "repercussions on the national economy", which were clearly pointed out in the legislative preparatory works.[28]

24 ICC, Judgment 194/2018, 12.3.
25 ICC, Judgment 173/2016, 11.1.
26 ICC, Judgment 250/2017, 10. See D'Onghia 2017, 103 and D'Onghia 2019, 284. Similarly, in other judgments the Court repeatedly stresses that the legislator is bound by the principle of reasonableness, see for instance, Judgment 194/2018, 9.3.
27 *E.g.* ICC, Judgment 223/2012 and ICC, Judgment 310/2013.
28 ICC, Judgment 178/2015, 12.2. Orlandini 2018, 27–28, critically observes that the Court departs from the questionable assumption that the suspension of collective bargaining procedure may be a reasonable mean to "solve the serious economic and financial situation of the country".

Indeed, the reasonableness of a provision may also reside in its rationale and be linked with the "overall legal-economic framework, both national and European".[29] Consistently, in order to be reasonable, the solidarity contribution scrutinised in Judgment 173/2016 shall not be "detached from the socio-economic reality",[30] it must result from a careful weighing of various factors such as "the international economic crisis and its impact on the national economy", it must be contextualised in the overall social security system's regime and it must constitute a measure which has the effect of supporting the most vulnerable part of the population.[31]

Often, a close relationship between reasonableness and appropriate justification of the contested provision can be observed. Judgment 70/2015 is emblematic, since the Court draws attention to the generic justification provided by the legislator for the contested norm, arguing that it fails to explain "why financial requirements should necessarily prevail over the rights affected by the balancing operation", nor it is supported by technical documents produced for this purpose, to conclude that the right of pensioners to maintain the purchasing power, protected by constitutional norms, "has been unreasonably sacrificed in the name of financial requirements which are not illustrated in detail",[32] while such appropriate justification (in the form of technical documents – see further in this section for a critique) is provided as regards the provision scrutinised in Judgment 250/2017, which, consequently, is found reasonable.

That the existence of a close relationship between justification and legal-economic context favours the reasonableness of a norm is unavoidable. Notably, what makes the first measure contested in Judgment 124/2017 (on the remuneration limits) reasonable is the objective pursued, that is the rationalisation of public spending, aimed to "guarantee the other constitutional interests concerned, given the limited resources".[33]

The value of the legal context in which the contested norm is placed emerges clearly in Judgment 194/2018, where the norm fails to pass the scrutiny because it fails to achieve the primary goal of the legal institute amended by the contested provision, that is "relief through compensation", which consists in an adequate compensation compared to the detriment suffered by the workers, in application of Art. 4.1 IC and Art. 35.1 IC.[34] This example demonstrates how the justification of the norm, consisting in the purpose "of enhancing opportunities for entry into the world of work by persons seeking employment", even if relevant, is not the sole element considered in the reasonableness scrutiny.

29 ICC, Judgment 310/2013, 13.4.
30 ICC, Judgment 173/2016, 11.
31 ICC, Judgment 173/2016, 11.1. According to D'Onghia 2019, 290, this ruling is exemplary of the interaction between the solidarity principle that holds the pension system and the economic downturn phase the country was undergoing.
32 ICC, Judgment 70/2015, 10.
33 ICC, Judgment 124/2017, 8.4.
34 ICC, Judgment 194/2018, 12.

Even though the principle of reasonableness, as applied in the selected cases, does include some steps which are common to the proportionality test, as the relationship means-aim, a systematic analogy with the principle of proportionality can hardly be observed. Perhaps, only in the evaluation of the norm's aim, which is often close to the suitability test, or in Judgment 178/2015 the proportionality test seems to lie behind the legal reasoning.[35] To the contrary, *proportionality* seems to be used by the Court as synonymous to strengthen and complement the concept of reasonableness, together with other concepts such as *adequacy*,[36] but it does not enjoy ontological autonomy.[37]

That the reasonableness criterion does not rigorously correspond to suitability either is shown by the moment in which the Italian Court declares inadmissible a question raised in the course of an entry of appearance, which was claiming that the contested provisions were unreasonable for an additional reason, namely that they were incapable of fulfilling the stated purpose of "enhancing opportunities for entry into the world of work by persons seeking employment", because it was not stated in the referral order.[38] If the reasonableness scrutiny corresponded to suitability, such an assessment would have been conducted by the Court independently from the referral order.

Notwithstanding that the Court refrains from referring to the three-prong test, a specific step of the legal reasoning in Judgment 250/2017 may help with reflecting on the necessity criterion. Here the Court emphasises that the technical reports, as well as any other document that elaborates upon the financial measures, "represent an instrument for the verification of the legislator's choices".[39] In fact, the possibility to accede to explanatory and technical documents seems crucial for the Court to rule for the constitutional legitimacy, *i.e.* the reasonableness, of the norms at issue.[40] Without going into detail, nor presenting any of the mentioned data, the Court concludes that the "Report", the "Technical Report" and the "Examination of the quantifications" provided by the legislator offer a comprehensive understanding of the amendments and highlight the "financial needs taken into account by the legislator in the exercise of its discretion". The choice of the Court to demand for and refer to an appropriate justification, or better to technical documents is extremely interesting, since in Judgment 70/2015 it had explicitly required the legislator to provide such documents.[41] At

35 Cartabia 2013 is one of the main authors that argue that the two principles are substantially very similar. Loi 2016, 87–90, reflects on Judgment 178/2015 by attempting to bring the various steps of the Court's legal reasoning back to the criteria provided by the proportionality test. See also Orlandini 2018, 27–28.

36 *E.g.* ICC, Judgment 124/2017.

37 Of a different view, Morelli 2015.

38 ICC, Judgment 194/2018, 4.

39 ICC, Judgment 250/2017, 6.5.1.

40 See also D'Onghia 2017, 98.

41 D'Onghia 2015, 341–342 underlines that attaching a technical report is a duty of the executive since it allows us to understand the balancing operated by the legislator. Cf. also Morelli 2015, 712; Guiglia 2016, 30. In a similar way, in ICC, Judgment 275/2016, 6.2, the Italian

first, the Court's request appears uncontroversial, since it seems obvious that the weaker the justification, the harder it is for the Court to conduct a supervision of the legislator's balancing. However, the judgment leaves the impression that it is sufficient that the data are provided for the justification to be proper. It is not clear whether the documents attached were just read and accepted or rather accurately analysed by the Court and, if so, by applying which criteria. A further elaboration on the reasons why these data can be considered a sufficient justification, which goes beyond the mere mentioning of the documents' names and the fact that they provide for accounting data, would have clarified which features make a technical document acceptable for justification purposes.[42] In this sense, the reference to the technical documents seems just a first attempt to consider the financial reasons of the legislator and a more extensive explanation would have been necessary to clarify which accounting data can justify an impact on the enforcement of fundamental social rights.[43] Moreover, if the Court decides to build its legal reasoning not only on the grounds of a proper enforcement of fundamental rights, but also on the basis of financial justifications,[44] it is legitimate to wonder whether it should also enter into the merit of the whole state expenditure, considering whether the resources taken at the detriment of labour rights could have been found somewhere else, for instance by cutting on expenditures which do not serve the purpose to implement a fundamental right. By applying, in other words, the *necessity test*. Conversely, we have already introduced the shortcomings in allowing a constitutional court to interfere in such matters, since it would inevitably go so far as to enter the legislator's discretional sphere.

Overall, although there is coherence as to the criterion applied, in terms of a logical flaw of the legal reasoning, a systematic consistency among the seven Italian judgments is missing.

The absence of a structured test is accepted by authoritative scholars, since the constitutional argumentation, which refers to binding legal norms, has a "dialectic way of arguing, not linked by deductive chains and certain procedural rules",[45] yet it is remarkable the attempt made by the Court, in certain rulings, to introduce and describe the argumentative structure it is going to apply, even if the theoretical structure and its operationalisation are not always coherent and consistent.

A remarkable example of structured legal reasoning, which, anyway, does not reflect the proportionality test structure, is offered by Judgment 70/2015. This complex legal reasoning can be systematised as follows. First, the Court

Court has identified in the technical reports an instrument to verify the legislator's choices, see Scagliarini 2019, 350.

42 With the addition of a further problematic element consisting in the politically oriented character of the data provided by the Presidency of Ministers, Troisi 2019, 364.

43 In a similar way, Longo 2017, 232, Cf. also Luciani 2016.

44 Even though they remain in the "backlight", Benvenuti 2012, 377, or "background", Sciarra 2018, 137.

45 Mengoni 1996a, 124.

identifies the rationale and aim of the automatic adjustment system provided for by the law reformed by the contested provision; second, it detects the constitutional principles that have been implemented by the affected system; third, it explains which criterion shall guide the legislator that, with its acts, imposes a sacrifice over those fundamental principles, that is the reasonableness criterion. Subsequently, it derives from Judgment 316/2010 the reasons that have justified – and may justify – the constitutionality of a measure which interferes with the automatic revaluation mechanism.[46] In the concluding paragraph, the Court illustrates which constitutionally protected interest has been violated by the contested norm and, in line with the mentioned case law, concludes that this sacrifice is in breach of the principle of reasonableness as assessed with reference to the fundamental labour principles enshrined in Articles 36.1 and 38.2 IC. Eventually, the Court points out that the "unreasonable sacrifice" of the constitutional right at stake is not supported by a sufficient justification. Therefore, as a last statement, it concludes for the unconstitutionality of the contested provision.[47]

It is noteworthy that in Judgment 194/2018 the legal reasoning which has led to the declaration of unconstitutionality of Art. 3.1 has been developed analogously to Judgment 70/2015.[48] Indeed, the Court, first, carefully reconstructs the rationale and the aim of the legal institute amended by Art. 3.1, Decree Law

46 According to D'Onghia, Judgment 316/2010 included a clear warning to the legislator and made clear that further suspensions of the revaluation mechanism could have infringed upon the principles of reasonableness and proportionality and this warning had to be taken into account by the legislator, who rather disregarded it, D'Onghia 2015, 331–332. The underestimation of this warning is identified by Giubboni as one of the main arguments supporting the Court's decision, together with the comparison with the previous cases of block of automatic revaluation. The precedents are crucial to, first of all, identify the function of the revaluation mechanism, that is to preserve the real value of the retirement benefits (to grant the enforcement of Art. 38.2 IC), see Giubboni 2015a, 527; Guiglia 2016, 24. To the contrary, others raise sharp criticism in relation to the use of legal precedents in Judgment 70/2015, see Lieto 2015; Anzon Demming 2015.

47 Another attempt to provide the legal reasoning with a systematic structure can be observed in Judgment 223/2012, where the Court identifies the abstract criteria to be applied to the case under assessment. Yet, when it comes to the analysis of the norm, it fails to apply the criteria with the same strictness. *A contrario*: according to Tega, the norm at stake was subject to a very strict scrutiny, which has led the Court to apply the equality and reasonableness principle differently from Judgment 310/2013 where a much weaker argumentation is developed: Tega 2014b, 55. While Loi points out that "the proportionality" is left aside in the legal reasoning of the Court, in Judgments 223/2012 and 310/2013, which does not make clear what are the argumentative steps that lead to the conclusion that the challenged norms are reasonable, Loi 2016, 90. Again a systematisation effort is observed in Judgment 173/2016.

48 The same provision had been challenged by the referring court also on other grounds, all of which were dismissed: the violation of the principle of equality due to, on the one hand, the application of the new regime solely to employees hired on or after 7 March 2015 and, on the other, the missed application of such regime to director workers; the violation of Art. 30 of the Charter of Fundamental Rights of the European Union and of ILO Convention n. 158.

81/2015, *i.e.* providing relief for unjustified dismissal. In the context of such argumentation, it elaborates on the constitutional principle implemented by the affected system, that is the right to work, as protected by Articles 4 and 35.1 IC. Subsequently and on the grounds of its case law, it identifies the constitutional norm that justifies a limit to the right to work, *i.e.* Art. 41 IC, by widely stressing the legislator discretional power in this domain, as well as the criterion that the legislator must follow when designing the regulation on protection for unjustified dismissal, which is, once again, the respect for the fundamental rights at issue and the related principle of reasonableness. Last, the Court explains which constitutional principle has been violated by the contested norm.

4.3.2 *The stone guest of the Spanish constitutional post-crisis case law: the principle of proportionality*

From the Spanish perspective, if coherence is a value for constitutional case law, Judgments 119/2014 and 8/2015 should be praised. Indeed, even if an apparent evolution marks the construction of the legal reasoning from Judgment 119/2014 to Judgment 8/2015, especially as far as concerns the proportionality test criteria,[49] a more attentive reading reveals that not only does the second ruling completely confirm the conclusions of Judgment 119/2014,[50] the two judgments are coherent also from the perspective of the legal technique applied: the only difference lies in the fact that in Judgment 8/2015 the Court mentions the three criteria, perhaps in order to satisfy the Spanish scholarship, which had strongly criticised the complete mis-consideration of the proportionality test in the first ruling.

The Court tends to adopt the same structure in the first phase of its argumentation: first, it identifies the constitutional article(s) allegedly violated; second, it discusses the aim of the norm; third, it evaluates if the aim is legitimate and if it implements a constitutional norm. While the following steps, as the distinction between the legitimacy of the aim and the legitimacy of the norm, are rather inconsistent.

Both rulings are built through a dialectic legal reasoning, and not even Judgment 8/2015 considers in a substantial manner the three criteria: suitability, necessity and balancing in a strict sense. Even though it widely refers to its case law on the merit of the issues raised, the Court builds the legal reasoning relying on a technique (if we can call "technique" what is applied here) which is not grounded upon a solid constitutional judicial history (nor theory).

The legal reasoning developed in Judgment 119/2014, except for the very first steps mentioned above, does not follow a clear path, neither in theory, nor in practice; it disregards completely the proportionality test and the respective

49 Fernández López 2015, 262, mentions the switch in the Court's argumentative path.

50 Emblematic is the cursory legal reasoning in Judgment 8/2015 to dismiss the newly raised question of constitutionality of Art. 14.2, Law 3/2012, see SCC, Judgment 8/2015, 6, b).

criteria and it seems to avoid systematically the use of terms such as "suitability" or "necessity", even where the scrutiny it claims to conduct may correspond to those criteria.[51] Whereas the legitimacy of the aim remains the cornerstone of its decisions to reject the questions of constitutionality (see the next section).

Surprisingly, the term *reasonableness* is particularly invoked by the Court, either alone or combined with proportionality, although its content as a hermeneutic criterion remains obscure.[52] Furthermore, the assessment of the justification's reasonableness and/or proportionality with the norm's reasonableness and/or proportionality is inconsistently alternated.[53]

Reasonableness is also used to allegedly review the legitimacy of the CAE probationary period in relation to ILO sources. This is not the place to review the misuse of ILO sources in the case law under assessment, but it is still worthwhile to underline that the Court has strategically used ILO Reports, by selecting the most convenient sentences and disregarding the whole reasoning supporting the ILO's conclusions.[54]

In Judgment 8/2015, the Court does refer to the three sub-criteria that compose the proportionality test: suitability, necessity and balancing in a strict sense, but, at the same time, it fails to apply them in a rigorous and structured way, where especially the assessment of the necessity of the contested norms is sacrificed.[55]

When the Court has to newly evaluate the legitimacy of Art. 4.3, Law 3/2012, it strongly reiterates the conclusions reached in Judgment 119/2014.[56]

51 *E.g.* SCC, Judgment 119/2014, 3, A, c), on the legitimacy of Art. 4.3., Law 3/2012 with regard to Art. 35.1 SC.

52 *E.g.*, in SCC, Judgment 119/2014, 3, C, b), where – mainly – the justification of the norm makes the latter "reasonable and proportionate".

53 Suarez Corujo 2015, 423, finds a new argumentative logic in the judgment. However, while looking at the legal reasoning, he does not address at all the issue of the application of the principle of reasonableness and proportionality by the Court. The fact that the author expressly mentions the test of constitutionality, as conducted with regard to the *contrato de apoyo*, which, in his view, implies an assessment of whether the norm purses a legitimate aim, and, if it is reasonable and proportionate, although the Court – differently from the dissenting opinion – never expressly refers to the test, demonstrates the mis-consideration given to this aspect by labour lawyers.

54 See, SCC, Judgment 119/2014, 3, A, e). Also, the misuse of ILO sources in Judgment 119/2014 suggests an a-critical attitude of the Court towards the legislator's choices. On the reasoning around ILO Convention 158, see, *inter alia*, Suarez Corujo 2015; Salcedo Beltrán 2014; García Murcia 2015, 301–303. Still, from a supranational perspective, Salcedo Beltrán 2014, 151, 157, highlights that no reference is made to the European Social Charter and the conclusions of the European Social Committee, which were relevant for the case at stake and were clearly arguing that the economic crisis cannot justify restrictions to social rights. Also, with regard to international norms, Valdés Dal-Ré's dissenting opinion differs consistently.

55 Even though the repeated reference made to reasonableness and proportionality may lead one to think that the Court has actually applied these principles, a more attentive assessment demonstrates the contrary, *inter alia*, González Beilfuss 2015.

56 SCC, Judgment 8/2015, 3.

Particularly, as regards the consistency with Art. 35 SC, the Court briefly concludes that the contested provision is in compliance with the *proportionality requirement*, since an appropriate balancing between the sacrifice imposed on the workers' guarantees and the individual and collective benefits of this provision is achieved and "the measure is, equally, necessary and suitable to achieve the legitimate aim". The Court justifies such a conclusion by arguing that the employer has a concrete chance to assess both the abilities of the workers and suitability of the job. What is surprising is not – only – the merit of the discourse, but especially the approximate use of criteria that had been "rejected" in the first part.

Suitability and necessity are vaguely mentioned and none of the arguments used to uphold the constitutionality of the contested provisions is properly and rigorously attached to such criteria. However, their misuse (or superficial use) is consistent with the premise to the proper rulings, where it is claimed that it is not up to the Court to assess whether other and better measures could have been approved.[57] Indeed, it is doubtful how the Court could *truly* assess suitability and necessity of a norm, without judging upon the "opportunity and efficacy" of the said norm.

Interestingly, the Court concludes by recognising that "the legislator could have adopted other alternative measures". However, it adds that "from a *strictly* constitutional perspective" (italics added), the one-year probationary period *ex* Art. 4.3 Law 3/2012 does not violate Art. 35.1 SC (while it legitimately implements Art. 40.1 SC).[58] The reasoning is, indeed, disorganised and while the Court admits that the legislator could have adopted different measures, it also denies any competence on this profile. Therefore, consistently with the premises of Judgment 8/2015, the Court fails to evaluate the necessity of the provision at stake.

As to the violation of Art. 37.1 SC, the Court just reiterates that also under this profile, the justification is legitimate, reasonable and proportionate.[59]

The Court equally begins the scrutiny of Art. 12.1, Law 3/2012, by introducing the criteria of the proportionality test that it is going to – allegedly – apply. This is the first, and only, time in the case law discussed that the Court expressly refers to the three criteria and frames them from a theoretical perspective, before proceeding with the legal reasoning. In particular, it states that "in order to demonstrate if it is proportionate to the aim pursued", it has to assess whether the norm is: (a) suitable to achieve the aim; (b) necessary, "in the sense that other measures, less harmful, do not exist to achieve the aim with the same effectiveness"; (c) balanced, in the sense that it brings more advantages to the "general interest" than prejudices to the constitutional interest at issue.

57 See para. 2, in this Chapter.
58 SCC, Judgment 8/2015, 2, b).
59 SCC, Judgment 8/2015, 3, c).

Nevertheless, the Court specifies that "the necessity evaluation is up to the legislator" and the Court can only assess whether the norm "has sacrificed in a clearly unnecessary way the constitutional rights",[60] which brings even more confusion to the attempt to define the necessity test.[61]

The conclusion is controversial also given that the collateral measures, which according to the Court function as shock absorbers, should rather refer to the extent of the impact the contested norm may have on the constitutional right allegedly violated and not on the suitability of the measure to achieve the aim pursued. Indeed, in order to explain the suitability of the norm the Court should have elaborated on the causal relationship between the aim of the norm and its content. For instance, given that the aim here is identified as "avoiding job losses, by adapting employment to the concrete companies' conditions/necessities", it is legitimate to wonder in what sense the judicial control (one of the collateral measures identified) could contribute to achieving it.

In addition, the necessity test is passed, according to the Court, because the contested provision has not created a "clearly unnecessary sacrifice of the constitutional rights". The necessity of the measure is explained by pointing out, first, the constraints to which the employer's power is subject and, second, the fact that this power is recognised to the employer only "following the failures of the negotiations with the employer's representatives". The relevance of this argument vacillates because the Court does not explain what is meant by failure and it completely disregards the fact that if the failure consists in not reaching an agreement within a certain time, this scenario can be easily achieved by the employer. Nor is it explained why the sacrifice imposed on the fundamental labour right concerned could not be considered "clearly unnecessary".

Last, the norm "passes the proportionality test in a strict sense, given that the measure is balanced", which is due to, first, the limits and guarantees provided for by the legislator; second, because its implementation implies more advantages to the right to work than disadvantages to the right to collective bargaining.[62] The conflict between the right to work and right to collective bargaining is controversial. Indeed, it justifies an understanding of the right to work exclusively in quantitative terms, differently from the right to a decent work, *i.e.* the right to work also in qualitative terms, which is granted precisely by the dialogue between social partners and, especially, by the workers representatives' role in collective bargaining and can hardly come into axiological conflict with the right to collective bargaining.

The Spanish Constitutional Court has been blamed for its misuse of the principle of proportionality, which cannot be understood as "a mere judgment

60 SCC, Judgment 8/2015, 4, a).

61 The application of the three criteria is conducted rather superficially and no assessment is done as to other alternative and less harmful measures that may equally achieve the aim, Sanguineti Raymond 2015.

62 SCC, Judgment 8/2015, 4, a).

of rationality or arbitrariness, that can be satisfied by the simple reference to the legitimate character of the aims". First, the suitability of the norm to achieve the aim is only based upon the fact that it pursues legitimate aims, no further assessment is made and reference to "economic crisis", "creation of stable employment", etc., seems enough to find the norm suitable. Similarly, on the necessity criteria, which should lead the judge to assess whether the challenged norm imposes a sacrifice upon fundamental rights which is not necessary, since alternative and less harmful means exist, the Court remains vague and solely focuses on the legitimate purpose of the norm.[63] Last, the key criterion of proportionality in a strict sense, which aims at understanding whether the constitutional sacrifices caused by a provision are justified by its beneficial effects, is not carefully addressed by the Court. As a result, it has been argued, this judgment has given the impression that the proportionality test is, in this case, only a "technical expedient used to elaborate a decision taken in advance".[64]

Formally, the technique used in the second judgment appears way more structured and respectful of the proportionality test, but in practice it is not more rigorous than in Judgment 119/2014. This – apparent – shift in the Court's approach, in the legal reasoning, may be due to the critiques raised against the 2014 Judgment. Indeed, not only the academic literature had expressed a clear dissent as to the missed application of the proportionality test, but especially the dissenting opinion of Judge Valdés Dal-Ré to that judgment, which to the contrary elaborates its counter-arguments by following the three criteria, may have pushed the Court, in this second occasion, to refer to the mentioned hermeneutic principles.[65]

63 Sanguineti Raymond 2015, 326–327.

64 Sanguineti Raymond 2015, 327–328.

65 Indeed, a large body of literature, besides reviewing the judgment, has focused on the dissenting opinion by Valdés Dal-Ré. This is due to the level of argumentation of the dissenting opinion, which, for that reason, has been compared to a proper and alternative judgment, albeit with no decisional power; see Senra Biedman 2014, 1, the author also conducts an accurate comparison between the Court's decision and the dissenting opinion; Diaz Aznarte 2015, mostly focuses on the dissenting opinion by Valdés Dal-Ré. The dissenting opinion, in her view, "expertly question, from the technical-juridical perspective the suitability, necessity and proportionality of the measures of Law 3/2012 challenged". However, the author's reflections are directed to the contents of the dissenting judgment, rather than on the reasoning of the judge on the three-prong test, Diaz Aznarte 2015, 203. Of a completely different view, Gómez Garrido 2015, mostly supportive towards the judgment, points out that Valdés Dal-Ré in his dissenting opinion has argued that the Court has applied a new canon of constitutionality and she argues that, instead, the Court has applied the traditional principle of proportionality with its three-prong test: Gómez Garrido 2015, 125. Cf. also Salcedo Beltrán 2014, 152–154; de Val Tena 2014, 466–478.

4.4 The terms balanced

The identification of the elements subject to the balancing exercise is useful to understand what role is recognised for the economic crisis argument and for constitutional interests and principles of an economic nature, by the Constitutional Judges. In this respect, two main profiles of inquiry emerge. First, the very opportunity of accepting a balancing between fundamental rights and interests or principles of an economic nature. Second, to what extent the arguments that have justified a limitation of the fundamental labour rights concerned are linked to the economic crisis and to what extent, instead, the economic crisis has just a marginal role, in a way that the Court's argument may be – potentially – applicable also in positive economic phases.

The Italian cases differ from the Spanish ones in the terms that are balanced against the relevant fundamental labour rights, even though they are both concerned with the economic and financial crisis context. The Italian norms are mostly intended to contain public spending, with the notable exception of Judgment 194/2018, the Spanish ones are adopted on the wave of the policy of flexibilisation of the labour market. Therefore, the legal reasoning is developed around fundamental labour rights and either constitutional norms that express public interests of an economic nature or fundamental economic rights.

4.4.1 The Italian post-crisis case law and the public financial contingencies

In Chapter 1, I argue that balancing can be conducted only between principles, which cannot be hierarchically ordered in absolute terms. These fundamental principles (expressed also as fundamental rights) cannot be hierarchically ordered in absolute terms because they express founding values of the legal system. Since no value can be considered completely overriding, in order to decide a case of conflict between principles that express values, those principles have to be discussed from a balancing perspective and only principles that express values have to be confronted on equal terms. Therefore, "constitutional balancing" is needed as long as we recognise that fundamental rights and principles are an expression of founding values, which begs the question: does the principle of balanced budget (enshrined in Art. 81 IC), for the only fact of being called "principle" and being entrenched in a constitutional article, belong to this dynamic? And, therefore, can it really be balanced against rights and principles which are the normative expression of values?

The problem raised by Luciani (balancing is possible only among equals)[66] may be solved precisely by referring to the main theoretical justification that underlies the balancing method and by looking at the very substance of constitutional rights and principles, that is if they are an expression of founding values.

66 Luciani 1995; albeit contested by other authoritative scholars, most recently, Bin 2018.

The "equal balancing" implicitly suggested by Luciani should not be understood in absolute terms, which in fact would empty its meaning, but from an axiological angle: the terms are equal, and therefore can be balanced, if they are both an expression of values (independently from whether they are named rights or principles). This approach, in the opinion of who is writing, excludes the possibility to balance fundamental labour rights with the principle of balanced budget (as widely discussed in relation to the Italian case law), inasmuch as the latest does not convey normatively a founding value, but rather crystalises a precise – and questionable – choice of political economy,[67] and the "institutional and ideological framework to which this (new) constitutional (and euro-unitarian) rule belongs is way different from our [the Italian] original constitutional pattern",[68] which explains why the reformed Art. 81 IC does not express a value consistent with the Italian constitutional system.

If it is shared that constitutional rights and principles must be balanced against on a case-by-case basis to solve possible conflicts, the assumption of legal dogmatics underpinning balancing should be equally accepted, that is that rights and principles interact through a balancing exercise – only – as long as they are the normative articulation of values.

In the post-crisis case law, the Italian Court is wavering between a cautious attitude towards the inclusion of Art. 81 IC in the legal reasoning[69] and a daring approach (still circumscribed), more prone to admit Art. 81 IC as a term of the constitutional balancing, although it is never presented in terms of value.

In a number of cases concerning public expenditure the Court appears careful in explicitly admitting the balancing between fundamental labour rights and the principle of balanced budget enshrined in the reformed Art. 81 IC. Indeed, the Court rather often recalls, by deploying various expressions, the general economic interest, as in Judgment 223/2012 where it broadly refers to the public financial reasons of the norm. In this occasion, the Court concludes its legal reasoning by stating that "[T]he *exceptionality of the economic situation* that the State has to face is such as to allow the legislator to make use of exceptional instruments, in balancing the *satisfaction of financial interests* and the guarantee for services and protection needed by every citizen".[70] Two main elements can be identified in this statement. First, the Court emphasises the economic context in which the measure has been approved and, second, it suggests that the terms of the balancing operated by the legislator are, on the one hand, the public financial interests, and, on the other, the social rights protected in the case at stake. Neither Art. 81 IC nor the principle of balanced budget are expressly mentioned. Given this methodological premise, the Court elaborates on the relationship between

67 Chessa 2018, 281, 282; Guazzarotti 2018.

68 Chessa 2016, 475.

69 As criticised by Anzon Demming 2015, in particular with regard to Judgment 70/2015, and, instead, praised by Cinelli 2015b.

70 ICC, Judgment 223/2012, 13.3, italics added.

fundamental rights and the economic and financial context: "it is up to the State to guarantee, also under these conditions, the compliance with the fundamental principles of the constitutional system, which, obviously, is not indifferent to the economic and financial circumstances, but, with just as much certainty, [the economic and financial circumstances] cannot allow to derogate from the principle of equality that grounds the constitutional system".[71] In this first ruling, the Court sets a clear boundary to the legislative action, by pointing out that the derogation from the founding constitutional principles on economic and financial grounds cannot be unlimited.

While at first sight Judgment 310/2013 seems to adopt a different approach, also in this case, "financial reasons", which have supported the contested measure, are not included among the terms of the constitutional balancing, whereas they are used to put emphasis on the economic and legal context in which the measure has been adopted, thus going beyond a purely *legal* approach. In a key paragraph of the judgment, we can observe how the principle of balanced budget is not clearly placed in the balancing framework, but is just *considered*: "there is no alternative *to consider* the evolution of the overall legal-economic framework, both national and European".[72] The Court continues by stating that "[T]he recent reform of Art. 81 Constitution [...] and the introduction of the expenditure rules, as well as Art. 119.1 Constitution, emphasise the duty of the public administrations to comply with the balanced budget, also in light of the general European economic context".[73] In addition, as a unique case in the post-crisis case law, the Court refers to Directive 2011/85/UE on requirements for budgetary frameworks of the Member States,[74] with the aim of drawing a clear picture of the legal European framework. In conclusion, still without referring to the balancing of conflicting values, the Court underlines that "the expenditure restraint and rationalization, that implements the *policy* of balanced budget, imply serious sacrifices, as those under assessment, that find justification in the context of economic crisis".[75]

Judgment 70/2015 takes a step further and points out that the mere generic reference to a "contingent financial situation" in the legislation under scrutiny is precisely the reason for the unconstitutionality of the contested provision, given that the legislator has failed to provide enough indications as to the terms that have been balanced in the process of approving the norm at stake. In addition,

71 ICC, Judgment 223/2012, 13.3.

72 ICC, Judgment 310/2013, 13.4, italics added. Troisi 2019, 366, similarly refers to the duty of the court as a duty to simply *consider* the economic context, where the latter has been detailed by the legislator.

73 Differently, according to Fontana, the Art. 81 IC, and therefore the Fiscal Compact and the commitments taken therein are used by the Court not as *obiter dictum*, but as proper legal grounds for the final decision in the application of what he calls the "reasonableness test", Fontana 2015; cf. also Faraguna 2016, 259.

74 ICC, Judgment 310/2013, 13.4.

75 ICC, Judgment 310/2013, 13.5, italics added.

in the introduction to the official English translation of the Judgment, it is specified that "the overall design of the legislation does not establish why financial requirements should necessarily prevail over the rights affected by the balancing operation, against which such highly invasive initiatives are adopted" and "[W]hilst the right to an adequate pension is not absolute, any sacrifice in the name of budgetary requirements must be justified in detail". Therefore, not only the broad reference to the financial situation, as a supposed parameter of the balancing, is criticised by the Court, but also the lack of sufficient justification for the sacrifice imposed upon the right to an adequate pension (Art. 38 IC), which is a counter-term of the balancing of interests, considered a source of illegitimacy of the contested measure.

Consistently, the Court does not dare to make explicit reference to Art. 81 IC. In fact, not even the legislator itself had referred to this parameter in the process of balancing conflicting interests and approving the contested measure.

Furthermore, differently from the cases considered so far, on this occasion the Constitutional Court does not even underline the peculiarity of the economic context, limiting itself to conduct a legal reasoning, based upon the *legal* sources put forward by the legislator.

Several authors have emphasised and criticised the total absence of any reference to Art. 81 IC in Judgment 70/2015, compared to the use made of this parameter in Judgment 10/2015. They critically observe that, while Judgment 10/2015 even intervened to regulate the temporal effects of the judgment, in order to avoid damages to the public finances, Judgment 70/2015 did not even mention Art. 81 IC and it did not take into account at all the public finance consequences.[76] The lack of reference to both Art. 81 IC and the consequences of the ruling in light of the "dramatic financial crisis of our country",[77] combined with the choice of basing the ruling upon the failure of the legislator to develop further the justifications, has been understood by a number of scholars as an *escamotage* to simplify the legal reasoning and avoid both having to deal with the issue of the economic consequences of the decision and to conduct the necessary balancing between the interests at stake, which would have required a careful consideration of the principle of balanced budget.[78]

76 Morelli 2015, 707, 708, *inter alia*, emphasises that the fact that Art. 81 IC has not been mentioned at all is in contrast with previous decisions, such as Judgments 10/2015, 304/2013 and 310/2013; Antonini considers the lack of reference to the constitutional norm a thunderous silence: Antonini 2015, 719; Anzon Demmig refers to an unusual seesaw of the case law about the weight of the constitutional principle of balanced budget in the judgment of constitutionality of ordinary norms: Anzon Demmig 2015, 679. The author is alarmed by several profiles of ICC, Judgment 70/2015, while in a previous article he had openly praised Judgment 10/2015, see Anzon Demmig 2015; cf. also Veronesi 2015.

77 Anzon Demmig 2015, 682.

78 Anzon Demmig 2015, 683, in particular uses the expression "*escamotage*"; of the same view, Veronesi also wonders whether the judges were aware of the "devastating economic situation of our country" Veronesi 2015, 695–696; Lieto concludes that the mis-consideration of the

Nonetheless, as properly noticed, Art. 81 IC and the principle of balanced budget cannot be considered a kind of "super constitutional value", as to make sure that all rights and principles are granted, particularly in light of the fact that the Constitution has to be considered as "homogeneous"[79] and, in this occasion, the Court has ruled consistently with its case law, thus considering the balanced budget issue, but without "deviating" its conclusions because of the economic contingency and by conducting a careful scrutiny that pays due attention to the enforcement of social rights.[80]

D'Onghia reminds that, although the Court surely must consider Art. 81 IC, it is not bound by the principle of balanced budget, otherwise the result would be a "complete assimilation of the Constitutional Court's rulings with the legislative acts". To keep its institutional role, the Court cannot be influenced by the costs of its decisions, since how to distribute the resources is a political matter.[81] Even if several fundamental social rights are inevitably influenced by the public financial situation, it is also true that their enforcement cannot be frustrated. Indeed, Art. 81 IC does not refer, either directly, or indirectly, to the duty of the lawmaker to upset the welfare state system in order to respect financial constraints. It is a matter of political choice the destination of the – even limited, but not null – resources to the welfare system. The Constitutional Court, which acts as a custodian of fundamental rights, is called upon to determine how far the economic reasons can go to the detriment of constitutionally protected rights.[82]

In Judgment 70/2015, by acting as a supervisor of the balancing, the Court has proven to be very attentive towards social security rights and careful in not allowing an "unequal balancing between rights of individuals and economic efficiency".[83]

balancing and Art. 81 IC has led to an "uncertain argumentation": Lieto 2015, 5; also Pin Longo 2015.

79 Cinelli 2015b, 444. It has been observed that the Court has not ignored Art. 81 IC, but it has referred to it when mentioning the financial requirements, and it has rather placed Art. 81 IC in the right perspective, that is in relation to Articles 3, 36 and 38 IC. In this respect, it is appreciated that the Court, while balancing the conflicting interests, has gone against the tendency to assign "a sort of prejudicial hierarchical prevalence to the principle of balanced budget", enshrined in the renovated Art. 81 IC. This has resulted in a renovated protection of welfare social rights, anchored to the principles of substantial equality and solidarity, that is Articles 2 and 3.2 IC, see Giubboni 2015a, 528, my translation.

80 D'Onghia 2015, 348–349. Barbieri and D'Onghia have edited a collective Working Paper, introduced by a telling statement: "some good reasons to discuss a good Judgment": Barbieri, D'Onghia 2015, 3.

81 D'Onghia 2015, 345–346, my translation; in a similar way Cinelli 2015b, 445, argues that the Court in Judgment 70/2015 has properly considered the economic context.

82 D'Onghia 2015, 326–328. The author refers to the "core content" of fundamental rights, a concept that is not adopted in this book, for the reasons explained in Chapter 1, para. 1.4.

83 D'Onghia 2015, 338, where the author in particular refers to the expression "unequal balancing" suggested by Luciani 1995, 126. In a similar way, Guiglia 2016, 25–30, argues that the unequal balancing conducted in ICC, Judgment 70/2015, which has not recognised in

Not even the legal reasoning of Judgment 250/2017 includes a reflection on the economic context. However, this ruling represents a remarkable case, given that, in the attempt to build a dialogue with the legislator, the Court emphasises that the legislation under scrutiny has expressly mentioned as a justification for the sacrifice imposed upon the pensioners' rights (in particular the right to an adequate pension at Art. 38.2 IC, as read jointly with Art. 36.1 IC, on the right to a fair remuneration) the principle of balanced budget (Art. 81 IC). The absence of any explicit reference to this constitutionally protected interest had been crucial for the declaration of unconstitutionality of the norm discussed in Judgment 70/2015 and the Court recognises that the legislator has properly understood the Court's guideline. As a result, Art. 81 IC enters into the legal reasoning as an external parameter.

It is noteworthy to underline that Judgment 173/2016 just refers to the "context of crisis of the welfare state system", without identifying a constitutional article that protects the interest pursued by the ordinary norm assessed. However, here the relevance of the financial context is highlighted when the Court points out that the legitimate expectation of the pensioners is not infringed upon if the solidarity contribution "is *not disconnected from the socio-economic reality*, of which the pensioners are aware and in which they are involved".[84] Therefore, no balancing occurs in this case, since the norms simply do not infringe upon a fundamental labour right and, hence, the balancing conducted by the legislator does not need to be scrutinised.

A less careful approach towards the inclusion of the principle of balanced budget among the terms of the constitutional balancing is adopted in Judgment 178/2015, on the freezing of collective bargaining in the public sector. This ruling raises a major issue as regards the status of the principle of balanced budget enshrined in the amended Art. 81 IC. To be balanced are, on the one hand, the rights protected under Art. 36.1 IC and Art. 39.1 IC against, and, on the other, "the collective interest of containing public spending", which, in turn, has to be addressed bearing in mind the "progressive deterioration of the equilibriums of the public finances". Although the Court had already addressed the legitimacy of a measure providing for collective bargaining suspension, caused by public financial constraints, it considers a careful evaluation of the specific case even more necessary given the recent reform of Art. 81 IC, from 2012, which has introduced into the Constitution the principle of balanced budget, by making "today's measures [...] more stringent".[85] In short, it follows from this premise to the Court's proper legal reasoning that the principle of balanced budget, which acquired constitutional status following the 2012 reform aimed at implementing the Europlus Pact, is going to be balanced against the fundamental

Art. 81 IC the role of super-parameter, cannot be considered a constant feature of the constitutional case law, since the balancing technique is structurally unstable.

84 ICC, Judgment 173/2016, 11.1, italics added.

85 ICC, Judgment 178/2015, 10.3.

rights protected under Articles 36.1 and 39.1 IC.[86] According to the Court, this evaluation is necessary to understand whether the protection of another constitutional "interest" justifies the sacrifice of the collective autonomy perpetrated by the ordinary norms under scrutiny. The Court clearly frames the dispute in terms of conflict between rights and interests, which therefore must be balanced in order to assess the constitutional legitimacy of the contested norm. Nevertheless, the Court is careful not to elevate the principle of balanced budget enshrined in Art. 81 IC to a proper value. In the concluding phase of the judgment, the Court states that a "coherent financial plan" expresses the "necessity to rationalise the allocation of resources and control of public expenditure (Art. 81.1 Italian Constitution)", thus clearly refusing to link Art. 81 IC to a constitutional value, while, in the same paragraph, it states that trade union freedom (Art. 39.1 IC) is "inextricably connected to other constitutional values".

The appropriateness of including in the legal reasoning an evaluation of the effects of the judgment over the public budget seems uncontroversial, although, it has been emphasised, this cannot lead the judge towards a political argument, nor the freedom to collective bargaining can be deprived of its protection and be structurally subject to financial arguments and interests.[87]

Remarkably, the ruling released two years later[88] is more careful in attaching to the recently introduced principle of balanced budget the status of *constitutional principle* – in neo-constitutional terms – representing perhaps an evolution in the Italian case law on the terms of the constitutional balancing. In this occasion, the Court recalls the need to consider, on the one hand, the "resources concretely available" and, on the other hand, the constitutionally protected value of highly professional jobs[89] and it implicitly suggests that the balancing must occur between the collective interest to an adequate management of public resources

86 Orlandini emphasises that, even though the challenged norms have been partially declared unconstitutional, in Judgment 178/2015 it is manifest that public budget constraints carry more weight than in the rest of the post-crisis judgments on labour rights. In particular, what strikes here is that the financial constraints do not concern *diritti di prestazione* (social rights that require a financial disbursement from the state), but a crucial collective labour right: the right to collective bargaining. The author is aware that this is not the first time in which the trade union freedom is balanced against "superior general interests", however, particularly this judicial case clearly demonstrates that these financial interests have acquired a different status following the 2012 constitutional reforms, Orlandini 2018, 25–27. See also Countouris 2020, 367, who, on the grounds of ICC, Judgment 178/2015, holds that the Italian Constitutional Court has reaffirmed the reforms promoted by the EU by means of judicial intervention.

87 In particular, Zoppoli 2017, 185 ff. and Occhino 2017, 9 ff., who addresses the topic of financial considerations with regard to the enforcement of social rights from a broader perspective; on the public budget constraints in the constitutional legal reasoning (on both ICC, Judgments 178/2015, ICC, Judgment 70/2015 and ICC, Judgment 10/2014) cf., *inter alia*, Butturini 2016; For a reflection on the renovated Art. 81 Italian Constitution and its impact on the constitutional case law see Madau 2015.

88 ICC, Judgment 124/2017.

89 ICC, Judgment 124/2017, 8.3.

and individual fundamental rights, which, we can infer from the text of the ruling, are the right to work (Art. 4 IC), the right to a fair remuneration (Art. 36.1 IC) and the right to an adequate pension (Art. 38.2 IC). The Court, by underlying the aim pursued by the contested provision, reiterates which is the element balanced against the fundamental labour rights and it does so, once again, only in general terms, by referring to the rationalisation of public spending.[90] Also in this case, the economic/financial argument is not relevant only as an element of the constitutional balancing, but it becomes part of the broad legal reasoning of the Court as well. Indeed, the limitedness of the resources plays a crucial role and justifies the comprehensive predetermination of the payments the public administration can guarantee, as provided for by the norm under scrutiny. The Court stresses the value of the peculiar context, which does not allow a relative consideration of retirement benefits, on the one hand, and remuneration, on the other.[91] Albeit it is not specified at this stage, from the above, "peculiar context" shall be likely understood in both economic and legislative terms, concerning both the limited public resources and the reforms of the latest years, which are leaning towards a reduction in public spending.

Next to the fact that in Judgment 124/2017 the Court never refers to Art. 81 IC, but it only mentions the need to consider the "resources concretely available", it develops a legal reasoning that seems to lean towards a less incisive strength of the economic principles constitutionalised by Constitutional Law 1/2012. Indeed, the Court indirectly provides some food for thought in relation to the weight of Art. 81 IC, by referring to Art. 97 IC, when it emphasises that constitutional principles are expressions of constitutional values, which have to coexist in the legal system. In particular, the Court refers to Art. 97 IC, for the part that provides for the general principle of *buon andamento* (smooth running) of the public administration, which is included among the norms as expressions of constitutional values. Whereas it does not refer in axiological terms to the first paragraph of the renovated Art. 97 IC, introduced by Constitutional Law 1/2012, which provides for the duty of the public administrations to ensure the balanced budget and the sustainability of the public debt, coherently with the EU legal order.

The Court takes a clear stand in including among the values, which are founding the Italian constitutional order, a principle that belongs to the Italian Constitution since its enforcement in 1948, and not that of balanced budget recently and offhandedly included following the international institutions' pressure, because of a contingent economic and political situation.

Notwithstanding the ambiguity in collocating Art. 81 IC in the legal reasoning of Judgment 178/2015 and the brave stand in Judgment 70/2015, this case law confirms, on the one hand, that economic and financial consequences are considered by the Court as *facts* to be considered in the fulfilment of its constitutional

90 ICC, Judgment 124/2017, 8.4.
91 ICC, Judgment 124/2017, 9.2.

role, and, on the other, that not all constitutional norms, not even all those which are labelled "principles", necessarily crystallise constitutional values.

4.4.2 The Spanish post-crisis case law and the overriding fight against unemployment

The Spanish Court often reiterates that constitutional labour rights can be limited by a norm that provides a "reasonable and proportionate justification and aims to guarantee other constitutional rights and goods".[92] Let us retrace these "other constitutional rights and goods" that admit a balancing against the right to work and the right to collective bargaining, in the post-crisis case law.

Art. 40.1 SC, which provides that public authorities "shall in particular carry out a policy aimed at full employment" is discussed in Judgment 119/2014, where it comes into conflict with Art. 35.1 SC (right to work).[93] Art. 40.1 SC, according to the Court, "shapes the collective dimension of the right to work" and can legitimate limitations to the fundamental right under assessment. The collective dimension, that founds the policy aimed at full employment, is a central element of the legal reasoning, since "a given restriction to the individual right to work 'is constitutional if it pursues the aim pursued by the employment policy: that is, in case of unemployment, it guarantees that with a given limitation is offered a job opportunity to the unemployed people, which could not lead, in any case, to a decrease in employment'".[94]

The Court elaborates on the reasons that justify the provision of the one-year probationary period, recalling Transitional provision 9, Law 3/2012, which, in the Court's view, confirms the strict link of the contested norm with its objectives. Transitional provision 9 limits the effectiveness of Art. 4.3, Law 3/2012, until the unemployment rate falls below 15%. The Court interprets this normative framework as perfectly consistent with the duty of public authorities to adopt a policy oriented to full employment, hence in line with Art. 40 SC, since: "[W]e are in front of a conjunctural measure, bound to a concrete situation of the labour market, of very high unemployment and that, beyond any doubt, is linked with the already mentioned duty of public authorities to realize a policy oriented toward full employment (Art. 40.1 Constitution)".[95] The main point is that the contested provision is legitimate, because it allegedly responds to the

92 *E.g.* in SCC, Judgment 119/2014, 3, A, c).

93 By explaining the scope of Art. 40 SC, the Court also traces the limits of Art. 35.1 SC (see Chapter 3, para. 3.1). The use of Art. 40 SC is considered a "new constitutional approach", which is found surprising, since, beforehand, the Court had never used the argument of a "policy oriented to a full employment" to overcome the enforcement of labour rights, as if the goal of full employment may justify any violation of labour rights. On the "full employment argument", see also Fernández López 2015, 262.

94 SCC, Judgment 119/2014, 3, A, c). The judgment quoted by the Court is SCC, Judgment 22/1981, 8 and 9.

95 SCC, Judgment 119/2014, 3, A, e).

"specific aim to foster the business initiative", which is consistent with Art. 41.1 SC that gives to the legislator the mandate to develop a policy oriented toward full employment.[96] The fact that Art. 41.1 SC relates to the duty of public authorities to implement a general interest and does not express a fundamental constitutional right does not hamper the Court to justify the prevalence of the latter over Art. 35.1 SC and the right to work enshrined therein, nor does the Court devote attention to this ontological distinction.

The Court summarises synthetically the legal reasoning developed as far as the violation of Art. 35.1 SC is concerned: it underlines the "serious economic crisis context" and the "high unemployment rate"; it recalls the duty of public powers to adopt a policy oriented to full employment (Art. 40.1 SC), which is an aim pursued by this measure; it stresses that the application of the contested provision is subject to certain legal limits.[97] While the "collective dimension of labour", as expressed by collective rights such as the right to collective bargaining is not mentioned at all.

To summarise, as far as concerns the scrutiny of Art. 4.3, Law 3/2012, the Court offers a clear picture of the rights that have been balanced against Art. 35.1 SC, *i.e.* Art. 38 SC (business freedom, see the next paragraph) and Art. 40.1 SC. However, Art. 38 SC seems to have a minor weight for the Court in the case at issue, given that when the Court links the aim of the Law with a constitutional norm it mostly refers to Art. 40.1 SC.

When assessing the possible violation of Art. 37 SC from other norms enshrined in Law 3/2012 the Court puts in the balance not only Art. 40.1 SC and Art. 38 SC,[98] but also the right to work (Art. 35.1 SC), which instead of the constitutional right allegedly violated, in this case, becomes, according to the Court, the right implemented by the contested norm.[99] On the basis of what is stated in the preamble, the main objectives pursued by the Law are "the defence of productivity and sustainability of the company and, eventually, employment". The Court plainly (in the sense that it does not analyse the various factors) states that a Law with an aim as such attempts to "facilitate the business sustainability and avoid recourse to dismissals". According to the Court, this is a "constitutionally legitimate aim" that implements three constitutional provisions: Art. 35.1 SC, the right to work; Art. 38 SC, the public powers' duty to protect productivity; Art. 40.1 SC, the duty to adopt policies oriented to full employment. In addition, the Court refers to a general "necessity to face the serious unemployment

96 SCC, Judgment 119/2014, 3, A, e).

97 SCC, Judgment 119/2014, 3, C, b).

98 As regards the right to collective bargaining, it has been argued that the Court ignores "the virtual character of the right to collective bargaining, which, paradoxically, does not seem to be well assessed, except for a comparison made with a hyper-realistic Art. 38 SC, combined with Art. 40 SC"; Fernández López 2015, 260–261, my translation; Suarez Corujo 2015, 424, 434.

99 Specifically on Art. 35.1 SC, see the next paragraph.

situation",[100] arguing that this aim is relevant especially because of the high number of small companies that characterise the Spanish system, which does not have workers' or employers' representations and therefore does not negotiate company-level agreements.[101]

Similarly, in Judgment 8/2015, Art. 37 SC is balanced against the same three constitutional norms. The Court takes into account, once again, the general aim of Law 3/2012, namely "to favour the internal flexibility of the companies as an alternative to job losses", which allows the companies to adjust their organisation to the "economic situation" and "the productive structures to the unexpected market evolutions". The Court argues that this aim is justified and legitimate because it implements "the citizens' right to work, through the adoption of a policy oriented to full employment, as well as the business freedom and the defence of productivity".[102]

In other words, in a conflict between the public bodies' duty and the right to collective bargaining (Art. 37.1 SC), the right to work (Art. 35.1 SC) is used to strengthen the duty of the legislator to adopt a policy of full employment (Art. 40.1 SC) to the detriment of the right to collective bargaining (Art. 37.1 SC). With the effect that, not only the general interest in full employment is placed in a higher position compared to the right to collective bargaining, but the same hierarchical relationship is established between the right to work and the right to collective bargaining, the individual dimension of labour is not recognised as inextricably linked to its collective dimension in the industrial relations' system and collective bargaining is not recognised as a necessary complement of the right to work or as a way to guarantee the right to a *decent* work.

While the "equal" value of the right to work and the right to collective bargaining, in constitutional terms, cannot be questioned (even though the fact that they are understood as conflicting elements is anything but uncontroversial), the public bodies' duty to pursue a policy aimed at full employment raises a major issue mainly as to the way in which a constitutional court can approach an aim as such in its scrutiny, especially because Art. 40.1 SC has a key role in legitimising the legislator's choices and fundamental labour rights have been balanced mostly against the general interest of full employment and the legislator's duty to pursue it.[103]

Indeed, the Court often stresses the legitimacy of the aim pursued by the legislator with Law 3/2012, which includes, *inter alia*, the purpose to provide a remedy to the serious unemployment situation. However, even leaving aside the core misunderstanding, that is that labour law serves the purpose to create

100 SCC, Judgment 119/2014, 5, A, a).
101 SCC, Judgment 119/2014, 6, c).
102 SCC, Judgment 8/2015, 4, a).
103 A decision defined as "paradoxical" by Judge Valdés Dal-Ré in his dissenting opinion, and incoherent with the Spanish Court's precedents, which identifies in Art. 40 SC a *principio rectore* of the legal system and, thereby, apt to support, rather than contrast with, fundamental labour rights, Masala 2017, 531, 532.

employment,[104] we should ask whether the Court, in assessing the legitimacy of the norm on grounds of its aim, should demand a demonstration of the causal link between, for instance, the one-year-long probationary period and the improvement in the employment levels. It would be legitimate for the Court to question such a nexus, considering that it is challenged worldwide at various levels.[105] However, this would mean assessing the suitability of the norm to achieve the aim pursued, which does not appear to be the objective of the Spanish Court. On the other hand, if the Court were to openly question such a causal link, as done by the ILO Committee, it would plainly enter into the merit of political choices. Nonetheless, the aim perpetrated by the challenged provisions, as a way to implement 40.1 SC, is widely emphasised by the Court and seems to constitute the key argument upholding the legitimacy of most of the norms. Still, all along the legal reasoning it is presented as a necessity rather than as the expression of a value and its extensive deployment by the Court sounds terribly strategic.[106]

4.4.3 The economic crisis argument, in the balance?

The use of the economic crisis argument in the judgments at issue cannot go unnoticed.[107] Both in the Italian and Spanish case law, it is extensively invoked by the Courts, mostly since it is expressly mentioned in the legislative texts, which often provide justifications linked to the economic crisis, using the concept with various shades.

Nevertheless, none of the courts has openly admitted a balancing between the fundamental labour rights concerned and the economic crisis. A remarkable aspect, that can be observed in some Italian and Spanish rulings, is the relevance of the temporal scope in relation to the economic crisis argument. The transitory and exceptional character of the challenged measure is crucial in the court's argumentation,[108] but only if, among the reasons that justify the contested

104 Of the same view, *inter alia*, Diaz Aznarte 2015. In Auto 43/2014, 4, A, b), the Court had recognised that the thesis according to which the reduction of the cost of dismissal can favour the labour market mobility is controversial, but "the truth is that this idea has been present in a good part of the reforms of our labor legislation since 1994" and is therefore, not in the Court's faculty to question the "*bondad técnica, la oportunidad, idoneidad o eficacia de las medidas introducidas*".

105 One for all, the ILO Committee, reporting precisely on the probationary period introduced by the CAE, has reminded us that "no direct link between the facilitation of dismissals and job creation has been demonstrated". Report of the Director-General, *Fourth supplementary report: Report of the Committee set up to examine the representation alleging non-observance by Spain of the Termination of Employment Convention, 1982 (No. 158), submitted under article 24 of the ILO Constitution by the Trade Union Confederation of Workers' Committees (CC.OO.) and the General Union of Workers (UGT)*. ILO Governing Body, 321st Session, Geneva, 13 June 2014).

106 On this line also Sanguineti Raymond 2015, who strongly raises the issue of the misuse of the proportionality principle as far as concerns SCC, Judgment 8/2015.

107 For all, Fontana 2015 and Loi 2016, on ICC, Judgment 178/2015.; Baylos Grau 2015.

108 As noticed, among others, by Tega 2014b.

measure, the economic crisis retains a prominent role.[109] In other words, if the norm is justified mainly on the grounds of the peculiar phase characterised by the economic crisis, its legitimacy is assessed in light of its temporal effects, which can be read – with an optimistic attitude – in the sense that both Courts are inclined to admit a sacrifice of fundamental labour rights in exceptional economic phases.[110]

In the Spanish ruling on the probationary period (Art. 4.3, Law 3/2012) the economic context is pervasive, and it is coupled with a quantitative data: the unemployment level.

It emerges as "unemployment situation" where the "context of serious economic crisis and high unemployment", together with the aim "to foster business initiative",[111] allows a limitation of the right to work,[112] or as "context of serious economic crisis",[113] but it is never used as a term of the balancing conducted by the legislator and its relevance is even minor in relation to collective bargaining.[114] Nevertheless, even if the Court does not envisage a constitutional balancing between the economic crisis and the fundamental labour rights concerned, it accepts that the economic circumstances play a decisive role in the legislator's decisions, which end up permeating the legal reasoning, to the point that it has been suggested that the Court has introduced a new adjudicating criterion: the economic crisis criterion, which goes to complement the others traditionally applied by the Court, such as the principle of proportionality.[115]

109 One for all, ICC, Judgment 178/2015 and SCC, Judgment 119/2014 and 8/2015 as far as concerns Art. 4.3, Law 3/2012.

110 Whether the crisis argument is conjunctural or structural and what consequences may derive by either of the two options is, indeed, a matter for discussion; *inter alia*, Benvenuti 2012, 407.

111 ICC, Judgment 119/2014, 3, A, e).

112 It has been underlined, the labour market problems that Spain was facing were not due to the labour law system – as it was before the latest reforms – but to the Spanish productive system, which means that the axiom *rigid labour rights entail unemployment* does not hold true, see Diaz Aznarte 2015, 203.

113 For instance as in SCC, Judgment 8/2015, 3.

114 The use of the economic crisis and high unemployment as a justification for the reduction of both individual and collective labour rights is criticised by Suarez Corujo 2015, 435. But Garcia Murcia 2015, 301, offers a different view. The author argues that an appropriate economic structure is necessary for the enjoyment of fundamental social rights and labour legislation cannot protect groups' interests, but the general interest of the whole society. Therefore, according to the author, it is not surprising that the Constitutional Court has balanced labour rights against the necessities of the "economic constitution", that is against Art. 38 Spanish Constitution.

115 Goig Martínez 2016, 140 ff., drawing on the dissenting opinion in SCC, Judgment 8/2015, the author points out that the axiological premise to constitutional balancing established by the Spanish Court does not allow the legislator to justify a reform simply upon the economic crisis argument, Goig Martínez 2016, 152. According to Salcedo Beltrán 2014, 152, the result is that labour rights are not "rights" in the strict sense anymore, but just prerogatives subject to the will of the legislator and the economic context. According to Sanguineti Raymond 2015, 325, the economic crisis has been a crucial trigger of the change in the constitutional case law approach: Judgment 119/2014 and Judgment

From a fundamental labour rights perspective, a reasoning as such may raise concern because, in fact, it admits a violation of the right at stake simply based upon contingent facts. Nonetheless, a comprehensive reading of the constitutional post-crisis case law suggests that, considering the extensive use of this argument made by the legislator *ab origine*, a proper consideration of this profile by the court cannot be excluded, and in the remote hypothesis to accept a restriction of fundamental labour rights based on contingent facts and aleatory choices of political economy, it would be desirable to have a strict evaluation and a clear explanation by the court of the reasons that have justified such conclusion, thereby ensuring non-generalisable conclusions and develop a legal reasoning that cannot be easily reiterated as regards norms approved without the economic crisis justification. It is, indeed, even worse when the limitation is recognised as structurally legitimate, as was the case for the right to collective bargaining in the Spanish judgments, seriously hindered by the main argument of the wide (nearly unlimited) discretional power of the legislator in this matter.

4.4.4 *An uncontroversial axiological term: the freedom to conduct a business*

The balancing between fundamental labour rights and the freedom to conduct a business does not pose the same criticalities, even though is not always uncontroversial, either.

Art. 38.1 SC, which provides for the freedom to conduct a business and entails a mandate to the public authority to guarantee both its exercise and the "defence of productivity", comes into conflict with the right to work in Judgment 119/2014. Among the legislator's duties stemming from Art. 38.1 SC is included the adoption of norms that provide the entrepreneur with a power of extinction of the contract of employment, as part of its managerial power, which must be exercised in compliance with the "necessary limits".[116] Although, technically, the balancing between the right to work and the business freedom appears uncontroversial, certain authors, as well as dissenting Judge Valdés Dal-Ré, have claimed that the judgment at stake has established as a cornerstone of the Spanish industrial relations system, Art. 38.1 SC, the freedom to conduct a business and the defence of productivity.[117] Indeed, even though the axiological

8/2015 are clear evidence of this tendency, as well as SCC, *Auto* 43/2014. In a similar way, Baylos Grau 2015, 28–29, points out that the economic crisis, and its consequences in terms of unemployment have been the core argument of this case law. It has been observed that the repeated use of the economic crisis as a key argument is in stark contrast to the ESCR, which has sharply rejected the economic crisis argument to justify the lowering of labour standards, Vallecillo Gámez 2015, 102.

116 SCC, Judgment 119/2014, 3, A, c).

117 This approach breaks with the past case law, which had declared the interest of the worker to keep their employment as a fundamental interest and converts labour law in the law that protects the business interests, Suarez Corujo 2015, 434–435. According to Judge Valdés

nature of the freedom to conduct a business in the Spanish legal system (as well as in the Italian legal system) is not under discussion, the criticalities raised as far as concerns the appropriateness of identifying a direct conflict between the right to work and, even more, the right to collective bargaining and the aforementioned freedom are plausible. What is contested is the selection of the balancing terms, not because of their nature, but on the grounds of the asserted absence of a conflict in this precise case, since not all measures that favour the employers' interest can be considered implementing Art. 38.1 SC. In particular, the competitiveness and sustainability of a company transcend the scope of protection of the latter constitutional provision, while the freedom to initiate and conduct a business in conditions of equality is included.[118]

As a consequence, to justify a measure limiting the right to work, and, even more, the right to collective bargaining exclusively upon the argument that it aims to favour the competitiveness of a company is disputable and equally questionable becomes the identification of a constitutional conflict between the different principles.[119]

In the field of dismissal reforms, the conflict between the business freedom and the right to work relies on a more solid basis, as well as on a rooted jurisprudence. The Italian post-crisis case law deals with the freedom to conduct a business (Art. 41 IC) in Judgment 194/2018, where the interests in play are plainly stated: "the freedom of organisation of the undertaking on the one hand and the protection of the unfairly dismissed worker on the other hand",[120] *i.e.* Articles 41 and 4IC, where "the balance between the values underlying Articles 4 and 41 of the Constitution [...] does not require a specific regime of protection to be adopted".[121] Two elements deserve to be emphasised in the reported sentence. First, the Court recognises the need to balance conflicting rights that are constitutionally protected. Second, the Court clearly understands the fundamental rights at issue as expressions of "values", a wording never used to describe "economic interests" or, even, Art. 81 IC.[122]

The ontological imbalance of powers within the employment contract is adjusted by the limits imposed on the employer's power of dismissal,[123] which, we can derive, is inherent to the freedom to conduct a business. On the other hand, even if a dismissal not based on "good cause" or "justified reason" is an "unlawful

Dal-Ré, Art. 38 SC is inappropriately used and the effect is that the economic context becomes a criterion to judge upon the constitutionality of an ordinary norm. Dissenting opinion by Judge Valdés Dal-Ré.

118 Dissenting opinion to SCC, Judgment 119/2018, by Judge Valdés Dal-Ré.

119 In a similar way, as concerns the Court of Justice judgments in *Laval* and *Viking*, where balancing is conducted between EU economic freedoms and the national rights to collective bargaining, Orlandini 2013, 49–61.

120 ICC, Judgment 194/2018, 12.

121 ICC, Judgment 194/2018, 9.2; cf. Maio 2022, 212–214.

122 In this respect, it is partially shared that ICC, Judgment 194/2018 "relaunches the value-thinking", Maio 2022, 218, my translation.

123 ICC, Judgment 194/2018, 9.1.

act",[124] the redress must be designed taking into account also the freedom of the undertaking, since, according to the Court, this is what makes the system of protection "balanced".[125]

Even though the Italian Court does not stress as much as the Spanish Court the "unemployment levels", in Judgment 194/2018, the aim of the norm, namely "enhancing opportunities for entry into the workplace by persons seeking employment", is one of the first elements addressed by the Court, notwithstanding that it is not attached to any constitutional norm balanced against the right to work. The purpose is plainly considered legitimate and consistent with the difference in treatment based on the passage of time, since a lower protection for workers hired after the entry into force of the Law is deemed coherent with the intention to encourage the creation of permanent jobs.[126] No further explanation is demanded from the legislator, nor is provided by the Court, to justify the causal link between the aim of the norm, encouraging permanent employment, and the means, lowering the protection for unjustified dismissal for newly hired workers,[127] which, as noted for the Spanish case law, would require further elaboration from the Court or a specific request to the legislator.

4.5 Conclusions

For the reasons illustrated above, a proper comparison among the judgments is not conceivable, yet it is noteworthy to observe the two groups of rulings on norms adopted under the pressure of EU institutions to manage the 2008 crisis and reflect on their structure and results.

The first, evident, common element among the judgments is the notable weight recognised in the justification that complements the challenged provisions. It is emblematic – and extreme – that the Spanish Court repeatedly stresses the faculty of the legislator to regulate the industrial relations system even limiting trade union rights, as long as such a limitation is justified. Where the "serious economic crisis context" or the "high unemployment rates", together with the enforcement of Art. 40.1 SC are enough to justify such a limitation.[128]

The justification is an effective means of communication between the Court and the legislator that allows the Court to both fulfil its role and appreciate the legislator's discretional power, considering that it contains (or may contain) all

124 ICC, Judgment 194/2018, 10.

125 ICC, Judgment 194/2018, 11.

126 For a critique, Giubboni 2018, 7 ff.

127 Speziale 2022, 152; Maio 2022, 214–218, reflects on "employment" as a constitutional value.

128 In the Spanish case, the Court has not even attempted to correct the – potential – "mistakes" that the legislator may have made in balancing the conflicting values and interests, mainly because it has rejected *ab origine* that the legislator has made any mistake, cf. Gonzalez 2003.

the elements that allow a Court to conduct its scrutiny. An exemplary, and brave, stand is found in the Italian case law, in Judgment 70/2015, where the Court has authoritatively reminded the legislator of its duty to carefully explain the linkages between reforms limiting the scope of fundamental labour rights and the economic and financial context.

The Italian Court particularly relies on the justification to apply the principle of reasonableness, that, notwithstanding the theoretical uncertainties and the lack of systematic character of its operationalisation,[129] has been applied in all judgments assessed.

Beyond any doubt, a scheme for the legal reasoning, explicitly described by the Court, helps the reader (legislator, scholar or civil society) to understand the judgment, to what extent the various elements have been considered by the Court and, hence, to increase its persuasiveness, as well as – if necessary – to accept an inevitable limitation of fundamental labour rights. Among the judgments addressed, some of the Italian cases have tried to provide such a systematisation, while, however, never applying the proportionality test. On the other hand, the Spanish case law, where one would have expected such clarity to stem directly from the application of the proportionality principle, does not help in this sense, because the Court has failed to apply the test.[130] As a consequence, these concluding reflections have to dispense with a "best practice" and the question as to whether a constitutional court can conduct a proper suitability and necessity test without going beyond its competences remains unanswered, as well as the doubt whether a faithful application of the proportionality test would be too invasive of the legislative prerogatives.

Nevertheless, the Italian case provides some cause for reflection also with regard to the proportionality test feasibility, especially about the evaluation of both suitability and necessity of the norm. Particularly, where the Court, first, demands technical documents from the legislator (ICC, Judgment 70/2015) and, second, acknowledges the existence of such documents in relation to following reforms (ICC, Judgment 250/2017). Indeed, the Court just states that these documents were provided and that they contained relevant data, but it does not go so far as to assess them and discuss their internal consistency and reliability, which may be due to two reasons: either, the Court does not want to enter the legislative merit, which may concern choices of economic policy and/or interests to be enforced in a priority way, or it does not possess enough technical means to conduct such an evaluation. In this second case, it is questionable whether it would be appropriate to advocate for providing the Court with the technical expertise to carry out a strictly economic assessment, considering that the main problem would remain anyway: technical documents inevitably draw on political

129 Baldassarre 1991, 656, a conclusion that still applies today.

130 If a dogmatic approach is not adopted the proportionality principle becomes an "empty category", see González Beilfuss 2015.

choices, which are not absolute and objective.[131] This is especially true when issues of economic policy are at stake.

However relevant is the discretional power of the legislator, it conversely entails a recognition of the Court's responsibility[132] and cannot become an excuse for the Court to avoid its responsibilities as warrantor of last instance of fundamental labour rights, as it apparently occurs in some moments of the Spanish judgments where the Court's main concern is solely to articulate the reasons why the legislator has full autonomy in regulating certain matters.

Indeed, not only the legislator, but also the courts retain a political responsibility, which requires them to consider also the factual – or environmental – circumstances.

The fulfilment of such responsibility is reached also by considering the economic and financial context, which is done in both the Italian and Spanish post-crisis case law, although in a controversial manner.

Particularly, the Italian Constitutional Court does consider the economic and financial context, which becomes part of the whole legal reasoning, but does not systematically attach them to a constitutional principle. These elements are acknowledged by the Court if they contribute to forming the justification elaborated by the legislator. This should not be enough to justify a constitutional balancing, precisely because they are not entrenched into constitutional principles expressing values, nonetheless both the Italian and the Spanish Courts occasionally admit such balancing.

Conversely, a norm can be reasonable and, hence, legitimate if it does not interfere with a fundamental labour right, as is apparently the case in ICC, Judgment 173/2016, which does not require *ab origine* a consideration of economic and financial factors, but it immediately entails the legitimacy of the contested norm.

For the court to proceed with the balancing scrutiny, the challenged provision must have an impact on a fundamental labour right protected and the other term of the balancing operated by the legislator must be clearly recognisable. Judgment 250/2017 is emblematic, since here the Italian Court admits the balancing with Art. 81 IC, because that was established by the legislator itself. For analogous reasons, in Judgment 178/2015, Art. 81 IC is also accepted as a balancing term, but, by contrast with Art. 39 IC, it is stressed that it does not entrench a value

131 Rivers 2006, 203–204, explains it in terms of "deference" to the legislator: "the occasion for deference is the court's acceptance that its judgement is more likely to be correct if it relies on some other authority's assessment of some relevant matter. It is about relative institutional competence. In respect of any question, it might seem that the court is competent or not. How could deference be a matter of degree? The answer lies in the confidence the court can place in the competence of the other body. It could simply accept the assertion of the public authority; it could demand such assertions under oath; it could require the authority to reveal the factual basis for its judgements; it could require a certain degree of rigour in the fact-finding process. In short, the degree of deference means the extent to which the court will demand that the authority puts procedural resources into answering the relevant questions reliably, and exposes that process to judicial scrutiny".

132 See Massa 2017.

of the Italian system. Indeed, the Court never refers to the principle of balanced budget introduced in 2012 in terms of values, although occasionally endorsing the balancing against fundamental labour rights.

Perhaps, such inconsistency can be explained by the choice of the Court to accept the peculiar contingency, in a tacit acknowledgement of the pressure that the Italian legislator was undergoing. A sort of, a-technically speaking, indulgent mood. Nevertheless, it is paramount to emphasise the lack of axiological character of the reformed Art. 81 IC, so that its inclusion in the constitutional balancing does not become a rooted precedent.

Judgment 127/2017 of the Italian Constitutional Court, which understands only the original provisions of Art. 97 IC as expression of values, and not also the dispositions reformed in 2012, confirms that an attentive reading of the constitutional norms leads to differentiating them, according to axiological arguments.

Differently, the Spanish Constitutional Court does not offer a value-based reflection, since it does not openly approach fundamental labour rights from an axiological perspective, but it rather sticks to the text of the provisions and to what is written in the constitutional articles. This explains why it easily comes to identify a constitutional conflict between the fundamental labour rights allegedly violated by the challenged norms, *i.e.* the right to work (Art. 35 SC) and the right to collective bargaining (Art. 37.1 SC) and, first, Art. 40.1 SC, which provides for public authorities to adopt policies aimed at full employment; second, the right to work, which is coupled with Art. 40.1 SC and the business freedom (Art. 38 SC). The paradox (reiterated in both Judgment 119/2014 and 8/2015) evidently lies in the conflict between the right to work and the right to collective bargaining, which – surprisingly – turns out to be disconnected from the right to work, thereby denying that the right to collective bargaining enforces the collective dimension of labour, which is rather regarded as expressed by the duty of the legislature to enact a policy of full employment.

To the contrary, the recognition that collective bargaining is an "essential tool to manage the employment relationship", as it contributes to improving working conditions and workers' lives desperately contradicts the possibility to envisage a conflict (even if just on a case-by-case basis) between the right to collective bargaining and the right work.[133]

In both cases, the justification of the challenged norms is attached by the Court to a constitutional article, which therefore frames the structure of the constitutional balancing.

The norms' justification retains again a key role as regards the value of arguments such as unemployment or economic crisis.

The economic crisis argument appears in both clusters of judgments, nonetheless it never achieves a major role, not becoming part of the constitutional balancing. Rather, it lingers in the legal reasonings, as if the Courts meant to demonstrate their awareness of the context in which the contested provisions

133 See Chapter 3.

have been adopted. Interestingly, it seems to be particularly considered when the constitutional legitimacy of the norm is attached – also – to its temporary character, meaning that it is destined to no longer produce effects as soon as the economic context has recovered.

The temporary (also called "exceptional" or "transitory") character of a measure that interferes with the enforcement of a fundamental labour right, as well as its generalised scope of application (meaning that it does not concern a single category of workers and/or pensioners) retain a central position in securing the constitutional legitimacy of the contested norms, notwithstanding its uncontroversial impact on a fundamental labour right. In the Italian judgments, the temporary character is particularly relevant when it comes to the suspension of economic rights, combined with the general character of the sacrifice. Which is true, especially, if the resources are limited, or, better, scarce (considering that the resources are ontologically limited).

It is rather arguable, instead, that also as far as concerns the right to employment stability a limitation to a fundamental labour right may become constitutional if both justified and destined to disappear with the passage of time, as supported by the Spanish Court.

Far from arguing that Constitutional Judges have a duty not to consider the national economic context, whether it concerns public budget factors, an economic crisis or the employment rate,[134] this work has used post-crisis judgments to reflect on the role of the court as, primarily, warrantor of fundamental – labour – rights.[135] In order to exercise this role properly, the court should give priority to the evaluation of the violation of fundamental rights and, on the other hand, be very cautious in entering into the merit of the normative means chosen by the legislator. Moreover, where a limitation is found justified by a peculiar economic context, this aspect should be elaborated in depth so as to circumscribe the accepted interference with the fundamental labour right concerned tightly. Subsequently, following the court's indications, the legislator should be able to guarantee the enforcement of such rights, in light of the available public resources or the industrial national context, by designing political and normative tools that do not violate, but rather promote fundamental rights.

134 In line with D'Onghia 2013 and consistently with the Italian judicial tradition of the Constitutional Court, see Romboli 1993.

135 *The* Constitutional Court role, according also to Sanguineti Raymond 2015.

Conclusions

The theoretical and operational questions *constitutional balancing* poses to lawyers are perennial and any ambition to provide definitive answers would be dystopic: not only unrealistic, as hardly achievable, but also undesirable, as general principles of law need to remain dynamic in order to fulfil their task to assist the interpreter in adjusting the static, written, norms to the social context. All that remains is to continue problematising a pivotal method that allows the coexistence and the enforcement – albeit necessarily partial – of an ample spectrum of rights and freedoms in pluralist legal systems, notwithstanding its shortcomings, or even failures, with the purpose of contributing to the construction of a hermeneutic pathway able to adapt the written norm to the course of history, so that the original sense of a text is mediated, but not distorted, by current times and by its necessities.

In confronting herself with constitutional balancing the labour lawyer carries along a peculiar sensitiveness, which derives from the very nature of fundamental labour rights that are meant to adjust the imbalance of powers inherent in the capitalist system and convey the values of modern societies, by articulating the principles of substantial equality and solidarity that permeate the social states, in the employment domain.

Only constitutional principles that express values can be subject to constitutional balancing and, therefore, a constraint of a fundamental labour right is possible solely if it is aimed to enforce other principles that equally entrench values. It follows that the latter cannot be balanced with contingent principles that, although enshrined in a constitutional norm, do not found the constitutional system and its social contract.[1]

1 The difference between the balancing addressed in this book and balancing operated by the legislator to manage the COVID-19 pandemic crisis is obvious. While in our case the elements that have triggered a reduction in the fundamental labour rights' scope, were, mostly, a constraint in public resources and a reduction in the economic growth, which invite the interpreter to question the legitimacy of a possible constitutional balancing under these terms; during the COVID-19 pandemic fundamental labour rights, as well as a number of personal liberties, were restricted in the name of the fundamental collective right to health, even defined in its highest version, as the right to life (for an idea of the national constraints this

DOI: 10.4324/9781003155362-6

The assumption underlying constitutional balancing – *i.e.* that balancing is functional to solve conflicts that occur in a constitutional system between fundamental principles that cannot be hierarchically ordered in absolute terms – raises serious doubts over the employment of such a method by the Court of Justice of the EU and the European Court of Human Rights, which are missing the legal dogmatics' assumptions that justify a court scrutinising ordinary norms by applying judicial balancing, especially when the constitutional balancing expressed by a norm is decided by the national legislator, and, consequently, the supranational court interferes in a significant manner with the political choices of elected representatives. Indeed, the flexible character of a hermeneutic principle cannot be enough to justify its indiscriminate use, since a court is not free to choose whatever adjudication method, but it is the legal system to which it belongs that implicitly dictates the available methods.[2]

Given the impact of the decisions of the Court of Justice over national constitutional equilibria, the most appreciable problems arise precisely through the application of balancing and the proportionality test by the Luxemburg Court.

Constitutional balancing is a method in the sense that it allows the court to supervise the balancing decided by the legislator and requires each court to select, or develop, a specific technique in order to be applied. This technique often takes the form of a criterion, or hermeneutic principle.

Every constitutional legal system has the faculty to select, or develop, the most appropriate balancing technique taking into account the national specificities and the relevant legal tradition. Still, the applicable technique can even be borrowed by other legal systems, as it was the case for the Spanish Constitutional Court, as long as the transplant does not cause rejections and the borrowing court is able to construct a coherent national understanding of the migrating criterion, where the case law remains, not immutable, but consistent (as was not the case for the latest Spanish constitutional case law).

Overall, however, the proportionality test as presented by the most accredited literature, composed of three rigorous sub-tests (suitability, necessity and balancing in a strict sense) does not convince, given that, if applied accordingly, the court's decision would result in a claim of absolute justice – even though still on a case-by-case basis – unbearable in a pluralist and democratic system. That justice may be equivalent to a mathematical formula must be averted, since it would entail, in the context of a constitutional ruling, that the constitutional judgment would be incontestable, even by the scholarship and/or the public

event has triggered, Carmona Cuenca 2021). The balancing terms are, therefore, substantially dissimilar from those relevant in the 2008 crisis management, and such conflict, not new to modern states (the Taranto (IT) experience is emblematic, see Laforgia 2018), evokes different questions and different assumptions of legal dogmatics, that this is not the place to analyse. In that respect it is suggested to read Habermas 2022.

2 And not even in the EU context, "the Courts' move to proportionality can be characterized as having 'constitutional' importance-or is inherently constitutional", as supported by Stone Sweet Mathews 2008, 144.

opinion. Whereas, to the contrary, the latter must be always entitled to contest even a constitutional ruling and bring forward the social and democratic dialectic.

The idea of an absolute, incontrovertible, hierarchy – even on a case-by-case basis – is inconsistent with a pluralist and democratic legal system. On the other hand, as we have observed, it is not enough to allegedly apply the proportionality test for a court to properly fulfil its role of warrantor of fundamental labour rights.

This does not imply compromising on clarity and rationality of the *ratio decidendi*, which can still be achieved, even without relying on rigid tests, but it does mean abandoning the search for an incontestable justice to be determined by the constitutional court and accepting that from the social and political responsibility, recognised to the constitutional court, inevitably derives also a circumscribed margin of discretion that shall be in constant dialogue with the discretional power of the legislative.[3]

In theory, whether the court fulfils the role of warrantor and guide with a proportionality test or other criteria is irrelevant. Indeed, it is not the principle *per se*, as a self-standing identity, but rather the use made of it by the court that makes the difference and allows the legislator to understand the limits of its action and the civil society to comprehend the reasons that may justify a limitation of the scope of fundamental labour rights.

As regards the proportionality test, the necessity sub-test is particularly puzzling. It is paradoxical to expect a constitutional court to truly and meaningfully assess if the norm is necessary to achieve the aim, or other, less harmful, options exist, without expecting that same court to overcome its powers and invade the legislator's discretion. The Italian constitutional post-crisis case law, with its superficial deployment of so-called "Technical documents", is telling of the structural boundaries a constitutional court may encounter in the attempt to scrutinise the necessity of a norm, unless, by necessity, the sub-test is meant to control the coherence and exhaustiveness of the justification to the contested norm articulated by the legislator.[4]

The justification, as we have observed in the post-crisis case law assessed, is an extremely relevant element for the court to elaborate its legal reasoning and enter into a constructive dialogue with the legislative power. First of all, it is decisive in the first critical phase of judicial balancing, which lies in the identification of the balancing terms that, as claimed above, can only be principles expressing values, because the conflicting principles balanced with a view to optimising both of them in the best possible way must be identified by the legislator in the genetic phase of the norm.

3 The general character of principles necessarily assigns to the judge the role to determine the precept as the answer can only derive from the evaluation of the concrete case, Lipari 2010, 638, 640, therefore "judges must regain, courageously, awareness of their role", Lipari 2010, 641.

4 Contiades Fotadou 2012, 676 ff., according to whom necessity means that the lawmaker has to demonstrate that he has looked for possible alternative measures.

The remaining factors that impact on the drafting of a legislative provision, such as the economic and social context or a constitutional principle that does not convey values, but is rather the constitutional endorsement of a contingency and, hence, does not retain an axiological character, can find a place in the legal reasoning, but cannot constitute the sole element determining a restriction, be it a suspension or a limitation, to a fundamental labour right.

In the Italian and Spanish constitutional post-crisis case law, the economic crisis is a recurrent element and the legal reasoning extensively takes into consideration the financial and economic contingencies that the legislator has invoked to justify the adoption of provisions impinging on fundamental labour rights. Depending on the judgment (and on the contested norm and the respective justification provided by the legislator) the economic crisis has been conveyed explicitly or by employing either the principle of balanced budget, especially Art. 81 IC, or the unemployment levels, in terms of duty of the Spanish public authorities to promote employment (Art. 41.1 SC).

However, even though in some instances a proper constitutional balancing between fundamental labour rights and either Art. 81 IC or Art. 41.1 SC can be observed, an attentive analysis demonstrates that none of the Courts has recognised an axiological character to the above-mentioned factors, which have admittedly found a notable space in the legal reasonings, but have not risen to the level of values in the respective legal systems. The fundamental labour rights concerned have remained, together with the freedom of enterprise, the sole value-based principles in the post-crisis case law.

The frequent reference to the "exceptional" or "transitory" character of a national measure violating a fundamental labour right, as features that justify the legitimacy of the contested norm witnessed in the judgments addressed in this book, is apparently reassuring as it may be functional to avoid their crystallisation and the structural reduction of the scope of the fundamental labour rights concerned. Nevertheless, on the one hand, the fact that neo-liberal economies are subject to cyclical crisis is renowned and, even accepting the "exceptionality argument", fundamental labour rights risk observing rare phases of tentative expansion, endangered by their continuous struggle to recover from a crisis, conversely, whether "exceptional" or "transitory", an infringement based upon contingencies has occurred, and solely for that reason the social contract that fundamental social rights express is broken. Infringed by a legislator that should retain the political power to counter the scarcity of public and private revenues by promoting a countless number of reforms (which are not in the court's faculty to address) that can preserve the social conquers and the path of modern societies towards the normative endorsement of equality and solidarity.[5]

5 Sharing the view that "[J]ustice conceived deontologically requires solidarity as its reverse side", Habermas 1989–90. The philosopher has, however, most recently rejected his claim; see the discussion by Pierce 2017.

Whether national legislators concretely retain the decisional power to enforce the respective constitutional principles, or, instead, are directed by other and external forces is legitimately questioned;[6] it is anyway incontestable that the political responsibility ultimately lies in the governing bodies.[7]

But while this is not the place to discuss similar arguments, it can, surely, be appreciated when constitutional courts, notwithstanding the ontological constrictions due to their institutional roles, engage in preserving the conquered scope of fundamental labour rights in a thorny dance of resistance to the decision-making bodies that sit far from democratic legitimisation and social conflicts.

Although, as a matter of fact, with regard to some of the contested norms, the courts have *considered*[8] the economic context enough for it to legitimise infringements upon fundamental labour rights, such as when the Spanish Court attempted to expand the meaning of Art. 41.1 SC or the Italian Court modulated the effects of its judgment not to excessively destabilise the public budget, a constructive attitude requires remaining focused on the exceptional character of such judicial choices, which creates a pattern to be followed by the same Courts in the scrutiny of future norms adopted under similar circumstances only to the extent that it reaffirms the ontological difference between fundamental rights and the remaining elements.

Notwithstanding the several critical profiles raised in this book, the Italian and Spanish case law deciding about norms adopted to manage the 2008 crisis corroborates the possibility to query the constitutional endorsement of the principle of balanced budget imposed by the EU institutions; it does not question the epistemological difference between fundamental labour rights and a public duty to promote employment; and confirms that the economic context remains a fact and, even in times of serious economic and financial constraints and high public debt, it must be considered by the constitutional court on a level with a substantive and transitory element that does not possess the authority to upset the original constitutional design and structurally impact on the nature and scope of fundamental labour rights.[9]

6 Bin 2007, 47.

7 Thompson 2009.

8 In italics to emphasise the a-technical character of this profile in the *ratio decidendi*.

9 "Constitutions, documents destined to last, cannot be changed under the impulse of the emergency – in an economic and financial crisis phase", Luciani 2011, 66.

Bibliography

Aa. Vv. (2002). *Corte costituzionale e principio di eguaglianza: atti del Convegno in ricordo di Livio Paladin*. Padova, 2 aprile 2001. Padova: CEDAM.

Aa. Vv. (2010). *Diversity of Social Rights in Europe(S): Rights of the Poor, Poor Rights*. University Paris Ouest Nanterre - European University Institute Social Law Working Group. EUI Working Paper, No. 2010/07.

Aa. Vv. (2013). *Las reformas del Derecho del Trabajo en el contexto de la crisis económica. La reforma laboral de 2012*. Valencia: Tirant lo Blanch.

Aa. Vv. (2014). *Reformas laborales frente a la crisis a la luz de los estándares de la OIT*. Lisboa: Juruá.

Adinolfi A. (2009). The Principle of Reasonableness in European Union Law. In: Bongiovanni G., Sartor G., Valentini C. (eds.), *Reasonableness and Law*. Berlin: Springer, 383 ff.

Aguiar de Luque L. (1993). Los limites de los derechos fundamentales. *Revista del Centro de Estudios Constitucionales*, 14: 9 ff.

Aleinikoff T. A. (1987). Constitutional Law in the Age of Balancing. *Yale Law Journal*, 96: 943 ff.

Ales E. (2015). Diritti Sociali e discrezionalità del legislatore nell'ordinamento multilivello: Una prospettiva giuslavoristica. *Giornale di Diritto del Lavoro e di Relazioni Industriali*, 147(3): 455 ff.

Ales E., Novitz T. (eds.), (2010). *Collective Action and Fundamental Freedoms in Europe: Striking the Balance*. Antwerp: Intersentia.

Alexy R. (2000). On the Structure of Legal Principles. *Ratio Juris*, 13(3): 294 ff.

Alexy R. (2003). On Balancing and Subsumption: A Structural Comparison. *Ratio Juris*, 16(4): 433 ff.

Alexy R. (2009). The Reasonableness of the Law. In: Bongiovanni G., Sartor G., Valentini C. (eds.), *Reasonableness and Law*. Berlin: Springer, 3 ff.

Alexy R. (2010a). *A Theory of Constitutional Rights*. Oxford: Oxford University Press.

Alexy R. (2010b). The Construction of Constitutional Rights. *Law & Ethics of Human Rights*, 4(1): 21 ff.

Alexy R. (2014). Constitutional Rights and Proportionality. *Revus: Journal for Constitutional Theory and Philosophy of Law*, 22: 66 ff.

Alexy R. (2021). Constitutional Rights, Porportionality and Argumentation. In: Sieckmann J. R. (ed.), *Proportionality, Balancing, and Rights Robert Alexy's Theory of Constitutional Rights*. Berlin: Springer, 1 ff.

Alon-Shenker P., Davidov G. (2013). Applying the Principle of Proportionality in Employment and Labour Law Contexts. *Mc Jill Law Journal*, 59(2): 375 ff.

Alston P. (ed.), (2005). *Labour Rights as Human Rights*. Oxford: Oxford University Press.
Álvarez Conde E., Suoto Galván C. (eds.), (2012). *La constitucionalización de la estabilidad presupuestaria*. Madrid: Istituto de Derecho publico-Universidad Rey Juan Carlos.
Amato G. (1967). *Individuo e autorità nella disciplina della libertà personale*. Milano: Giuffrè.
Andrade Neto J. (2016). The Debatable Universality of the Proportionality Test and the Wide-Scope Conception of Fundamental Rights. *Revista Brasileira de Direito*, 12(1): 4 ff.
Andrade Neto J. (2018). *Borrowing Justification for Proportionality: On the Influence of the Principles Theory in Brazil*. Berlin: Springer.
Andreoni A. (2006). *Lavoro, diritti sociali e sviluppo economico*. Torino: Giappichelli.
Antonini L. (2015). Forzatura dei principi versus modulazione temporale degli effetti della sentenza. *Quaderni Costituzionali*, 3: 718 ff.
Anzon A. (1990). Modi e tecniche del controllo di ragionevolezza. In: Romboli R. (ed.), *La giustizia costituzionale a una svolta*. Atti del Convegno di Pisa del 5 maggio 1990. Torino: Giappichelli, 31 ff.
Anzon Demmig A. (2015). Un'inedita altalena nella giurisprudenza della Corte sul principio dell'equilibrio di bilancio. *Quaderni Costituzionali*, 3: 679 ff.
Aparicio Wilhelmi M. (2019). La reforma del art. 135 CE como dispositivo de desposesión constitucional. *Jueces para la democracia*, 95: 17 ff.
Arroyo Jiménez L., Ortega Carballo C. (2014). Towards the Modernization of the Appeal for Constitutional Protection of Fundamental Rights in Spain. *European Public Law*, 20(19): 31 ff.
Atkinson J. (2018). Human Rights as Foundations for Labor Law. In: Collins H., Lester G., Mantouvalou V. (eds.), *Philosophical Foundations of Labour Law*. Oxford: Oxford University Press, 122 ff.
Baccelli L. (2013). *I diritti dei popoli*. Bari: Editori Laterza.
Baccelli L. (2014). Welfare, diritti sociali, conflitti. Ci salveranno i barbari? *Ragion pratica*, 42(1): 87 ff.
Bäcker C. (2021). Limited Balancing: The Principle of Human Dignity and Its Inviolability. In: Sieckmann J. R. (ed.), *Proportionality, Balancing, and Rights Robert Alexy's Theory of Constitutional Rights*. Berlin: Springer, 85 ff.
Baldassarre A. (1989). *Diritti sociali, Enciclopedia giuridica*. Roma: Treccani.
Baldassarre A. (1991). Costituzione e Teoria dei Valori. *Politica del Diritto*: 639 ff.
Ballestrero M. V. (2000). Brevi osservazioni su costituzione europea e diritto del lavoro italiano. *Lavoro e Diritto*, XIV(4): 547 ff.
Ballestrero M. V. (2008). Le sentenza Viking e Laval: la Corte di giustizia "bilancia" il diritto di sciopero. *Lavoro e Diritto*, XXII(2): 371 ff.
Ballestrero M. V. (2019). La Corte costituzionale censura il d.lgs. n. 23/2015: ma crescono davvero le tutele? *Lavoro e Diritto*, XXXIII(2): 243 ff.
Barak A. (2012). *Proportionality: Constitutional Rights and Their Limitations*. Cambridge: Cambridge University Press.
Barbera A. (2015). La sentenza relativa al blocco pensionistico: Una brutta pagina per la corte. *Rivista dell'Associazione Italiana dei Costituzionalisti*, 2: 1 ff.
Barberis M. (2011). Diritto e morale: La discussione odierna. *Journal for Constitutional Theory and Philosophy of Law: Revus*, 16: 55 ff.

Barberis M. (2013). Eguaglianza, ragionevolezza e diritti. *Rivista di filosofia del diritto*, 1: 191 ff.

Barbieri M. (2017). Giurisprudenza costituzionale ed effetti temporali delle sentenze. *Giornali di Diritto del Lavoro e di Relazioni Industriali*, 153: 167 ff.

Barbieri M., D'Onghia M. (2015). La sentenza n. 70/2015 della Corte Costituzionale. *WP CSDLE "Massimo D'Antona". Collective Volumes* - 4.

Barile P. (1994). Il principio di Ragionevolezza della giurisprudenza della Corte Costituzionale. In: Aa. Vv., *Il principio di ragionevolezza nella giurisprudenza della Corte costituzionale: riferimenti comparatistici*. Atti del seminario svoltosi in Roma, Palazzo della Consulta, nei giorni 13 e 14 ottobre 1992. Milano: Giuffrè, 21 ff.

Barnard C. (2012). *EU Employment Law*. Oxford: Oxford University Press. 4th Edition.

Barnard C. (2014). EU Employment Law and the European Social Model: The Past, the Present and the Future. *Current Legal Problems*, 67: 199 ff.

Barnard C. (2020). Are Social 'Rights' Rights? *European Labour Law Journal*, 11(4): 351 ff.

Barnes J. (1998a). El Principio de proporcionalidad. Estudio preliminar. *Cuadernos de Derecho Publico*, 5: 15 ff.

Barnes J. (1998b). Jurisprudencia constitucional sobre el principio de proporcionalidad en él ambito de los derechos y libertades. *Cuaderno de Derecho Publico*, 5: 333 ff.

Bavaro V. (2018). Lineamenti sulla costituzione materiale dei diritti sociali del lavoro. *Lavoro e Diritto*, XXXII(2): 243 ff.

Baylos Grau A. (2012a). Crisis y Derecho del Trabajo o el Derecho del Trabajo en Crisis. Sobre la reforma laboral española de 2012. *Derecho Laboral*, 245: 1 ff.

Baylos Grau A. (ed.), (2012b). *Políticas de Austeridad y Crisis en las Relaciones Laborales: La Reforma del 2012*. Albacete: Bomarzo.

Baylos Grau A. (2015). La proteccion de los derechos fundamentales por el Tribunal Constitucional espanol: Auge y declive de la function de tutela. *Revista de Derecho Social*, 69: 17 ff.

Baylos Grau A. (2017). Poteri privati e diritti fondamentali dei lavoratori. *Lavoro e Diritto*, 1: 7 ff.

Baylos Grau A. (2022). Un primo approccio alla riforma del lavoro spagnola. *Giornale di Diritto del Lavoro e di Relazioni Industriali*, 174(2): 225 ff.

Baylos Grau A., Trillo Párraga F. (2013). *El Impacto de Las Medidas Anti-Crisis y La Situacion Social y Laboral: España. Estudio*. Bruxelles: Comité Económico y Social Europeo.

Baz Rodríguez R. (2012). El contrato de trabajo indefinido de apoyo a los emprendedores. Análisis crítico de una apuesta por la flexi-seguridad. *Revista de Derecho Social*, 59: 98 ff.

Belavusau U. (2008). The Case of Laval in the Context of the Post-Enlargement EC Law Development. *German Law Journal*, 9(12): 2279 ff.

Benvenuti M. (2012). La Corte Costituzionale. In: Aa. Vv., *Il diritto alla prova della crisi economica. Atti del convegno di Roma, 26–27 Aprile 2012*. Napoli: Jovene Editore, 115 ff.

Bercusson B. (2009). *European Labour Law: Law in Context*. Cambridge: Cambridge University. 1st Edition.

Bergonzini C. (2016). The Italian Constitutional Court and Balancing the Budget. *European Constitutional Law Review*, 12: 177 ff.

Bernal Pulido C. (2005). *El principio de proporcionalidad y los derechos fundamentales.* Madrid: Centro de Estudios Políticos y Constitucionales. 2nd Edition.
Bernal Pulido C. (2007). *El principio de proporcionalidad y los derechos fundamentales.* Madrid: Centro de Estudios Políticos y Constitucionales. 3rd Edition.
Bernal Pulido C. (2013). The Migration of Proportionality Across Europe. *NZ J Public Int Law*, 11(3): 483 ff.
Bernal Pulido C. (2014). *El principio de proporcionalidad y los derechos fundamentales.* Bogotà: Univesrsidad Externado de Colombia. 4th Edition.
Biasi M. (2014). The Effect of the Global Crisis on the Labor Market: Report on Italy. *Comparative Labour Law & Policy Journal*, 35: 371 ff.
Bilchitz D. (2014). Socio-Economic Rights, Economic Crisis, and Legal Doctrine. *International Journal of Constitutional Law*, 12(3): 710 ff.
Bin R. (1992). *Diritti e Argomenti. Il bilanciamento degli interessi nella giurisprudenza costituzionale.* Milano: Giuffrè.
Bin R. (2007). Che cos'è la Costituzione? *Quaderni costituzionali*, 1: 11 ff.
Bin R. (2015). Quando i precedenti degradano a citazioni e le regole evaporano in principi. *Forum dei Quaderni Costituzionali*, 4: 1 ff.
Bin R. (2018). *Critica della teoria dei diritti.* Milano: Franco Angeli Editore.
Bobbio N. (1997). *Il positivismo giuridico.* Torino: Giappichelli.
Böckenförde E.-W. (1993). *Escritos sobre derechos fundamentales.* Baden-Baden: Nomos Verlagsgesellschaft.
Bogg A. (2017). Labour, Love and Futility: Philosophical Perspectives on Labour Law. *The International Journal of Comparative Labour Law and Industrial Relations*, 33(1): 7 ff.
Bolego G. (2016). Il licenziamento immotivato nel d.lgs. 23/2015. *Giornale di Diritto del Lavoro e di Relazioni Industriali*, 150: 317 ff.
Bomhoff J. (2013). *Balancing Constitutional Rights: The Origins and Meanings of Postwar Legal Discourse.* Cambridge: Cambridge University Press.
Bonardi O. (2012). La Corta Vita dei Contributi di Solidarietà. *Argomenti di diritto del lavoro*, 6: 1233 ff.
Bongiovanni G. (2001). Diritti dallo «statuto» difficile. Aspetti del dibattito italiano sui diritti sociali nel secondo dopoguerra. *Scienza e Politica*, 24: 75 ff.
Bongiovanni G., Sartor G., Valentini C. (eds.), (2009). *Reasonableness and Law.* Berlin: Springer.
Borowski M. (2021). Limited Review in Balancing Constitutional Rights. In: Sieckmann J. R. (ed.), *Proportionality, Balancing, and Rights: Robert Alexy's Theory of Constitutional Rights.* Berlin: Springer, 135 ff.
Brkan M. (2018). The Concept of Essence of Fundamental Rights in the EU Legal Order: Peeling the Onion to Its Core. *European Constitutional Law Review*, 14: 332 ff.
Bruun N., Hepple B. (2009). Economic Policy and Labour Law. In: Hepple B., Veneziani B. (eds.), *The Transformation of Labour Law in Europe: A Comparative Study of 15 Countries 1945–2004.* Oxford and Portland: Hart Publishing, 31 ff.
Bruun N., Lorcher K., Schoemann I. (eds.), (2014). *The Economic and Financial Crisis and Collective Labour Law.* Oxford and Portland: Hart Publishing.
Buecker A., Dorssemont F., Warneck W. (2011). The Search for a Balance: Analysis and Perspectives. In: Buecker A., Warneck W. (eds.), *Reconciling Fundamental Social Rights and Economic Freedoms after Viking, Laval and Rueffert.* Baden-Baden: Nomos.

Buekers T., De Witte B., Kilpatrick C. (eds.), (2017). *Constitutional Change Through Euro-Crisis Law*. Cambridge: Cambridge University Press.

Busch K. Hermann C., Hinrichs K., Thorsten S. (2013). *Euro Crisis, Austerity Policy and the European Social Model: How Crisis Policies in Southern Europe Threaten the EU's Social Dimension*. Bonn: Friedrich Ebert Stiftung.

Butturini D. (2016). Il diritto della crisi economico-finanziaria tra ragioni dell'emergenza e giudizio di costituzionalità. *Osservatorio Costituzionale*, 3: 1 ff.

Camardi C. (2017). Brevi riflessioni sull'argomentazione per principi nel diritto privato. *Rivista di Diritto Civile*, 5: 1130 ff.

Carbas D. (2013). La legge di attuazione del principio costituzionale del pareggio di bilancio. *Quaderni Costituzionali*, 1: 124 ff.

Caredda M. (2019). *Giudizio incidentale e vincoli di finanza pubblica. Il giudice delle leggi prima e dopo la crisi*. Torino: Giappichelli.

Caretti P., Tarli Barbieri G. (2017). *I diritti fondamentiali: Libertà e diritti sociali*. Torino: Giappichelli. 4th Edition.

Carinci F., De Luca Tamajo R., Tosi P., Treu T. (2016). *Diritto del Lavoro. 1. Il diritto sindacale*. Milano: UTET Giuridica.

Carinci M. T. (2015). "In the Spirit of Flexibility". An Overview of Renzi's Reforms (the so-called Jobs Act) to 'Improve' the Italian Labour Market. *WP CSDLE "Massimo D'Antona".IT* – 285.

Carinci M. T. (2018). La Corte costituzionale n. 194/2018 ridisegna le tutele economiche per il licenziamento individuale ingiustificato nel "Jobs Act", e oltre. *WP CSDLE "Massimo D'Antona".IT* – 378.

Carmona Cuenca E. (1994). El principio de igualdad material en la jurisprudencia del Tribunal Constitucional. *Revista de Estudios Políticos (Nueva Época)*, 4: 265 ff.

Carmona Cuenca E. (2021). Estado de alarma, pandemia y derechos fundamentales ¿limitación o suspensión? *Revista de Derecho Político*, 112: 13 ff.

Cartabia M. (2013). *I principi di ragionevolezza e proporzionalità nella giurisprudenza costituzionale italiana*. Roma, Palazzo della Consulta 24–26 ottobre 2013, Conferenza trilaterale delle Corte costituzionali italiana, portoghese e spagnola.

Caruso B. (2015). Nuove traiettorie del diritto del lavoro nella crisi europea. Il caso italiano. In: Caruso B., Fontana G. (eds.), *Lavoro e diritti sociali nella crisi europea*. Bologna: Il Mulino, 57 ff.

Caruso B. (2016). Impresa, lavoro, diritto nella stagione del Jobs Act. *Giornale di Diritto del Lavoro e di Relazioni Industriali*, 150: 255 ff.

Caruso B., Del Punta R. (2016). Il diritto del lavoro e l'autonomia perduta. *Lavoro e Diritto*, 4: 645 ff.

Caruso B., Del Punta R., Treu T. (eds.), (2020). *Il diritto del lavoro e la grande trasformazione*. Bologna: Il Mulino.

Caruso B., Fontana G. (2015). *Lavoro e diritti sociali nella crisi europea. Un confronto fra costituzionalisti e giuslavoristi*. Bologna: Il Mulino.

Casas Baamonde M. E. (2014). La eficacia y la eficiencia del derecho del trabajo: Reflexiones sobre un derecho cuestionado por la economía y el desempleo. *Revista universitaria de ciencias del trabajo*, 15: 67 ff.

Casas Baamonde M. E., Rodríguez-Piñero y Bravo-Ferrer M., Valdés Dal-Ré F. (2012). La nueva reforma laboral. Relaciones laborales. *Revista crítica de teoría y práctica*, 5: 1 ff.

Castelli L. (2021). Alla ricerca del "limite dei limiti": Il «contenuto essenziale» dei diritti Fondamentali nel dialogo fra le corti. *Rivista Associazione Italiana dei Costituzionalisti*, 1: 454 ff.

Cerri A. (2016). Spunti e riflessioni sulla ragionevolezza nel diritto. *Diritto Pubblico*, 2: 625 ff.

Cheli E. (1999). *Il giudice delle leggi*. Bologna: Il Mulino.

Cheli E. (2011). *Stato costituzionale e ragionevolezza*. Lezioni magistrali, 45. Napoli: Editoriale Scientifica.

Chessa O. (2016). Pareggio strutturale di bilancio, keynesismo e unione monetaria. *Quaderni Costituzionali*, 3: 455 ff.

Chessa O. (2018). La dogmatica costituzionale dei diritti sociali tra struttura e sovrastruttura. *Lavoro e Diritto*, 2: 269 ff.

Chiassoni P. (2015). *Neoconstitucionalismo, positivismo jurídico y modernidad*. Manuscrito inédito.

Chieco P. (2015). "Riforme strutturali" del mercato del lavoro e diritti fondamentali dei lavoratori nel quadro della nuova governance economica europea. *Giornale di Diritto del Lavoro e di Relazioni Industriali*, 147: 359 ff.

Cinelli M. (2015a). Jobs Act e dintorni. Appunti sulle metamorfosi in progress nel sistema delle tutele sociali. *Rivista di Diritto della Sicurezza Sociale*, 2: 285 ff.

Cinelli M. (2015b). Illegittimo il blocco della indicizzazione delle pensioni: Le buone ragioni della Corte (Corte cost. 30 aprile 2015, n. 70). Con nota. *Rivista del Diritto della Sicurezza Sociale*, 2: 429 ff.

Cinelli M. (2015c). Sostenibilità economica e sostenibilità sociale nella recente giurisprudenza costituzionale. In: Barbieri M., D'Onghia M. (eds.), *La sentenza n. 70/2015 della Corte Costituzionale. WP CSDLE "Massimo D'Antona".Collective Volumes* – 4.

Cinelli M. (2022). Solidarietà intergenerazionale uso e abuso di un sintagma polisemico. *Rivista Italiana di Diritto del Lavoro*, 2(I): 157 ff.

Ciolli I. (2012a). *Le Ragioni dei Diritti e il Pareggio di Bilancio*. Roma: Aracne editrice.

Ciolli I. (2012b). I paesi dell'eurozona e i vincoli di bilancio. Quando l'emergenza economica fa saltare gli strumenti normativi ordinari. *Rivista Associazione Italiana dei Costituzionalisti*, 1: 1 ff.

Ciolli I. (2012c). I diritti sociali. In: Aa. Vv., *Il diritto alla prova della crisi economica. Atti del convegno di Roma, 26–27 Aprile 2012*. Napoli: Jovene Editore, 83 ff.

Clasen J., Clegg D., Kvist J. (2012). *European Labour Market Policies in (the) Crisis*. Working Paper 12. Brussels: ETUI

Clauwaert S. Schömann I. (2012). *The Crisis and National Labour Law Reforms: A Mapping Exercise*. Working Paper 04. Brussels: ETUI.

Clérico L. (2018). Proportionality in Social Rights Adjudication: Making It Workable. In: Duarte D., Sampaio J. S. (eds.), *Proportionality in Law*. Berlin: Springer, 25 ff.

Collins H., Lester G., Mantouvalou V. (eds.), (2018). *Philosophical Foundations of Labour Law*. Oxford: Oxford University Press, 122 ff.

Colombo S., Regalia I. (2016). Changing Joint Regulation and Labour Market Policy in Italy during the Crisis: On the Edge of a Paradigm Shift? *European Journal of Industrial Relations*, 22(3): 295 ff.

Comella V. F. (2004). The European Model of Constitutional Review of Legislation: Toward Decentralization? *International Journal of Constitutional Law*, 2(3): 461 ff.

Contiades X., Fotiadou A. (2012). Social Rights in the Age of Proportionality: Global Economic Crisis and Constitutional Litigation. *International Journal of Constitutional Law*, 10(3): 660 ff.

Contiades X., Fotiadou A. (2014). Socio-Economic Rights, Economic Crisis, and Legal Doctrine: A Reply to David Bilchitz. *International Journal of Constitutional Law*, 12(3): 740 ff.

Costa P. (1997). All'origine dei diritti sociali: "Arbeitender Staat" e tradizione solidaristica. In: Gozzi G. (ed.), *Democrazia, diritti, costituzione. I fondamenti costituzionali delle democrazie contemporanee*. Bologna: Il Mulino, 277 ff.

Countouris N., Freedland M. (2013). *Resocialising Europe in a Time of Crisis*. Cambridge: Cambridge University Press.

Countouris N. (2020). The Narrowing Constitution: European Constitutionalism, the Social Market Economy, and the Principle of Accommodation. In: Bogg A., Rwobottom J., Young A. L. (eds.), *The Constitution of Social Democracy: Essays in Honour of Keith Ewing*. Oxford and Portland: Hart Publishing, 357 ff.

Craig P. P. (2013). The Nature of Reasonableness Review. *Oxford Legal Studies Research Paper*, 78: 1 ff.

Cruces Aguilera J., Lago Peñas J. M., Moreno Preciado R., Rocha Sánchez F., Sanz Berzal E. (2016). *El Impacto de la Reforma Laboral de 2012 en la Negociación Colectiva* [2013–2015]. Confederación Sindical de CCOO. Available at: https://www.ccoo.es/1981389654947ddbb89316fc085d6669000001.pdf (last access: 15 February 2023).

Cruz Villalón J. (1989). Formación y evolución de los derechos fundamentales. *Revista Española de Derecho Constitucional*, 9(25): 35 ff.

Cruz Villalón J. (2012). El descuelgue de condiciones pactadas en convenio colectivo tras la reforma de 2012. In: Baylos Grau A. (ed.), *Politicas de Austeridad y Crisis en las Relaciones Laborales: la Reforma del 2012*. Albacete: Bomarzo Editorial.

Cruz Villalón J. (2015). Interrogantes y equívocos de la jurisprudencia constitucional, sobre la reforma laboral de 2012. *Derecho de las relaciones laborales*, 3: 304 ff.

Cruz Villalón J. (2016). La nuova disciplina della contrattazione collettiva in Spagna: Verso una flessibilità senza consenso. *Giornale di diritto del lavoro e di relazioni industriali*, 149: 35 ff.

D'Onghia M. (2013). *Diritti Previdenziali e Compatibilità Economiche nella Giurisprudenza Costituzionale*. Bari: Cacucci Editore.

D'Onghia M. (2015). Sostenibilità economica versus sostenibilità sociale. La Corte costituzionale, con la sentenza n. 70/2015, passa dalle parole (i moniti) ai fatti. *Rivista di Diritto della Sicurezza Sociale*, 2: 320 ff.

D'Onghia M. (2017). Welfare e vincoli economici nella più recente giurisprudenza costituzionale. *Lavoro e Diritto*, 1: 93 ff.

D'Onghia M. (2019). Retroattività e diritti previdenziali fra (presunta) intangibilità dei cd. diritti quesiti e solidarietà intergenerazionale. *Rivista del Diritto della Sicurezza Sociale*, 2: 275 ff.

Dalfino D. (2017). L' "incostituzionalità differita" dietro quella (asseritamente) "sopravvenuta" (a proposito di Corte cost. 178/2015). *Giornali di Diritto del Lavoro e di Relazioni Industriali*. 153: 168 ff.

Davidov G. (2016). *A Purposive Approach to Labour Law*. Oxford: Oxford University Press.

Davidov G., Langille B. (2011). *The Idea of Labour Law*. Oxford: Oxford University Press.

Davies A. (2008). One Step Forward, Two Steps Back? The Viking and Laval Cases in the ECJ. *International Law Journal*, 37(2): 126 ff.

Dawkins C., Dawkins C. (2022). Disciplining the Notion of "Labour Rights as Human Rights". *Global Labour Journal*, 13(1): 2 ff.

Dawson M., Lynskey O., Muir E. (2019). What is the Added Value of the Concept of the "Essence" of EU Fundamental Rights? *German Law Journal*, 20: 763 ff.

De Angelis G. (2022). A New Role for the European Stability Mechanism in Post-COVID-19 EMU? Explaining the Failure of the Pandemic Crisis Support and Assessing Ways Forward. *International Journal of Political Economy*, 51(1): 18 ff.

De Búrca G. (1993). The Principle of Proportionality and its Application in EC Law. *Yearbook of European Law*, 13(1):105 ff.

De la Quadra-Salcedo Janini T. (2020). El Tribunal Constitucional español ante la crisis económica: La inexistencia de límites al legislador derivados del reconocimiento de derechos sociales en la CE. *Federalismi.it*, 13: 61 ff.

De Fazio F. (2021). Proportionality Test and Constitutional Social Rights. In: Sieckmann J.-R. (ed.), *Proportionality, Balancing, and Rights*. Berlin: Springer, 197 ff.

De Shutter O., Tulkens F. (2008). Rights in Conflict: The European Court of Human Rights as a Pragmatic Institution. In: Brems E. (ed.), *Conflicts between Fundamental Rights*. Cambridge: Intersentia, 169 ff.

De Stefano V. (2013). A Tale of Oversimplification and Deregulation: The Mainstream Approach to Labour Market Segmentation and the Recent Responses to the Crisis in European Countries. *WP CSDLE "Massimo D'Antona".INT* – 102.

De Val Tena A. L. (2014). La Constitucionalidad de la Reforma Laboral de 2012. Comentario a la STC 119/2014. *Foro, Nueva época*, 17(2): 437 ff.

de Vries S. A. (2013). Balancing Fundamental Rights with Economic Freedoms According to the European Court of Justice. *Utrecht Law Review*, 9(1): 169 ff.

De Vries S. A., Groussot X., Thor Petursson G. (2012). *Balancing Fundamental Rights with the EU Treaty Freedoms: The European Court of Justice as 'Tightrope' Walker*. The Hague: Eleven International Publishing.

De Witte B. (2009). Balancing of Economic Law and Human Rights by the European Court of Justice. In: Dupuy P. M., Petersmann E.-U., Francioni F. (eds.), *Human Rights in International Investment Law and Arbitration*. Oxford: Oxford University Press, 197 ff.

De Witte B., Beukers T. (2013). The Court of Justice Approves the Creation of the European Stability Mechanism Outside the EU Legal Order. *Common Market Law Review*, 50: 805 ff.

Del Punta R. (2019). Valori del diritto del lavoro ed economia di mercato. *WP CSDLE "Massimo D'Antona".IT* – 395.

Del Punta R. (ed.), (2022a). *Valori e tecniche nel diritto del lavoro*. Florence: Firenze University Press.

Del Punta R. (2022b). Introduzione. In: Del Punta R. (ed.), *Valori e tecniche nel diritto del lavoro*. Florence: Firenze University Press, 7 ff.

Del Punta R. (2022c). Diritto del lavoro e valori. In: Del Punta R. (ed.), *Valori e tecniche nel diritto del lavoro*. Florence: Firenze University Press, 21 ff.

Della Torre G. (2008). Libertà di coscienza e di religione. *Stato, Chiese e Pluralismo confessionale*, 4: 1 ff.

Di Gregorio L. (2002). L'identità strutturale tra il principio di ragionevolezza e il Verhältnismässigkeitsgrundsatz. In: La Torre M., Spadaro A. (eds.), *La ragionevolezza nel diritto*. Torino: Giappichelli, 237 ff.
Diaz Aznarte M. T. (2015). Cuando la crisis económica se convierte en un argumento jurídico. La jusriprudencia constitucional avala la reforma. *Derecho de las relaciones laborales*, 2: 195 ff.
Doorey D. J. (2017). Just Transitions Law: Putting Labour Law to Work on Climate Change. *Journal of Environmental Law and Practice*, 30(2): 201 ff.
Dorssemont F. (2014). Collective Action against Austerity Measures. In: Bruun N., Lorcher K., Scheomann I. (eds.), *The Economic and Financial Crisis and Collective Labour Law*. Oxford and Portland: Hart Publishing, 171 ff.
Dorssemont F., Lörcher K., Clauwaert K., Schmitt M. (eds.), (2019). *The Charter of Fundamental Rights of the European Union and the Employment Relation*. Dublin: Bloomsbury.
Dorssemont F., Lörcher K., Schoemann I. (eds.), (2013). *The European Convention on Human Rights and the Employment Relation*. Dublin: Bloomsbury.
Duarte D. (2018). Gains and Losses in Balancing Social Rights. In: Duarte D., Sampaio J. S. (eds.), *Proportionality in Law*. Berlin: Springer, 49 ff.
Duarte D. (2021). From Constitutional Discretion to the Positivist Weight Formula In: Sieckmann J. R. (ed.), *Proportionality, Balancing, and Rights Robert Alexy's Theory of Constitutional Rights*. Berlin: Springer, 11 ff.
Duarte D., Silva Sampaio J. (eds.), (2018). *Proportionality in Law: An Analytical Perspective*. Berlin: Springer.
Dukes R. (2014). *The Labour Constitution: The Enduring Idea of Labour Law*. Oxford: Oxford University Press.
Dworkin R. (1967). The Model of Rules. *University of Chicago Law Review*, 35(1): 14 ff.
Dworkin R. (1977). *Taking Rights Seriously*. Cambridge: Harvard University Press.
Eklund R. (2007–2008). A Swedish Prespective on Laval. *Comparative Labour Law & Policy Journal*, 29: 551 ff.
Emiliou N. (1996). *The Principle of Proportionality in European Law: A Comparative Study*. London: Kluwer Law International.
Ewing K. D. (2012). Economic Rights. In: Rosenfeld M., Sajó A. (eds.), *The Oxford Handbook of Comparative Constitutional Law*. Oxford: Oxford University Press, 1037 ff.
Ewing K. D. (2015). The Death of Social Europe. *King's Law Journal*, 26(1): 76 ff.
Ewing K. D., John Hendy Q. C. (2010). The Dramatic Implications of Demir and Baykara. *Industrial Law Journal*, 39(1): 2 ff.
Faraguna P. (2016). The Economic Crisis as a Threat to the Stability of Law Recent Developments in the Case Law of the Italian Constitutional Court. *The Hague Journal on the Rule of Law*, 8: 249 ff.
Fasone C. (2014). *Constitutional Courts Facing the Euro Crisis: Italy, Portugal and Spain in a Comparative Perspective*. EUI Working Paper, 25.
Fernández López M. F. (2015). El Derecho del Trabajo en la jursprudencia constitucional. *Derecho de las relaciones laborales*, 3: 248 ff.
Fernández Segado F. (1993). La teoría jurídica de los derechos fundamentales en la doctrina constitucional. *Revista española de derecho constitucional*, 13(39): 195 ff.
Ferrajoli L. (2001). *Diritti fondamentali. Un dibattito teorico*. Bologna: Laterza.

Ferrajoli L. (2010). Costituzionalismo principialista e costituzionalismo garantista. *Giurisprudenza costituzionale*, 55(3): 2771 ff.

Ferrante V. (2014). Diritto al giusto salario e lavoro pubblico, ovvero del fascino dell'antico. *Forum di Quaderni costituzionali*. Available at: https://www.forumcostituzionale.it/wordpress/images/stories/pdf/documenti_forum/giurisprudenza/2013/0037_nota_310_2013_ferrante.pdf (last access: 15 February 2023).

Fiorillo L. (2015). Contrattazione collettiva e lavoro pubblico: Una nuova interpretazione sistematica della Corte costituzionale. *Giurisprudenza Costituzionale*, 5: 1679 ff.

Fontana G. (2015). I giudici europei di fronte alla crisi economica. In: Caruso B., Fontana G. (eds.), *Lavoro e diritti sociali nella crisi europea*. Bologna: Il Mulino, 123 ff.

Fontana G. (2017). Le politiche di austerity e i diritti sociali fondamentali. *WP CSDLE "Massimo D'Antona".INT* – 140.

Fontana G. (2022). Il diritto del lavoro e i valori nella crisi. In: Del Punta R. (ed.), *Valori e tecniche nel diritto del lavoro*. Florence: Firenze University Press, 81 ff.

Frosecchi G. (2016). The Supremacy of the Right to Collective Bargaining: A Judgment of the Italian Constitutional Court on Austerity Measures. *International Labour Rights Case Law Journal*, 2: 313 ff.

Frosecchi G. (2019). European Social Charter in the Constitutional Review of National Laws: The Decisive Application of Art. 24 by the Italian Constitutional Court. *International Labour Rights Case Law Journal*, 5: 182 ff.

Frosecchi G. (2022). L'esercizio della libertà religiosa nuovamente alla prova della neutralità aziendale: Un percorso a ostacoli tra discriminazione diretta, discriminazione indiretta e bilanciamento dei diritti. *LABOR. Il lavoro nel diritto*, 1: 81 ff.

Frosecchi G., Orlandini G. (2020). An Internationally Oriented Interpretation of EU Law on Public Procurement: Strengthening Labour Clauses Through ILO Convention No. 94. *WP C.S.D.L.E. "Massimo D'Antona".INT* – 153.

Fudge J. (2015). Constitutionalizing Labour Rights in Canada and Europe: Freedom of Association, Collective Bargaining, and Strikes. *Current Legal Problems*, 68(1): 267 ff.

Gaeta L. (ed.), (2003). *Costantino Mortati e il "Lavoro nella Costituzione": Una rilettura*. Milano: Giuffrè.

Gallo D., Cisotta R. (2014). The Portuguese Constitutional Court Case Law on Austerity Measures: A Reappraisal. In: Kilpatrick C., De Witte B. (eds.), *Social Rights in Times of Crisis in the Eurozone: The Role of Fundamental Rights' Challenges*. EUI Law Department Research Paper, 05.

Garben S. (2020). Balancing Social and Economic Fundamental Rights in the EU Legal Order. *European Labour Law Journal*, 11(4): 364 ff.

Garben S., Kilpatrick C., Muir E. (2017). Towards a European Pillar of Social Rights: Upgrading the EU Social Acquis. *College of Europe Policy Brief*, 1: 1 ff.

Garcia Blasco J. (2012). La Contratacion Laboral en la Reforma Legal de 2012: Entre el estimulo de la Contratacion Indefinida y la Preocupacion por el Empleo. *Documentación Laboral*, 95–96: 7 ff.

García Murcia J. (2015). La reforma laboral de 2012 ante el Tribunal Constitucional. *Derecho de las relaciones laborales*, 3: 283 ff.

Gardbaum S. (2010). A Democratic Defense of Constitutional Balancing. *Law & Ethics of Human Rights*, 4(1): 79 ff.

Gerards J. (2013). How to Improve the Necessity Test of the European Court of Human Rights. *International Journal of Constitutional Law*, 11(2): 466 ff.

Gerstenberg O. (2019). *Euroconstitutionalism and Its Discontents*. Oxford: Oxford University Press.

Gertensberg O. (2020). Fundamental Rights and Democratic Sovereignty in the EU: The Role of the Charter of Fundamental Rights of the EU (CFREU) in Regulating the European Social Market Economy. *Yearbook of European Law*, 39(1): 199 ff.

Ghera F. (2003). *Il principio di eguaglianza nella Costituzione italiana e nel diritto comunitario*. Padova: CEDAM.

Ghera E. (2022). Le tre sentenze della Corte costituzionale sul regime sanzionatorio del licenziamento illegittimo. Interrogativi e prospettive. *Rivista Italiana di Diritto del Lavoro*, 1(I): 3ff.

Gil y Gil J. L. (2014). Strengthening the Power of Dismissal in Recent Labor Reforms in Spain. *Comparative Labour Law and Policy Journal*, 35: 413 ff.

Giubboni S. (2006). Il primo dei diritti sociali. Riflessioni sul diritto al lavoro tra Costituzione italiana e ordinamento europeo. *WP CSDLE "Massimo D'Antona". INT* – 46.

Giubboni S. (2013). Cittadinanza, lavoro e diritti sociali nella crisi europea. *WP CSDLE "Massimo D'Antona".INT* – 100/2013.

Giubboni S. (2015a). La perequazione automatica delle pensioni tra legislatore e giudice costituzionale. *Politiche Sociali*, 3: 523 ff.

Giubboni S. (2015b). Profili costituzionali del contratto di lavoro a tutele crescenti. *WP CSDLE "Massimo D'Antona".IT* – 246.

Giubboni S. (2016). Il diritto del lavoro nella crisi europea (a proposito di un recente volume). *WP CSDLE "Massimo D'Antona".INT* – 126.

Giubboni S. (2017). *Diritto del Lavoro europeo. Una introduzione critica*. Padova: CEDAM.

Giubboni S. (2018). Il licenziamento del lavoratore con contratto «a tutele crescenti» dopo l'intervento della Corte costituzionale. *WP CSDLE "Massimo D'Antona". IT* – 379.

Giubboni S. (2022). *Solidarietà. Un itinerario di ricerca*. Napoli: Editoriale Scientifica.

Giubboni S., Lo Faro A. (2013). Crisi finanziaria, governance economica europea e riforme nazionali del lavoro: Quale connessione? In: Aa. Vv. (ed.), *Nuove regole dopo la legge 92/2012 di riforma del mercato del lavoro, competizione versus-garanzie?* Torino: Giappichelli, 41 ff.

Giubboni S., Orlandini G. (2018). Dentro la Crisi. Spunti Comparati sull'Impatto delle «Riforme Strutturali» nel Diritto del Lavoro in Italia, Portogallo e Spagna. *Rivista Giuridica del Lavoro e della Previdenza Sociale*, 4: 643 ff.

Gluckman, M. (1963). *Order and Rebellion in Tribal Africa*. New York: Free Press.

Goig Martínez J. M. (2016). La crisis económica y el principio de «adecuación a las decisiones políticas» como nuevo canon de constitucionalidad. Límites a la interpretación constitucional. *Anuario Iberoamericano de Justicia Constitucional*, 20: 117 ff.

Gómez Garrido L. M. (2015). Los pronunciamentos del Tribunal Constitutcional en Tiempo de Crisis. *Nueva Revista Española de Derecho del Trabajo*, 178: 101 ff.

Gómez-Millán Herencia M. J. (2012). Crisis económica y reformas en materia de empleo: objerivos e instrumentos utilizados para la activación del mercado laboral, la igualdad de oportinidades y la flexibilidad interna de las empresas. *Temas laborales: Revista andaluza de trabajo y bienestar social*, 114: 79 ff.

González Beilfuss M. (2015). *El Principio de Proporcionalidad en la Jurisprudencia del Tribunal Constitucional.* Madrid: Aranzadi.
González Pascual M. (2014). Welfare Rights and Euro Crisis - The Spanish Case. In: Kilpatrick C., De Witte B. (eds.), *Social Rights in Times of Crisis in the Eurozone: The Role of Fundamental Rights' Challenges.* EUI Department of Law Research Paper, 05.
Grandi M. (2006). Lavoro e valori: Note sulla prospettiva assiologica di Luigi Mengoni. *Jus*, II/III: 359 ff.
Grimm D. (2007). Proportionality in Canadian and German Constitutional Jurisprudence. *The University of Toronto Law Journal*, 57(2): 383 ff.
Grimm D. (2019). Constitutionalisation without Constitution: A Democracy Problem. In: Barber N. W., Cahill M., Ekins R. (eds.), *The Rise and Fall of the European Constitution.* Oxford and Portland: Hart Publishing, 23 ff.
Guarriello F. (2016). Crisi economica, contrattazione collettiva e ruolo della legge. *Giornale di Diritto del Lavoro e di Relazioni Industriali*, 149: 3 ff.
Guastini R. (2010). Le fonti de diritto. Fondamenti teorici. In: Schlesinger P. (ed.), *Trattato di diritto civile e commerciale.* Milano: Giuffrè.
Guazzarotti A. (2013). Giustizia costituzionale e regime economico: Fluidificare o resistere? *Lavoro e Diritto*, XXXII(1): 55 ff.
Guazzarotti A. (2018). Giustizia costituzionale e regime economico: Fluidificare o resistere? *Lavoro e Diritto*, XXXII(1): 55 ff.
Guazzarotti M. (2013). Crisi economica e ruolo delle Corti: Quali contrappesi alla governance europea e internazionale? *Diritto pubblico*, 3: 1011 ff.
Guiglia G. (2016). La Corte costituzionale e l'adeguatezza delle pensioni al tempo della crisi. *Federalismi.it* – 18, 1 ff.
Gutiérrez-Fons J. A. (2021). The Margin of Appreciation in the Case Law of the Court of Justice: Proportionality and Levels of Fundamental Rights Protection. In: Izquierdo-Sans C., Martínez-Capdevila C., Nogueira-Guastavino M. (eds.), *Fundamental Rights Challenges.* Berlin: Springer, 231 ff.
Habermas J. (1989–90). Justice and Solidarity: On the Discussion Concerning Stage 6. *The Philosophical Forum*, XXI(1–2): 32 ff.
Habermas J. (1996). *Between Facts and Norms: Contributions to a Discourse Theory of Law and Democracy.* Cambridge: Polity Press.
Habermas J. (2022). *Proteggere la vita. I diritti fondamentali alla prova della pandemia.* Bologna: Il Mulino.
Harbo T.-I. (2010). The Function of the Proportionality Principle in EU Law. *European Law Journal*, 16(2): 158 ff.
Hartzén A.-C., Iossa A., Karageorgiou E. (2022). *Law, Solidarity and the Limits of Social Europe. Constitutional Tensions for EU Integration.* Cheltenham: Edward Elgar.
Hickman T. R. (2004). The Reasonableness Principle: Reassessing Its Place in the Public Sphere. *The Cambridge Law Journal*, 63(1): 166 ff.
Horwitz L., Myant M. (2012). *Spain's Labour Market Reforms: The Road to Employment – Or to Unemployment?* Working Paper 30. Brusells: ETUI.
Ichino P. (2015). *Il lavoro ritrovato.* Milano: Mondadori.
Ichino P. (2018). Il rapporto tra il danno prodotto dal licenziamento e l'indennizzo nella sentenza della consulta. *Rivista Italiana di Diritto del Lavoro*, 4: 1050 ff.
Izquierdo-Sans C., Martínez-Capdevila C. and Nogueira-Guastavino M. (eds.), (2021). *Fundamental Rights Challenges.* Berlin: Springer.

Jacobs F. G. (1999). Recent Developments in the Principle of Proportionality in EC Law. In: Ellies E. (ed.), *The Principle of Proportionality in the Laws of Europe*. Dublin: Bloomsbury, 1 ff.

Jestaedt M. (2012). The Doctrine of Balancing – Its Strengths and Weaknesses. In: Klatt M. (ed.), *Institutionalized Reason: The Jurisprudence of Robert Alexy*. Oxford: Oxford University Press, 152 ff.

Juan Moreso J. (2012). Ways of Solving Conflicts of Constitutional Rights: Proportionalism and Specificationism. *Ratio Juris*, 25(1): 31 ff.

Jung C., Hirschl R., Rosevear E. (2014). Economic and Social Rights in National Constitutions. *The American Journal of Comparative Law*, 62(4): 1043 ff.

Kahn-Freund O. (1974). On Uses and Misuses of Comparative Law. *The Modern Law Review*, 37(1): 1 ff.

Katsaroumpas I. (2018). De-Constitutionalising Collective Labour Rights: The Case of Greece. *Industrial Law Journal*, 47(4): 465 ff.

Khosal M. (2010). Proportionality: An Assault on Human Rights? A Reply. *International Journal of Constitutional Law*, 8(2): 298 ff.

Kilpatrick C. (2015). *Constitutions, Social Rights and Sovereign Debt States in Europe: A Challenging New Area of Constitutional Inquiry*. EUI Working Paper, 34.

Kilpatrick C. (2018). The Displacement of Social Europe: A Productive Lens of Inquiry. *European Constitutional Law Review*, 14(1): 62 ff.

Kilpatrick C., De Witte B. (eds.), (2014). *Social Rights in Times of Crisis in the Eurozone: The Role of Fundamental Rights' Challenges*. EUI Department of Law Research Paper, 05.

King J. (2012). *Judging Social Rights*. Cambridge: Cambridge University Press.

Korda M., Schoukens P. (2006). The EU Constitution: What Went Wrong for 'Social Protection'? *European Journal of Social Security*, 8(1): 7 ff.

Kott S., Droux J. (eds.), (2013). *Globalizing Social Rights: The International Labour Organization and Beyond*. Geneve: ILO.

Kumm M. (2004). Constitutional Rights as Principles: On the Structure and Domain of Constitutional Justice. *International Journal of Constitutional Law*, 2(3): 574 ff.

Künkler M., Stein T. (2017). *Böckenförde, E-W. Constitutional and Political Theory: Selected Writings*. Vol. 1. Oxford: Oxford University Press.

Laforgia S. (2018). *Diritti fondamentali dei lavoratori e tecniche di tutela. Discorso sulla dignità sociale*. Napoli: Edizioni Scientifiche Italiane.

Lenaerts K. (2019). Limits on Limitations: The Essence of Fundamental Rights in the EU. *German Law Journal*, 20: 779 ff.

Langford M. (2008). The Justiciability of Social Rights: From Practice to Theory. In: Langford M. (ed.), *Social Rights Jurisprudence*. Cambridge: Cambridge University Press, 3 ff.

Lassandari A. (2015). L'ordinamento perduto. *Lavoro e Diritto*, 1: 63 ff.

Leccese V. (2012). Il diritto sindacale al tempo della crisi. Intervento eteronomo e profili di legittimità costituzionale. *Giornale di Diritto del Lavoro e di Relazioni Industrili*, 136: 479 ff.

Leschke J. (2012). *Has the Economic Crisis Contributed to More Segmentation in Labour Market and Welfare Outcomes?* Working Paper 02. Brussels: ETUI.

Lieto S. (2015). Trattare in modo eguale i diseguali? Nota alla sentenza n. 70/2015. *Forum dei Quaderni Costituzionali*: 1 ff. Available at https://www.forumcostituzionale.it/wordpress/wp-content/uploads/2015/05/lieto-sent.70-2015.pdf (last access: 15 February 2023).

Lipari N. (2010). Diritti fondamentali e ruolo del giudice. *Rivista di Diritto Civile*, 5: 635 ff.

Lipari N. (2016). Intorno ai "principi generali del diritto". *Rivista di Diritto Civile*, 1: 28 ff.

Lo Faro A. (2014a). Fundamental Rights Challenges to Italian Labour Law Developments in the Time of Economic Crisis: An Overview. In: Kilpatrick C. De Witte B. (eds.), *Social Rights in Times of Crisis in the Eurozone: The Role of Fundamental Rights' Challenges*. EUI Department of Law Research Paper, 05.

Lo Faro A. (2014b). Compatibilità economiche, diritti del lavoro e istanze di tutela dei diritti fondamentali: Qualche spunto di riflessione dal caso italiano. *Giornale di Diritto del Lavoro e di Relazioni Industriali*, 142(2): 279 ff.

Lock, T. (2020). The Future of EU Human Rights Law: Is Accession to the ECHR Still Desirable? *Journal of International and Comparative Law*, 7(2): 427 ff.

Loi P. (2011). The Reasonableness Principle in the European Court of Justice Age Discrimination Cases. In: Moreau M.-A. (ed.), *Before and After the Economic Crisis What Implications for the 'European Social Model'*? Cheltenham: Edward Elgar, 141 ff.

Loi P. (2016). *Il principio di ragionevolezza e proporzionalità nel diritto del lavoro*. Torino: Giappichelli.

Longo E. (2017). I diritti sociali nella Costituzione italiana: Un percorso di analisi. *Rivista di Diritto della Sicurezza Sociale*, XVII(2): 202 ff.

Losurdo F. (2016). *Lo Stato sociale condizionato. Stabilità e crescita nell'ordinamento*. Torino: Giappichelli.

Lourenço L. (2019). Religion, Discrimination and the EU General Principles' Gospel: Egenberger. *Common Market Law Review*, 56(1): 193 ff.

Luciani M. (1994). Lo spazio della ragionevolezza nel giudizio costituzionale. In: *Il principio di ragionevolezza nella giurisprudenza della Corte costituzionale*. Atti del seminario svoltosi in Roma, Palazzo della Consulta, 13–14 ottobre 1992, Milano: Giuffré, 246 ff.

Luciani M. (1995). *Sui diritti sociali*. In: Aa. Vv (ed.), *Scritti in onore di Manlio Mazziotti di Celso*. Padova: CEDAM, 101 ff.

Luciani M. (2011). *Unità nazionale e struttura economica. La prospettiva della Costituzione repubblicana*, presented at: Convegno annuale AIC su Costituzionalismo e Costituzione, 28 October 2011, Torino.

Luciani M. (2016). Diritti sociali e livelli essenziali delle prestazioni pubbliche nei sessant'anni della Corte Costituzionale. *Rivista Associazione Italiana dei Costituzionalisti*, 3: 1 ff.

Lyon-Caen G. (1991). *Le droit du travail non salarié*. Paris: Edition Sirey.

Maccormick N. (1978). *Legal Reasoning and Legal Theory*. Oxford: Oxford University Press.

Madau L. (2015). L'incidenza del nuovo Articolo 81 Cost. sui giudizi di legittimità costituzionale: Prime osservazioni. *Contabilità-pubblica.it*. Available at http://www.contabilita-pubblica.it/Dottrina2015/3.Madau1.pdf (last access: 15 February 2023).

Maduro M. (1999). Striking the Elusive Balance between Economic Freedom and Social Rights in the European Union. In: Alston P., Cassese A., Lalumière C., Leuprecht P. (eds.), *An EU Human Rights Agenda for the New Millennium*. Oxford: Hart Publishing, 449 ff.

Maio V. (2022). Valori e tecniche nell'assetto dei licenziamenti ergente dopo la sentenza della Corte Costituzionale n. 194 del 2018. In: Del Punta R. (ed.), *Valori e tecniche nel diritto del lavoro*. Florence: Firenze University Press, 201 ff.

Magnani M. (2019). Il "Jobs Act" e la Corte costituzionale. Riflessioni su Corte cost. n. 194/2018. *Diritto delle Relazioni Industriali*, 2: 1 ff.

Mancini M. (2013). Le prestazioni di fine servizio dei dipendenti pubblici alla luce della sentenza della Corte costituzionale n. 223/2012. *Rivista del Diritto della Sicurezza Sociale*, 2: 379 ff.

Maniaci G. (2007). Quale razionalità per risolvere i conflitti tra diritti? *Ragion Pratica*, 2: 339 ff.

Mantouvalou V. (2012). Are Labour Rights Human Rights?. *European Labour Law Journal*, 3(2): 151 ff.

Mantouvalou V. (2013). Labour rights in the European Convention on Human Rights: An Intellectual Justification for an Integrated Approach to Interpretation. *Human Rights Law Review*, 13(3): 529 ff.

Maresca A. (2019). Licenziamento ingiustificato e indennizzo del lavoratore dopo la sentenza della Corte costituzionale n. 194/2018 (alla ricerca della norma che non c'è). *Diritto delle Relazioni Industriali*, 1: 228 ff.

Mariucci L. (2015). Il diritto del lavoro al tempo del renzismo. *Lavoro e Diritto*, 1: 13 ff.

Marshall S. (2014). Shifting Responsibility: How the Burden of the European Financial Crisis Shifted Away from the Financial Sector and onto Labour. *Cmparative Labour Law and Policy Journal*, 35: 449 ff.

Martín y Pérez de Nanclares J. (2019). La Unión Europea como comunidad de valores: A vueltas con la crisis de la democracia y del Estado de Derecho. *Teoría y realidad constitucional*, 43: 121 ff.

Martìnez Pujalte A. L. (1997). *La garantìa del contenudo esencial de los derechos fundamentals*. Madrid: CEC.

Marx K. (1974). *Il 18 Brumaio di Luigi Bonaparte*. Roma: Editori Riuniti.

Masala P. (2017). La giurisprudenza del Tribunale costituzionale spagnolo sul "nuovo diritto del lavoro": due modelli di giudizio alternativi di fronte alle riforme "flessibilizzatrici" in Europa. *DPCE Online*, 2: 517 ff.

Massa M. (2017). Discrezionalità, sostenibilità, responsabilità nella giurisprudenza costituzionale sui diritti sociali. *Quaderni Costituzionali*, 1: 73 ff.

Mazzù C. (2008). *Compatibilità economica e società pluralista*. Milano: Giuffrè Editore.

McBride J. (1999). Proportionality and the European Convention on Human Rights. In: Ellies E. (ed.), *The Principle of Proportionality in the Laws of Europe*. Dublin: Bloomsbury, 24 ff.

Medina Guerrero M. (1996). *La vinculación negativa del legislador a los derechos fundamentales*. Madrid: McGraw-Hill Interamericana de España.

Medina Guerrero M. (1998). El principio de proporcionalidad y el legislador de los derechos fundamentales. *Cuaderno de Derecho Publico*, 5: 119 ff.

Medina Guerrero M. (2008). Articulo 53.1. La eficacia vinculante de los derechos frente a los poderes pùblicos; en especial, frente al legislador. In: Casas Baamonde M. E., Rodriguez-Pinero y Bravo-Ferrer M. (eds.), *Comentarios a la Constitucion espanola*. Alphen aan den Rijn: Wolters Kluwer, 1456 ff.

Medina Guerrero M. (2012). La reforma del artículo 135 Ce. *Teoría y Realidad Constitucional*, 29: 131 ff.

Meilán Delgado S. (2016). La comisión consultiva nacional de convenios colectivos en la inaplicación de condiciones de trabajo de convenios colectivos. *Revista de información laboral*, 2: 57 ff.

Mengoni L. (1986). Spunti per una teoria delle clausole generali. (Originally in *Rivista Critica di Diritto Privato)*. In: Castronovo C., Albanese A., Nicolussi A. (eds.), (2011). *Scritti I. Metodo e teoria giuridica*. Milano: Giuffrè, 165 ff.

Mengoni L. (1992). I principi generali del diritto e la scienza giuridica. (Originally in Scritti in onore di Renato Scognamiglio, 1992, Roma, 317–328). In: Castronovo C., Albanese A., Nicolussi A. (eds.), (2011) *Scritti I. Metodo e teoria giuridica*. Milano: Giuffrè, 239 ff.

Mengoni L. (1993). Per una dogmatica dei diritti fondamentali. (Originally in Giornate in onore di Angelo Falzea, Milano 1993). In: Castronovo C., Albanese A., Nicolussi A. (eds.), (2011) *Scritti I. Metodo e teoria giuridica*. Milano: Giuffrè, 255 ff.

Mengoni L. (1996a). *L'argomentazione nel diritto costituzionale*. In: *Ermeneutica e Dogmatica Giuridica. Saggi*. Milano: Giuffrè.

Mengoni L. (1996b). *Ermeneutica e dogmatica giuridica*. Milano: Giuffré.

Mengoni L. (1998). Fondata sul lavoro: La Repubblica fra diritti inviolabili dell'uomo e doveri inderogabili di solidarietà. In: Napoli M. (ed.), *Costituzione, lavoro, pluralismo sociale*. Roma: Vita e Pensiero, 7 ff.

Menéndez Menéndez A. J. (2012). La mutación constitucional de la Unión Europea. *Revista Espanola de Derecho Constitutional*, 96: 41 ff.

Merino Segovia A. (2012). La reforma de la negociación colectiva en el RDL 3/2012: Las atribuciones al convenio de empresa y novedades en la duración y vigencia de los convenios colectivos. *Revista de Derecho Social (monográfico sobre La reforma laboral)*, 57: 249 ff.

Messineo D. (2010). *Garanzia del Contenuto Essenziale e Tutela Multilivello dei Diritti Fondamentali*. Macerata: Edizioni Simple.

Mezzanotte C. (2014). *Corte costituzionale e legittimazione politica*. Napoli: Editoriale Scientifica.

Mezzetti L. (2010). Legittimazione democratica e tecniche interpretative della Corte Costituzionale italiana. *Pensamiento Constitucional*, 14(4): 69 ff.

Miani Canevari F. (2015). Giurisprudenza costituzionale 2014–2015 sulla sicurezza sociale. *Rivista del Diritto della Sicurezza Sociale*, XV(3): 594 ff.

Miriello C. (2014). La sentenza n. 310 del 2013 della Corte costituzionale e l'adeguamento retributivo dei docenti universitari: *Quantum mutatus ab illo*! *Forum di Quaderni Costituzionali*. Available at: https://www.forumcostituzionale.it/wordpress/images/stories/pdf/documenti_forum/giurisprudenza/2013/0045_nota_310_2013_miriello.pdf (last access: 15 February 2023).

Mocchegiani M. (2015). La tecnica decisoria della sentenza 178 del 2015: Dubbi e perplessità. *Forum di Quaderni costituzionali*. Available at: https://www.forumcostituzionale.it/wordpress/wp-content/uploads/2015/10/nota_178_2015_mocchegiani.pdf (last access: 15 February 2023).

Modugno F. (1982). Corte costituzionale e potere legislativo. In: Barile P., Cheli E., Grassi S. (eds.), *Corte costituzionale e sviluppo della forma di governo in Italia*. Bologna: Il Mulino.

Modugno F. (2007). *La ragionevolezza nella giustizia costituzionale*. Napoli: Editoriale Scientifica.

Modugno F. (2008). *Scritti sull'interpretazione costituzionale*. Napoli: Editoriale Scientifica.
Montoya Melgar A. (2011). Introducción: Crisis económica y reforma laboral. In: Montoya Melgar A., Cavas Martínez F. (eds.), *Comentario a la reforma laboral de 2010. Ley 35/2010, de 17 de septiembre, de medidas urgentes para la reforma del mercado de trabajo*. Navarra: Aranzadi.
Morelli A. (2015). La Corte nel gioco dei bilanciamenti. *Quaderni Costituzionali*, 3: 707 ff.
Moreno Fernández L. (2013). *La Europa asocial. Crisis y Estado del bienestar*. Barcelona: Ediciones Península.
Moreno Vida M. N. (2013). La Reforma de la Contratación Laboral: De Nuevo el Fomento del Empleo a Través de la Precariedad. *Revista General de Derecho del Trabajo y de la Seguridad Social*, 34.
Morrone A. (2001). *Il custode della ragionevolezza*. Milano: Giuffrè.
Morrone A. (2002). Principio di ragionevolezza e definizione di "Diritto". In: La Torre M., Spadaro A. (eds.), *La ragionevolezza nel diritto*. Torino: Giappichelli.
Morrone A. (2014). Pareggio di Bilancio e Stato Costituzionale. *Rivista Telematica Giuridica dell'Associazione Italiana dei Costituzionalisti*, 1 Available at: https://www.rivistaaic.it/images/rivista/pdf/1_2014_Morrone.pdf (last access: 15 February 2023).
Morrone A. (2015a). Ragionevolezza a rovescio: L'ingiustizia della sentenza n. 70/2015 della Corte costituzionale. *Federalismi.it* – 10, 1 ff.
Morrone A. (2015b). Le conseguenze finanziarie della giustizia costituzionale. *Quaderni costituzionali*, 3: 575 ff.
Mortati C. (1970). Appunti per uno studio sui rimedi giurisdizionali contro comportamenti omissivi del legislatore. Il Foro Italiano, 93(9): 153 ff.
Mortati C. (1998). *La Costituzione in senso materiale*. Milano: Giuffré.
Moscarini A. (1996). *Ratio legis e valutazioni di ragionevolezza della legge*. Torino: Giappichelli.
Naômé C. (2008). EU enlargement and the European court of Justice. In: Best E., Christiansen T., Settembri P. (eds.), *The Institutions of the Enlarged European Union: Continuity and Change*. Cheltenham: Edward Elgar, 100 ff.
Navarro Nieto F. (2013). El Régimen de Inaplicación y Modificación de Convenios Colectivos. *Temas Laborales*, 120: 233 ff.
Nimmer M. (1968). The Right to Speak from Times to Time: First Amendment Theory Applied to Libel and Misapplied to Privacy. *Californian Law Review*, 56: 935 ff.
Nogler L. (2006). L'itinerario metodologico di Luigi Mengoni. *WP C.S.D.L.E. "Massimo D'Antona".IT* – 47.
Nogler L. (2009). Cosa significa l'Italia e una Repubblica "fondata sul lavoro"? *Lavoro e Diritto*, XXIII(3): 427 ff.
Nogler L. (2015). I licenziamenti per giustificato motivo soggettivo o per giusta causa nel d.lgs. 23 del 2015. *Argomenti di Diritto del Lavoro*, 3: 507 ff.
Nogler L. (2020). Dal principio lavorista al diritto costituzionale sull'attività umana: primo abbozzo. Della Morte M., De Martino F.R., Ronchetti L. (eds.), *L'attualità dei principi fondamentali della Costituzione dopo settant'anni*. Bologna: Il Mulino, 145 ff.
Occhino A. (2017). I diritti sociali nell'interpretazione costituzionale. *Rivista del Diritto della Sicurezza Sociale*, 1: 3 ff.

Ojeda Avilés A. (2013). The Primacy of Company-Level Agreements in Spain: An Unusual Approach for Continental Europe. *E-Journal of International and Comparative Labour Studies*, 2(2): 1 ff.

Onida V. (1993). Giudizio di costituzionalità delle leggi e responsabilità finanziaria del Parlamento. In: Aa. Vv., *Le Sentenze della Corte Costituzionale e l'Art. 81, U.C., della Costituzione. Atti del Seminario. Roma, 8–9 novembre 1991*. Milano: Giuffrè, 19 ff.

Orlandini G. (2008). Trade Union Rights and Market Freedoms: The European Court of Justice Sets Out the Rules. *Comparativ Labour Law & Policy Journal*, 29: 573 ff.

Orlandini G. (2013). *Mercato unico dei servizi e tutela del lavoro*. Milano: Franco Angeli Editore.

Orlandini G. (2018). Libertà di circolazione e dimensione sociale europea: Storia di un'integrazione mancata. *Rivista del Diritto della Sicurezza Sociale*, 4: 655 ff.

Orlandini G. (2019). Il licenziamento dopo la sentenza della Corte costituzionale n. 194/18, tra vincoli costituzionali e fonti internazionali: la partita resta aperta. *Lavoro Diritti Europa*, 1: n.p..

Paladin L. (1992). Esiste un "principio di ragionevolezza" nella giurisprudenza costituzionale? In: *Il principio di ragionevolezza*. Milano: Enciclopedia del Diritto, Aggiornamento, I.

Palombella G. (2015). Principles and Disagreements in International Law (with a View from Dworkin's Legal Theory). In: Pineschi L. (ed.), *General Principles of Law – The Role of the Judiciary*. Berlin: Springer, 3 ff.

Palomeque López M. C. (1983). El derecho constitucional de igualidad en las relaciones de trabajo. *Documentacion Laboral*: 8, 7 ff.

Palomeque López M. C. (1991). *Los derechos laborales en la Constitución Española*. Madrid: Centro de Estudios Políticos y Constitucionales.

Palomeque López M. C. (2004). Un compañero de viaje histórico del Derecho del Trabajo: la crisis económica. In: *Derecho del Trabajo y Razón Critica: libro dedicado al profesor Manuel Carlos Palomeque López en su vigésimo aniversario como catedrático*. Salamanca: Caja Duero, 29 ff.

Palomeque López M. C., Alvarez de la Rosa M. (2014). *Derecho del Trabajo*. Madrid: Universitaria Ramon Areces. 22nd Edition.

Parejo Alfonso L. (1981). El contenido esencial de los derechos fundamentales el la jurisprudencia constitucional; a proposito de la sentencia del Tribunal Constitucional de 8 Abril de 1981. *Revista Espanola de Derecho Constitucional*, 1(3): 169 ff.

Paul Jacqué J. (2011). The Accession of the European union to the European Convention on Human Rights and Fundamental Freedoms. *Common Market Law Review*, 48: 995 ff.

Pedullà L. (2016). Le "pensioni d'oro" quale paradigma del difficile bilanciamento tra diritti di prestazione sociale ed equilibrio economico-finanziario. *Forum dei Quaderni Costituzionali*. Available at: https://www.forumcostituzionale.it/wordpress/wp-content/uploads/2016/01/nota_173_2016_pedulla.pdf (last access: 15 February 2023).

Pennacchi L. (2018). *De valoribus disputandum est. Sui valori dopo il neoliberismo*. Milano: Mimesis Edizioni.

Pepe I. (2017). Costituzionalmente legittimi gli interventi sulle pensioni d'oro per il triennio 2014/2016. *Il lavoro nella giurisprudenza*, 1: 37 ff.

Pereira Sáez C. (2004). Una contribución al estudio del empleo del principio de proporcionalidad en la jurisprudencia reciente del Tribunal Constitucional Español. *Anuario da Facultade de Dereito da Universidade da Coruña*, 8: 1043 ff.

Perello Domenech I. (1997). El principio de proporcionalidad y la jurisprudencia constitucional. *Jueces para la democracia*, 28: 69 ff.

Perez F. (2014). La interpretacion de la Constitucion. *Nueva Revista Espanola de Derecho del Trabajo*, 169: 21 ff.

Pérez Rey J. (2012). Un Nuevo contrato Estrella: La modalidad contractual de apoyo a los emprendedores. In: Baylos Grau A. (ed.), *Politicas de Austeridad y Crisis en las Relaciones Laborales: la Reforma del 2012*. Albacete: Bomarzo Editorial, 75 ff.

Pérez-Luno A. E. (2017). *DDHH, Estado y Constitucion*. Madrid: Editorial Tecnos.

Persiani M. (2017). Sulla garanzia costituzionale dei mezzi adeguati alle esigenze di vita. *Giornale di Diritto del Lavoro e di Relazioni Industriali*, 154: 281 ff.

Perulli A. (2005). Razionalità e proporzionalità nel diritto del lavoro. *Giornale di diritto del lavoro e di relazioni industriali*, 105: 1 ff.

Perulli A. (2015). Il contratto a tutele crescenti e la Naspi: Un mutamento di "paradigma" per il diritto del lavoro? In: Fiorillo L., Perulli A. (eds.), *Contratto a tutele crescenti e Naspi. Decreti legislativi 4 marzo 2015, n. 22 e n. 23*. Torino: Giappichelli Editore, 3 ff.

Perulli A. (2018). I valori del diritto e il diritto come valore. economia e assiologia nel diritto del lavoro neomoderno. *Rivista Giuridica del Lavoro e della Previdenza Sociale*, LXIX(4): 681 ff.

Perulli A. (2021). Il "trittico" della Corte costituzionale sulla disciplina licenziamento. Dalla law&economics ai principi di tutela del lavoro. *Lavoro Diritti Europa*, 3: 1 ff.

Perulli A., Speziale V. (2022). *Dieci tesi sul diritto del lavoro*. Bologna: Il Mulino.

Perulli A., Sychenko E. (2018). Recent Jurisprudence of the European Court of Human Rights Relevant to Employment Law. *European Labour Law Journal*, 9(3): 287 ff.

Petersen N. (2020). Alexy and the "German" Model of Proportionality: Why the Theory of Constitutional Rights Does Not Provide a Representative Reconstruction of the Proportionality Test. *German Law Journal*, 21: 163 ff.

Pierce A. J. (2017). Justice without Solidarity? Collective Identity and the Fate of the 'Ethical' in Habermas' Recent Political Theory. *European Journal of Philosophy*, 26(1): 546 ff.

Pin A., Longo E. (2015). Dalla sentenza n. 10 alla n. 70 del 2015: Quando la giustizia costituzionale diventa imprevedibile. *Quaderni Costituzionali*, 3: 697 ff.

Pinardi R. (2019). Diritti e risorse finanziarie: Il ruolo della Corte costituzionale. *Rivista del Diritto della Sicurezza Sociale*, 2: 107 ff.

Pino G. (2007). La «lotta per i diritti fondamentali» in Europa Integrazione europea, diritti fondamentali e ragionamento giuridico. In: Trujillo I., Viola F. (eds.), *Identità, diritti, ragione pubblica in Europa*. Bologna: Il Mulino, 109 ff.

Pino G. (2008). *Diritti fondamentali e ragionamento giuridico*. Torino: Giappichelli.

Pino G. (2009). Principi e argomentazione giuridica. *Ars Interpretandi*, XIV: 131 ff.

Pino G. (2014). Proporzionalità, diritti, democrazia. *Diritto e Società*, 3: 597 ff.

Pino G. (2016). Diritti sociali. Per una critica di alcuni luoghi comuni. *Ragion pratica*, 2: 495 ff.

Pirker B. (2013). *Proportionality Analysis and Models of Judicial Review*. Zutphen: Europa Law Publishing.

Pirozzoli A. (2011). Il Vincolo Costituzionale del Pareggio di Bilancio. *Rivista Associazione Italiana dei Costituzionalisti*, 4: 1 ff.

Pizzoferrato A. (2015). The Economic Crisis and Labour Law Reform in Italy. *The International Journal of Comparative Labour Law and Industrial Relations*, 31(2): 187 ff.

Preciado Domènech C. H. (2016). Interpretcioòn de los Derechos Humanos y los Derechos Fundamentales. In *Cuadernos Aranzadi del Tribunal Constitucional.* Madrid: Thomson Reuters Aranzadi.

Prieto Sanchís L. (2000). La limitación de los derechos fundamentales y la norma de clausura del sistema de libertades. *Derechos y libertades: Revista del Instituto Bartolomé de las Casas*, 5(8): 429 ff.

Prieto Sanchís L. (2001). Neoconstitucionalismo Y ponderación judicial. *Anuario de la Facultad de Derecho de la Universidad Autónoma de Madrid*, 5: 201 ff.

Prieto Sanchís L. (2003). *Justicia Constitucional y derechos fundamentales.* Madrid: Trotta.

Prieto Sanchís L. (2016). Los derechos sociales como derechos fundamentals. In: Aa. Vv (ed.), *Liber amicorum. Homenaje al profesor Luis Martínez Roldán.* Oviedo: Ediciones de la Universidad de Oviedo, 589 ff.

Procopio M. A. (2016). La legittimità costituzionale delle pensioni d'oro: Il singolare 'dietrofront' operato dal giudice delle leggi. *Rivista di giurisprudenza tributaria*, 11: 836 ff.

Pugiotto A. (2015). Un inedito epitaffio per la pregiudizialità costituzionale. *Forum di Quaderni costituzionali.* Available at: https://www.forumcostituzionale.it/wordpress/wp-content/uploads/2014/12/nota_10_2015_pugiotto.pdf (last access: 15 February 2023).

Ramião R. (2018). Some Fundamental Problems Concerning Alexy's Notion of Legal Principles. In: Duarte D., Silva Sampaio J. (eds.), *Proportionality in Law: An Analytical Perspective.* Berlin: Springer, 157 ff.

Ratti G. B. (2015). Neoconstitucionalismo negativo y Neoconstitucionalismo positive. *Ius Humani. Revista de Derecho*, 4: 227 ff.

Reich N. (2008). Free Movement v. Social Rights in an Enlarged Union: The Laval and Viking Cases Before the European Curt if Justice. *German Law Journal*, 9(2): 125–161.

Rey Pérez J. L. (2007). La naturaleza de los derechos sociales. The Nature of Social Rights. *Derechos y Libertade*, 16(II): 137 ff.

Ricci G. (2014). La retribuzione in tempi di crisi: Diritto sociale fondamentale o variabile dipendente? *WP CSDLE "Massimo D'Antona".IT* – 113.

Ridaura Martínez M. J. (2012). La reforma del artículo 135 de la Constitución Española : ¿pueden los mercados quebrar el consenso constitucional? *Teoría y Realidad Constitucional*, 29: 237 ff.

Rivera I. (2016). Il sindacato di ragionevolezza quale strumento di controllo della razionalità (formale e pratica) della norma. Brevi osservazioni a margine della sentenza n. 113 del 2015. *Forum di Quaderni Costituzionali.* Available at: https://www.forumcostituzionale.it/wordpress/wp-content/uploads/2016/02/nota_113_2015_rivera.pdf (last access: 15 February 2023).

Rivers J. (2006). Proportionality and Variable Intensity of Review. *The Cambridge Law Journal*, 65(1): 174 ff.

Rivers J. (2014). The Presumption of Proportionality. *Modern Law Review*, 77(3): 409 ff.

Roca Trias E. (2013). *Los principios de razonabilidad y proporcionalidad en la jurisprudencia constitucional española.* Reunión de Tribunales Constitucionales de italia, portugal y españa. Roma - octubre.

Rocha F. (2014). Crisis and Austerity Policies in Spain: Towards an authoritarian model of industrial relations. In: Rocha F. (ed.), *The New Economic Governance and its Impact on the National Collective Bargaining System.* Madrid: Fundacion 1° de Mayo.

Rodotà S. (2011). *Diritti e libertà nella storia d'Italia.* Roma: Donzelli Editore.

Rodotà S. (2012). *Il diritto di avere diritti.* Bari: Laterza.

Rodríguez M. L. (2014). Labour Rights in Crisis in the Eurozone: The Spanish Case. In: Kilpatrick C., De Witte B. (eds.), *Social Rights in Times of Crisis in the Eurozone: The Role of Fundamental Rights' Challenges.* EUI Department of Law Research Paper, 05.

Rodríguez Ruiz B. (1999). El caso valenzuela contreras y nuestro sistema de derechos Fundamentales. *Revista Española de Derecho Constitucional,* 19(56): 223 ff.

Rodríguez-Armas M. L. (1996). El problema del contenido esencial de los derechos fundamentales en la doctrina española y su tratamiento en la jurisprudencia constitucional. *Anales de la Facultad de Derecho. Universidad de La Laguna,* 13: 41 ff.

Rogowski R. (2013). *Reflexive Labour Law in the World Society.* Cheltenham: Edward Elgar.

Rogowski R. (2016). *The European Social Model and Transitional Labour Markets.* London: Routledge.

Rogowski R. (2019). The European Employment Strategy, the European Social Pillar and Their Impact on Labour Law Reform in the European Union. *International Journal of Comparative Labour Law and Industrial Relations,* 35(3): 283 ff.

Romboli R. (1992). Il significato essenziale della motivazione per le decisioni della Corte costituzionale in tema di diritti e libertà pronunciate a seguito di bilanciamento tra valori costituzionali contrapposti. In: Angiolini V (ed.), *Libertà e giurisprudenza costituzionale.* Torino: Giappichelli, 206 ff.

Romboli R. (1993). Il principio generale di equilibrio finanziario nell'attività di bilanciamento dei valori costituzionali operata dalla Corte. In: Aa. Vv., *Le Sentenze della Corte Costituzionale e l'Art. 81, U.C., della Costituzione.* Atti del Seminario. Roma, 8–9 novembre 1991. Milano: Giuffrè, 185 ff.

Romboli R. (2000). Giudicare la legge? La legge "giusta" nello stato costituzionale. In: Ripepe E. (ed.), *Interrogativi sul diritto "giusto".* Pisa: SEU, 99 ff.

Romboli R. (2015). L' "obbligo" per il giudice di applicare nel processo a quo la norma dichiarata incostituzionale ab origine: natura incidentale del giudizio costituzionale e tutela dei diritti. *Forum di Quaderni costituzionali.* Available at: https://www.forumcostituzionale.it/wordpress/wp-content/uploads/2014/12/nota_10_2015_romboli.pdf (last access: 15 February 2023).

Rossano C. (1994). "Ragionevolezza" e fattispecie di eguaglianza. In: Aa. Vv., *Il principio di ragionevolezza nella giurisprudenza della Corte Costituzionale. Riferimenti comparatistici.* Milano: Giuffrè, 171 ff.

Ruggeri A. (2003). Balances' entre valores constitucionales y teorìa de las fuentes. *Teorìa e Realidad Constitucional,* 12–13: 155 ff.

Ruggeri A. (2015). Sliding doors per la incidentalità del processo costituzionale (a margine di Corte cost. n. 10 del 2015). *Forum di Quaderni costituzionali.* Available at: https://www.forumcostituzionale.it/wordpress/wp-content/uploads/2014/12/nota_10_2015_ruggeri.pdf (last access: 15 February 2023).

Ruiz Miguel A. (1994). Derechos liberales y derechos Sociales. *Doxa*, 15–16: 651 ff.

Russels B. (2017). *In Praise of Idleness*. New York: St. Martins Press, Macmillan.

Sagan A. (2018). Article 11 ECHR Freedom of Assembly and Association. In: Ales E., Bell M., Deinert O., Robin-Olivier S. (eds.), *International and European Labour Law*. Varese: Nomos, 1513 ff.

Salazar C. (2013). Crisi economica e diritti fondamentali. *Rivista dell'Associazione Italiana dei Costituzionalisti*, 4: 1 ff.

Salcedo Beltrán M. C. (2014). De nuevo sobre el período de prueba tras la doctrina del Tribunal Constitucional: El necesario respeto a las normas internacionales (a propósito de la SJS nº 3 de Barcelona de 5 de noviembre de 2014). *Revista de Derecho Social*, 68: 143 ff.

Sánchez Gonzalez G. (2003). De la imponderable ponderaciòn y otras artes del Tribunal Constitucional. *Teoria y Realidad Constitucional*, 12–13: 351 ff.

Sandulli A. M. (1975). Il Principio di Ragionevolezza nella Giurisprudenza Costituzionale. (Originally published in *Diritto e Società*, 3). In: Aa. Vv (ed.), (1990) *Scritti Giuridici. Diritto Costituzionale*. Napoli: Jovene Editore, 678 ff.

Sandulli P. (2016). La Corte costituzionale orienta il legislatore delle pensioni. A proposito delle sentenze nn. 173 e 174/2016. *Rivista del Diritto della Sicurezza Sociale*, 4: 687 ff.

Sanguineti Raymond W. (2012). L reforma flexibilizadora de las modigicaciones sustancialesde las condiciones de trabajo y sus lìmites inmanentes. In: Baylos Grau A. (ed.), *Politicas de Austeridad y Crisis en las Relaciones Laborales: la Reforma del 2012*. Albacete: Bomarzo Editorial, 125 ff.

Sanguineti Raymond W. (2015). Sentencia del Tribunal Constitucional 8/2015, de 22 de enero [boe n.º 47, de 24-II-2015]. *Trabajo y Seguridad Social*, 3: 325 ff.

Sartor G. (2010). Doing Justice to Rights and Values: Teleological Reasoning and Proportionality. *Artificial Intelligence and Law*, 18: 175 ff.

Saura Estapà J. (2011). La exigibilidad jurídica de los derechos humanos: Especial referencia a los derechos económicos, sociales y culturales (DESC). *Papeles el tiempo de los derechos*, 2: 53 ff.

Sauter W. (2013). Proportionality in EU Law: A Balancing Act? In: Barnard C., Llorens A. A., Gehrin M., Schütze R. (eds.), *The Cambridge Yearbook of European Legal Studies. Volume 15*. Cambridge: Cambridge University Press, 439 ff.

Scaccia G. (2000). *Gli strumenti della ragionevolezza nel giudizio costituzionale*. Milano: Giuffrè.

Scaccia G. (2019). Proportionality and the Balancing of Rights in the Case-Law of European Courts. *Federalismi.it*, 4: 1 ff.

Scagliarini S. (2015). Diritti e risorse: Il ragionevole equilibrio raggiunto dalla Corte. *Giurisprudenza italiana*, 52: 2705 ff.

Scagliarini S. (2019). Il bilanciamento tra diritti e risorse finanziarie nella più recente giurisprudenza costituzionale. *Rivista del Diritto della Sicurezza Sociale*, 2: 331 ff.

Scalia A. (1989). Originalism: The Lesser Evil. *University of Cincinnati Law Review*, 57: 849 ff.

Scharpf F. W. (2002). *The European Social Model: Coping with the Challenges of Diversity*. MPIfG Working Paper, No. 02/8. Cologne: Max Planck Institute for the Study of Societies.

Schiek D. (2017). Towards More Resilience for a Social EU – The Constitutionally Conditioned Internal Market. *European Constitutional Law Review*, 13: 611 ff.

Schoemann I. (2014). Changes in the General European Legal Framework. In: Bruun N., Loercher K., Schoemann I. (eds.), *The Economic and Financial Crisis and Collective Labour Law*. Oxford and Portland: Hart Publishing.

Schwarze J. (2006). *European Administrative Law*. London: Sweet & Maxwell.

Sciarra S. (2005). Fundamental Labour Rights after the Lisbon Agenda. *WP C.S.D.L.E. "Massimo D'Antona" .INT* – 36.

Sciarra S. (2008). Viking and Laval: Collective Labour Rights and Market Freedoms in the Enlarged EU. *Cambridge Yearbook of European Legal Studies*, 10: 563 ff.

Sciarra S. (2013). *L'Europa e il lavoro. Solidarietà e conflitto in tempi di crisi*. Bari: Laterza.

Sciarra S. (2014). Social Law in the Wake of the Crisis. *WP CSDLE "Massimo D'Antona".INT* – 108/2014.

Sciarra S. (2015). Il diritto sociale europeo al tempo della crisi. *Il Diritto dell'Unione Europea*, 757 ff.

Sciarra S. (2016). Prove di razionalità per il diritto del lavoro della crisi. *Argomenti di Diritto del Lavoro*, 21(1): 5 ff.

Sciarra S. (2017). I diritti sociali e i dilemmi della giurisprudenza costituzionale. *Rivista Italiana di Diritto del Lavoro*, I: 347 ff.

Sciarra S. (2018). *Solidarity and Conflict: European Social Law in Crisis*. Cambridge: Cambridge University Press.

Sciarra S. (2019a). Prove di solidarietà in alcune sentenze della Corte Costituzionale. *Rivista del Diritto della Sicurezza Sociale*, 2: 261 ff.

Sciarra S. (2019b). *Solidarity and Conflict: European Social Law in Crisis*. Cambridge: Cambridge University Press.

Sciarra S., Nicastro G. (2016). A New Conversation: Preliminary References from the Italian Constitutional Court. *Maastricht Journal of European and Comparative Law*, 23: 195 ff.

Sen A. (2006). Human Rights and the Limits of Law. *Cardozo Law Review*, 27(6): 2913 ff.

Senra Biedma R. (2014). El Derecho del Trabajo de la Crisis y la Crisis del Derecho del Trabajo el Recurso de Inconstitucionalidad del Parlamento de Navarra Contra Varios Preceptos de la Reforma Laboral 2012. Comentario a la Sentencia del Tribunal Constitucional (Pleno) 119/2014, De 16 Julio. *IUSLabor*, 3: 1 ff.

Shambaugh J. C. (2012). The Euro's Three Crisis. *Brookings Papers on Economic Activity*, 43(1): 157 ff.

Sieckmann J. R. (2018). Proportionality as a Universal Human Rights Principle. In: Duarte D., Silva Sampaio J. (eds.), *Proportionality in Law: An Analytical Perspective*. Berlin: Springer, 3 ff.

Sieckmann J. R. (2021). To Balance or Not to Balance: The Quest for the Essence of Rights. In: Sieckmann J. R. (ed.), *Proportionality, Balancing, and Rights Robert Alexy's Theory of Constitutional Rights*. Berlin: Springer, 113 ff.

Sieckmann J. R. (ed.), (2021). *Proportionality, Balancing, and Rights Robert Alexy's Theory of Constitutional Rights*. Berlin: Springer.

Silva Sampaio J. (2018). Proportionality in Its Narrow Sense and Measuring the Intensity of Restrictions on Fundamental Rights. In: Duarte D., Silva Sampaio J. (eds.), *Proportionality in Law: An Analytical Perspective*. Berlin: Springer, 72 ff.

Silva Sampaio J. (2021). Brute Balancing, Proportionality and Meta-Weighing of Reasons. In: Sieckmann J. R. (ed.), *Proportionality, Balancing, and Rights Robert Alexy's Theory of Constitutional Rights*. Berlin: Springer.

Silvestri G. (1993). Relazioni e interventi. In: *Le sentenze della Corte costituzionale e l'art. 81, U.C., della Costituzione. Atti del Seminario. Roma, 8–9 novembre 1991.* Milano: Giuffrè, 77 ff.

Simoncini A. (2003). La riforma del Titolo V ed il «modello costituzionale di welfare» in Italia. *Diritto del Mercato del Lavoro*, 3: 100 ff.

Sinzheimer H. (2022). Il problema dell'essere umano nel diritto. *Giornale di Diritto del Lavoro e di Relazioni Industriali*, 173(1): 39 ff.

Solozabal Echavarria J. J. (1991). Algunas cuestiones básicas de la teoría de los derechos. *Revista de estudios políticos*, 71: 87 ff.

Sorace D. (1984). Note in tema di sentenze della Corte Costituzionale che importano nuove o maggiori spese e art. 81 Cost. nota a C. Cost. 27 maggio 1982, No. 102. *Il foro italiano*, 1(I): 42 ff.

Speziale V. (2022). Il 'diritto dei valori'. La tirannia dei valori economici e il lavoro nella Costituzione e nelle fonti europee. In: Del Punta R. (ed.), *Valori e tecniche nel diritto del lavoro*. Florence: Firenze University Press, 125 ff.

Startin N., Krouwel A. (2013). Euroscepticism Re-galvanized: The Consequences of the 2005 French and Dutch Rejections of the EU Constitution. *Journal of Common Market Studies*, 51(1): 65 ff.

Stone Sweet A., Mathews J. (2008). Proportionality Balancing and Global Constitutionalism. *Columbia Journal of Transnational Law*, 47: 72 ff.

Suarez Corujo B. (2015). La Constitucionalización de la Ruptura Laboral. *Revista jurídica Universidad Autónoma de Madrid*, 31: 419 ff.

Supiot A. Meadows P. (2001). *Beyond Employment: Changes in Work and the Future of Labour Law in Europe*. Oxford: Oxford University Press.

Taschini L. (2019). *I diritti sociali al tempo della condizionalità*. Torino: Giappichelli.

Tega D. (2014a). Welfare e crisi davanti alla Corte Costituzionale. *Giornale di Diritto del Lavoro e di Relazioni Industriali*, 142(2): 303 ff.

Tega D. (2014b). Welfare Rights in Italy. In: Kilpatrick C., De Witte B. (eds.), *Social Rights in Times of Crisis in the Eurozone: The Role of Fundamental Rights' Challenges*. EUI Department of Law Research Paper, 05.

Tesauro G. (2012). Reasonableness in the European Court of Justice Case-Law. In: Court of Justice of the European Union (ed.), *The Court of Justice and the Construction of Europe: Analyses and Perspectives on Sixty Years of Case-Law*. The Hague: T.M.C. Asser Press, 307 ff.

Thielbörger P. (2019). The "Essence" of International Human Rights. *German Law Journal*, 20: 924 ff.

Thompson E. (2009). The Political Origins of the Financial Crisis: The Domestic and International Politics of Fannie Mae and Freddie Mac. *The Political Quarterly*, 80(1): 17 ff.

Tridico P. (2013). The Impact of the Economic Crisis on EU Labour Markets: A Comparative Perspective. *International Labour Review*, 152(2): 175 ff.

Tridimas T. (1996). The Principle of Proportionality in Community Law: From the Rule of Law to Market Integration. *Irish Jurist*, 31: 83 ff.

Tridimas T. (2006). *The General Principles of EU Law*. Oxford: Oxford University Press. 2nd Edition.

Tridimas T., Gentile G. (2019). The Essence of Rights: An Unreliable Boundary? *German Law Journal*, 20: 794 ff.

Tsakyrakis S. (2009). Proportionality: An Assault on Human Rights? *International Journal of Constitutional Law*, 7(3): 468 ff.

Tosi P. (2019). La sentenza n. 194/2018 della Corte costituzionale e il suo “dopo”. *Diritto delle Relazioni Industriali*, 1: 244 ff.

Troisi M. (2019). La quantificazione del «costo» delle pronunce della Corte costituzionale in materia di diritti. *Rivista del Diritto della Sicurezza Sociale*, 2: 353 ff.

Tuori K., Tuori K. (2014). *The Eurozone Crisis: A Constitutional Analysis*. Cambridge: Cambridge Studies in European Law and Policy.

Valdés Dal-Ré F. (2012). La reforma de la negociación colectiva de 2012. *Relaciones laborales: Revista crítica de teoría y práctica*, 23–24: 221 ff.

Valdés Dal-Ré F. (2013). La reforma laboral de 2012. (Notas sobre su texto -sistemática interna y calidad técnica- y su contexto -la falta de correspondencia entre el objetivo proclamado y los objetivos realmente perseguidos-). *Relaciones Laborales*, 2: 1–10.

Vallauri M. L. (2010). L’argomento della “dignità umana” nella giurisprudenza in materia di danno alla persona del lavoratore. *Giornale di Diritto del Lavoro e di Relazioni Industriali*, 128(4): 659 ff.

Vallecillo Gámez M. (2015). Política de empleo y periodo de prueba de un año: Crítica desde la doble perspectiva constitucional e internacional. *Temas laborales: Revista andaluza de trabajo y bienestar social*, 129: 79 ff.

Van Peijpe T. (2009). Collective Labour Law after Viking, Laval, Rüffert, and Commission v. Luxemburg. *International Journal of Comparative Labour Law And Industrial Relations*, 25(2): 81 ff.

Vaughan-Whitehead D. (2003). *EU Enlargement Versus Social Europe? The Uncertain Future of the European Social Model*. Cheltenham: Edward Elgar.

Vaughan-Whitehead D. (2015). The European Social Model in Times of Crisis: An Overview. In: Vaughan-Whitehead D. (ed.), *The European Social Model in Crisis: Is Europe Losing Its Soul?* Geneva: International Labor Office, 1 ff.

Veneziani B. (2016). Del contenuto essenziale dei diritti dei lavoratori: Spunti per una ricerca. *Diritti Lavori Mercati*, 2: 229 ff.

Veronesi P. (2015). La coerenza che non c’è: Sugli effetti temporali delle pronunce d’accoglimento (e sulla sorte dell’«equilibrio di bilancio») dopo le sentenze nn. 10 e 70 del 2015. *Quaderni Costituzionali*, 3: 692 ff.

Vicente Palacio A. (2012). El Real Decreto-Ley 3/2012, de 10 de Febrero, De Medidas Urgentes Para la Reforma del Mercado Laboral (Una Breve Presentación de la Reforma en el Ámbito del Derecho Individual). *Revista General de Derecho del Trabajo y de la Seguridad Social*, 31: 58 ff.

Vigneau C. (2018). Social Dumping at the Core of National Labour Law Reforms. *Giornale di Diritto del Lavoro e di Relazioni Industriali*, 160(4): 871 ff.

Villaverde I. (2008). La resolución de conflictos entre derechos fundamentales. El principio de proporcionalidad. In: Carbonnell M. (ed.), *El principio de proporcionalidad y la interpretación constitucional*. Ecuador: Quito, 175 ff.

Viola F. (1989). *Diritti dell’uomo, diritto naturale, etica contemporanea*. Torino: Giappichelli.

Voogsgeerd H. (2012). The EU Charter of Fundamental Rights and Its Impact on Labor Law: Plea for Proportionality-Test Light. *Goettingen Journal of International Law*, 4(1): 293 ff.

Weiler J., Lockhart N. (1995). Taking Rights Seriously: The European Court and Its Fundamental Rights Jurisprudence - Part I. *Common Market Law Review*, 32: 51 ff.

Young K. G. (2008). The Minimum Core of Economic and Social Rights: Concept in Search of Content. *Yale Journal of International Law*, 33(1): 113 ff.

Young K. G. (2017). Proportionality, Reasonableness, and Economic and Social Rights. In: Jackson V. C., Mark Tushnet M. (eds.), *Proportionality: New Frontiers, New Challenges.* Cambridge: Cambridge University Press, 248 ff.

Zagrebelsky G. (1992). *Il diritto mite.* Torino: Einaudi.

Zagrebelsky G. (1993). Problemi in ordine ai costi delle sentenze costituzionali. In: Aa. Vv., *Le Sentenze della Corte Costituzionale e l'Art. 81, U.C., della Costituzione. Atti del Seminario. Roma, 8–9 novembre 1991.* Milano: Giuffrè, 99 ff.

Zagrebelsky G. (1994). Su tre aspetti della ragionevolezza. In: Aa. Vv., *Il principio di ragionevolezza nella giurisprudenza della Corte Costituzionale. Atti del seminario. Roma, 13–14 ottobre 1992.* Milano: Giuffrè, 179 ff.

Zagrebelsky G. (1998). *Giustizia Costituzionale.* Bologna: Il Mulino.

Zagrebelsky G. (2008). *La legge e la sua giustizia.* Bologna: Il Mulino.

Zahn R., De Witte B. (2011). La prospettiva dell`Unione europea: Dare preminenza al mercato interno o rivedere la dottrina Laval? *Giornale di diritto del lavoro e di relazioni industriali*, 131(3): 433 ff.

Zoppoli L. (2017). Una sentenza interpretativa di accoglimento con manipolazioni temporali relative allo *ius novum*. *Giornali di Diritto del Lavoro e di Relazioni Industriali*. 153: 183 ff.

Zoppoli L. (2019). Il licenziamento "de-costituzionalizzato": Con la sentenza n. 194/2018 la Consulta argina, ma non architetta. *Diritto delle Relazioni Industriali*, 1: 277 ff.

Index